Key Concepts 2

Reading and Writing Across the Disciplines

First Edition

Barbara Smith-Palinkas

Kelly Croghan-Ford

D1608989

HEINLE
CENGAGE Learning

Australia • Brazil • Japan • Korea • Mexico • Singapore • Spain • United Kingdom • United States

HEINLE
CENGAGE Learning

Key Concepts 2
Reading and Writing Across the Disciplines
Barbara Smith-Palinkas, Kelly Croghan-Ford

Publisher: Sherrise Roehr

Acquisitions Editor: Tom Jefferies

Associate Development Editor: Sarah Sandoski

Director of Global Marketing: Ian Martin

Director of US Marketing: Jim McDonough

Marketing Manager: Caitlin Driscoll

Senior Content Project Manager:
 Dawn Marie Elwell

Senior Print Buyer: Betsy Donaghey

Cover Designer: Lisa Mezikofsky

Compositor: Pre-PressPMG

Cover photo: © Shutterstock/Yurchyks

For product information and technology assistance, contact us at
Cengage Learning Customer & Sales Support, 1-800-354-9706
For permission to use material from this text or product,
submit all requests online at **cengage.com/permissions**
Further permissions questions can be emailed to
permissionrequest@cengage.com

Library of Congress Control Number: 2008937896

ISBN-13: 978-0-618-47462-2

ISBN-10: 0-618-47462-5

Heinle
20 Channel Center St.
Boston, MA 02210
USA

Cengage Learning is a leading provider of customized learning solutions with office locations around the globe, including Singapore, the United Kingdom, Australia, Mexico, Brazil, and Japan. Locate your local office at:
international.cengage.com/region

Cengage Learning products are represented in Canada by Nelson Education, Ltd.

Visit Heinle online at **elt.heinle.com**

Visit our corporate website at **www.cengage.com**

Printed in Canada
2 3 4 5 6 7 8 9   14 13 12 11 10 09

Acknowledgments

We would like to express our gratitude to Tom Jefferies, Acquisitions Editor, and Sarah Sandoski, Associate Development Editor, at Cengage Learning, who provided support and guidance to us throughout the entire process.

We also wish to convey our thanks to Susan Maguire and Kathy Sands-Boehmer, from Houghton Mifflin, with whom we first worked to develop *Key Concepts*. It was their initial encouragement that kept this project alive.

We want to express our appreciation to our ESL colleagues who shared their expertise and ideas with us as we developed the activities for the book. Their insights were invaluable, and their continued interest in the project provided us with much-appreciated moral support.

We are grateful to the many students in the English for Academic Purposes Program at Hillsborough Community College, Ybor Campus, who provided us with "real-time" feedback as we developed and tested the contents of the book.

In addition, we thank the following reviewers of the entire *Key Concepts* series, whose comments and suggestions helped bring the books to their final form:

Carol Auerbach
Northern Virginia Community College

Anne Bachman
Clackamas Community College

Michael Berman
Montgomery College

Keri Bjorklund
Laramie Community College

Mary B. Caldwell
El Paso Community College

Richard Cervin
Sacramento City College

Gwendolyn Charvis
North Harris College

Maggie Discont
West Hills College

Cynthia Dunham-Gonzalez
Seminole Community College

Mark Ende
Onondaga Community College

Kathy Flynn
Glendale Community College

Beverly Gandall
Santa Ana College

Elizabeth Gilfillan
Houston Community College

Margo Harder
South Seattle Community College

Carolyn Ho
Cy Fair College

Michael Khirallah
Oakland Community College

Carole Marquis
Santa Fe Community College

Michelle Naumann

Esther Robbins
Prince George's Community College

Dan Smolens
Roxbury Community College

Shirley Terrell
Collin County Community College

Donna M. Tortorella

Kent Trickel
Westchester Community College

Barbara Smith-Palinkas
Kelly Croghan-Ford

Contents

CHAPTER 2 ● **From the Social Sciences: Cultural Anthropology   41**

Key Concepts 2: Reading and Writing Across the Disciplines

Contents   **vii**

CHAPTER 7 ● From the Physical Sciences: Physics   233

Key Concepts 2 Skills Overview

In each Reading section, students practice surveying, predicting, summarizing, and the Academic Word List. In each Writing section, students revise, edit, and proofread their work.

Chapter	Reading Skills and Strategies	Writing Skills and Strategies	The Process
1	• reading and understanding test questions • identifying text structure: introduction to outlining • using context to guess meaning: contrast	• the grammar of conditionals • dependent and independent clauses • simple and compound sentences	• timed writing • overview of process: • key words • planning/writing a response • editing and proofreading • respond to short answer/essay questions
2	• stated main idea • identifying text structure: summary • using context to guess meaning: definition	• the grammar of noun clauses • complex and compound-complex sentences	• structure of a paragraph • paraphrasing and summarizing • synthesizing • paragraph of summary
3	• implied main idea • identifying text structure: cause/effect • using context to guess meaning: synonyms/antonyms	• the grammar of parallelism • clause relationships	• structure of an essay • introduction • thesis statement • overview of writing process • essay of cause/effect
4	• making inferences: tone and figurative language • identifying text structure: literature • using context to guess meaning: inference	• the grammar of participial adjectives • sentence errors: fragments, run-on sentences, comma splices	• body and support sentences • topic sentences • general and specific support • quotations • citations and references • synthesizing • essay of reaction/response
5	• reading details: tables, charts, and graphs • identifying text structure: exemplification • using context to guess meaning: examples	• the grammar of adjective clauses • dependent clauses: adjective clauses	• body and support sentences • facts and opinions • statistics and details from graphics • synthesizing • essay of exemplification/illustration
6	• drawing conclusions: logical fallacies • identifying text structure: argument/persuasion • using context to guess meaning: surrounding sentences	• the grammar of adverb clauses • dependent clauses: adverb clauses	• body and support sentences • examples as support • conclusions • synthesizing • essay of argument/persuasion
7	• understanding referents • identifying text structure: process • using context to guess meaning: review of strategies	• the grammar of modals • dependent clauses: noun clauses	• unity and coherence • text structure and logical order • key words, synonyms, and pronouns • transitions • consistency in verb tense and point of view • essays with combined text structure • essay of process

Introduction

The *Key Concepts* series takes a content-based approach to teaching students the academic skills they need to participate successfully in college or university classes in English. The series is designed for mid- and high-intermediate level students, and each level includes two books: *Listening, Note Taking, and Speaking* and *Reading and Writing.*

The books in the series may be used separately, each offering an integrated-skills approach to listening, note taking, and speaking or to reading and writing. Because the corresponding chapters at each level address the same academic disciplines, however, using both books in the level results in a fully integrated four-skills approach to teaching academic English.

Key Concepts 2: Reading and Writing Across the Disciplines is the second of a two-volume series that focuses on the academic skills of reading and writing. The subject matter of the readings, along with the writing focus, centers on one of the following academic disciplines: college success, social science, business, mathematics, physical science, and humanities. As students encounter recurring concepts and vocabulary, they build on their knowledge of academic subjects and use of academic language in English.

The chapters of *Key Concepts 2* include the topics from the following college disciplines:

- Social Sciences: Cultural Anthropology

- Business: Business Ethics

- Language Arts: English Literature

- Mathematics: Applied Mathematics

- History: American History

- Physical Sciences: Physics

In addition to presenting discipline-specific vocabulary from the readings, identified as Key Concept Words, each chapter of *Key Concepts* also introduces students to and offers practice with twenty vocabulary items from Averil Coxhead's Academic Word List. These words are the most frequently used vocabulary in college texts, and the words practiced in *Key Concepts* are taken directly from the chapter readings. In addition, vocabulary exercises in *Key Concepts* build the student's vocabulary by focusing on word forms and help the student discern differences in meaning by focusing on context and usage. A list of Glossed Words follows the concept words and assists the students with comprehension of the material by defining words that are likely to be unfamiliar to them.

The content-based approach of *Key Concepts* promotes the integration of reading and writing skills, and each chapter helps students make the connection by drawing and/or reinforcing parallels between the two. The first chapter of *Key Concepts 2* reinforces students' test-taking skills as they read about different types of tests, practice reading and understanding test questions, and write timed responses. The readings in subsequent chapters mirror and serve as models for the methods of development students will use in their writing assignments. *Key Concepts 2* includes summary writing as well as the patterns of cause/effect, reaction/response, exemplification/illustration, argument/persuasion, and process.

Key Concepts 2 simulates the university experience by offering high-intermediate-level students reading and writing activities with similar academic content. The experience of interacting with academic texts can provide students a better sense of what to expect in a college or university course. *Key Concepts* offers students this experience.

Text Organization

The first half of each chapter is devoted to reading skills. Students are introduced to the reading skills and strategies of surveying, predicting, and summarizing through presentation of an academic passage averaging approximately 800 words. Following the reading, students practice using words from the Academic Word List, which are contained in the reading. In addition to identifying text structure and guessing meaning from context, each chapter focuses on one of the following reading skills: outlining as a study tool, identifying stated and implied main idea, making inferences, understanding details, drawing conclusions, and understanding referents. Students are then given a second reading averaging approximately 1,000 words and are asked to practice their reading skills "on their own."

The second half of each chapter is devoted to writing skills. The writing section opens with a short grammar focus on a structure common to the academic readings in the chapter. This is followed by a section on sentence essentials, focusing on sentence types (simple, compound, complex, and compound-complex). Chapter 1 presents an overview of the timed-writing process, Chapter 2 an overview of the process of paragraph writing, and Chapter 3 an overview of the process of essay writing. Subsequent chapters address writing thesis statements; general and specific support including quotations, facts, opinions, and statistics (from charts and graphs); and conclusions. Unity and coherence are addressed in the final chapter of the book. Students are guided through the writing skills of brainstorming, narrowing the topic, writing a topic sentence or thesis statement, supplying details, writing a conclusion, and outlining before they are asked to write a paragraph or essay "on their own." The reading passages in each chapter serve as models for the paragraph or essay types students are asked to write. They include summary, cause/effect, reaction/response, exemplification/illustration, argument/persuasion, and process.

The appendices include a comprehensive list of words from the readings that appear on the Academic Word List; samples of different types of brainstorming; lists of conjunctions, transition words, and key words for specific text structures; additional writing topics; a glossary of reading and writing terms; a glossary of essay prompt terms; and samples of APA citations.

Contents of a Chapter

Reading 1: Skills and Strategies

Students are introduced to the first reading via two activities: Get Ready to Read, which activates their background knowledge about the topic, and Surveying and Predicting. After the reading, students do a Summarizing activity and Comprehension activity and are then introduced to ten words from the reading that appear on the Academic Word List. Students practice the vocabulary through different exercise types. Next, a reading strategy is introduced and practiced. The reading strategy is followed by an introduction to a specific text structure and the key words associated with it. Students then practice using the key words.

Reading 2: On Your Own

As with the first reading, students are introduced to the second reading via the Get Ready to Read and Surveying and Predicting activities. After the reading, they complete a Summarizing activity and Comprehension activity, followed by the introduction to a new set of ten words from the reading that appear on the Academic Word List. Students again practice the vocabulary through different exercise types. This is followed by a vocabulary exercise to practice guessing meaning from context.

Writing 1A: Skills and Strategies

Students are presented with a short introduction to the grammar of a structure found in the readings. After practice recognizing and/or using the structure, students work on Sentence Essentials. This section focuses on specific sentence types, sentence connectors, sentence errors, or sentence punctuation.

Writing 1B: The Process

Students are introduced to the writing process via Get Ready to Write, which addresses timed writing in Chapter 1, summary paragraphs in Chapter 2, and essay structure in Chapter 3. In this section, students also are introduced to planning a response to an essay question, paraphrasing and summarizing, synthesizing, writing an introduction and a thesis statement, writing the body and support sentences, as well as unity and coherence in writing.

After practicing the specific writing skill, students are presented with How Did They Do That?, an interactive activity that requires them to follow the steps the writer took to develop a summary paragraph or an essay. The paragraph or essay models the specific text structure introduced in the readings and practiced in the Reading 1: Skills and Strategies section.

Writing 2: On Your Own

In this section, students are asked to write a summary paragraph or essay of their own, using the text structure presented in the Writing 1B: The Process section. After students write their paragraph or essay, they use the checklist in the Revising activity to make any changes in their work. Finally, they use the checklist in the Editing and Proofreading activity to make final changes to their writing before handing it in.

Online Resources

Additional Web Activities for Students

The *Key Concepts* series offers additional materials for students and teachers that they can access online by logging onto *http://elt.heinle.com/keyconceptsrw.*

Assessment

Students using the *Key Concepts* series can practice the Academic Word List vocabulary with flashcards. Web Quizzes test the students' comprehension of Readings 1 and 2, as well as their mastery of the writing skills addressed in that chapter.

Instructor Manual and Answer Keys

Answer Keys are available for every activity in the *Key Concepts* series. Teachers will also find chapter notes written by the authors that include brief guides to the activities in addition to summaries of each reading.

1 The Student Experience: Success in College

Taking exams is a part of college life, just as attending classes, making new friends, and using the library are. Although there are many ways instructors can evaluate their students' progress, exams are still one of the most commonly used methods.

Using your general knowledge and experience of taking exams, discuss the following questions with a partner or in a small group.

- What are the different types of exams instructors use?
- What kind of exams do you prefer to take?
- What specific strategies do you use when taking exams?

This chapter will help you understand some of the **key concepts** in test-taking skills such as

- subjective vs. objective tests
- strategies for test-taking
- timed writings
- prompts for essay exams

Get Ready to Read

Effective or Ineffective

Read the following test-taking strategies and decide if they are effective or ineffective strategies. Share your answers with a classmate.

1. Answer the parts of the exam worth the most points first.　　　　　EFFECTIVE　　INEFFECTIVE

2. Leave answers you are unsure of blank.　　　　　EFFECTIVE　　INEFFECTIVE

3. Save time by not reading the directions.　　　　　EFFECTIVE　　INEFFECTIVE

4. Answer multiple-choice questions "in your head" first, then look at the choices on the test.　　EFFECTIVE　　INEFFECTIVE

5. Skim the entire test before answering any questions.　　　　　EFFECTIVE　　INEFFECTIVE

Surveying and Predicting

Survey and Predict

> **Survey:** to look at the parts of a text to get an idea of the topic

A. Follow the steps below to survey Reading 1 below.

1. Read the title. Write it here. _____

2. Read the first paragraph. Write one or two words that tell the topic or what the paragraph is about. _____
_____

3. Write the main idea, what the writer wants you to know about the topic, here.
_____

4. Read the headings, the titles of the sections in the reading. Write them here.
_____
_____

5. Look for any graphic or visual aids in the reading. Graphic aids are charts, graphs, pictures, maps, diagrams, etc. Describe them here. _____
_____

6. Look for key (important) terms related to the topic. They are usually in **bold**. List them here. _____
_____

7. Read the last paragraph. It is a summary of the entire reading.

B. Share your survey answers with a partner and discuss what you think the reading will be about. Then circle the number of the statement below that matches your prediction.

1. The passage will outline test-taking skills for different kinds of tests.

2. The passage will explain strategies for scoring well on objective tests.

3. The passage will describe how to study to take an objective test.

C. Now read the passage to see if your prediction is correct. Try to read as quickly as you can. Do not stop to look up words in your dictionary.

Taking Objective Tests

Instructors commonly test students on subject knowledge with **objective** and/or **subjective** tests. Objective exams include true/false, multiple-choice, and matching; subjective exams include short answer and essays. No matter how well you understand a subject or how well you prepare for an exam, poor test-taking skills could lead to earning a *C* instead of an *A* on an exam. There are several strategies that can help you reduce errors and score better on objective tests.

Overview of Exam

First, once you receive the exam, take a few minutes to get an overview of the entire test. Skim each part of the test, noting which parts contain questions easy to answer and which parts contain more difficult questions. Pay attention to the **point value** for each section of the test, noting which sections are worth the most points. Note if there is any overlapping—that is, if different parts of the test cover the same material or address the same topic. If so, you may find the answer to a question in another part of the test.

Plan Approach

After you have skimmed the test, read the directions for the entire test to understand what you are expected to do. Then plan your approach: allocate time for each section of the test. Allocating your time will allow you to do two things: go back to review questions you are unsure of and make sure you have answered all the questions on the exam.

Where you start on the test is up to you. You may choose to start at the beginning and work your way straight through to the end. You may decide, however, to focus on the easy sections first, saving the hard ones for later. Alternatively, you may elect to answer the questions worth the most points first and save the ones with lower point values for last, answering first the easy questions and later the difficult ones. Most experts recommend taking this approach as it ensures that you have correctly answered the questions with the most point values. Do what feels comfortable and gives you the most confidence.

Whichever approach you take, re-read the directions for each part of the test before you begin

that part. When you finish the test, don't be in a hurry to leave the room! Check to make sure you have answered every question. Never leave a test answer blank unless there is a penalty for wrong answers. Never change your answers unless you know they are definitely wrong.

Specific Strategies

The above strategies apply for objective tests in general; each type of objective exam also requires a specific approach. For example, when taking true/false exams, read the entire statement first. If any part of the statement is false, then the answer is *false*. Read statements containing **qualifying words** such as *never, always, none, all,* and *every* carefully. Chances are that statements with those qualifiers are false. In contrast, statements which contain the qualifiers *some, sometimes, a few,* or *occasionally* are often true.

A different approach is required for answering **multiple-choice questions**: Read the question or statement and, without looking at the choices offered, answer the question. Then choose the option offered that matches your answer. If none of the options matches your answer, skip that question and go on to the next one. When you reach the end of the section, go back to the question(s) you skipped. Try to eliminate choices you know are incorrect. Again, look for the qualifying words *never, always, none, all,* and *every,* and eliminate answers that contain them. Underline phrases such as *not, except,* or *all but one* to make sure you do not misread the question and choose the wrong answer. It may also help to underline a key word or phrase in the question to help you recall the correct answer. If you cannot eliminate all but one answer, try to narrow your choices to two and then guess. Mark the question and go back to it if you have time; you may find the answer to it in another part of the test or another question in the same section.

The approach to answering **matching questions** is to first survey the list of terms and the list of definitions or matching statements. Match the ones you know first, crossing out the definitions or statements as you use them. This prevents you from using the same definition twice and lets you know which choices are still available. If you are unsure of a term, read the statement or definition first and then try to define it with one of the terms. Sometimes matching parts of speech may help you find the right answer. For example, match nouns with nouns and verbs with verbs: *statement = a declaration* vs. *state = to declare*.

Reading assigned chapters, attending class, taking notes, and reviewing are all active ways to learn and remember the **subject matter** of a class. Tests show what you have learned and remembered. The better your test-taking skills, the better your grade.

Key Concept Words

matching questions – (n.) questions that require choosing a term from one column and pairing it with an answer from a second column

multiple-choice questions – (n.) questions which typically offer three or four answers from which to choose

objective tests – (n.) tests with questions that offer one or more answers from which to choose

point value – (n.) how many points each question or section is worth

qualifying words – (n.) words which limit an answer, for example, *always, never,* or *not*

subjective tests – (n.) tests which require the test-taker to supply the entire answer

subject matter – (n.) the topic or content of a class, book, or article

Glossed Words

earning – (n.) receiving; **overview** – (n.) a general look at an entire test; **penalty** – (n.) punishment, for example, a loss of points; **skim** – (v.) to read or look over quickly; **skip** – (v.) to pass over, not read; **strategy** – (n.) a plan or technique

Summarizing

Share What You Read

Use two or three sentences to tell your partner what you thought the reading was about. Then listen to your partner's sentences. Next, read the following statements and circle the number of the statement that best summarizes the reading.

1. When taking an objective test, there are specific strategies that will help you score better.

2. When taking an objective test, there is a specific approach to answering certain questions.

3. When taking an objective test, poor test-taking skills could result in your receiving a low grade.

Check Your Comprehension

Read the following statements about taking objective tests and put an X in front of any that do not belong in the category.

1. Overview of Exam
   _____ a. Skim each part of the test.
   _____ b. Note which parts are easy and hard.
   _____ c. Pay attention to point values.
   _____ d. Underline qualifying words.

2. Plan Approach

_____ a. Read the directions for the entire test.

_____ b. Answer the questions you know right away.

_____ c. Decide how much time to spend on each section.

_____ d. Answer the multiple-choice questions in your head first.

3. Specific Strategies

_____ a. Pay attention to qualifying words in true/false statements.

_____ b. If none of the multiple-choice options matches the answer "in your head," skip it.

_____ c. Guess at answers if you cannot eliminate all but one.

_____ d. Start the test at the beginning.

Academic Word List

In *Key Concepts,* you will practice many vocabulary words from the Academic Word List, which contains the most frequently used vocabulary words found in college-level textbooks. You may already be familiar with some of the vocabulary words.

Scan: to find specific information in a text by reading quickly

Scan and Define

A. Look at the ten words listed below. Scan the reading and underline the words from the list. Write the definitions for the words you know. Do not use a dictionary.

1. allocate *to plan or set aside something, usually time or money* _____

2. alternatively _____

3. approach (n.) _____

4. assigned (adj.) _____

5. definitely _____

6. ensure _____

7. expert (n.) _____

8. overlapping (n.) _____

9. specific _____

10. survey (v.) _____

B. Share your definitions with a partner and then with the rest of your classmates. As a group, try to complete the definitions for all ten words. Use a dictionary to check the definitions if you are unsure about them. Then complete the vocabulary activity.

ACTIVITY 6   *Vocabulary Challenge*

A. Using your dictionary, work with a partner to find the missing word forms and complete the chart. If no form exists, draw a line in the space. The first one has been done for you.

Noun	Verb	Adjective	Adverb
1. *allocation*	allocate	allocated, allocating	---------
2.			alternatively
3. approach			
4.		assigned	
5.			definitely
6.	ensure		
7. expert			
8. overlapping			
9.		specific	
10.	survey		

B. Substitute one of the words from the Academic Word List for the underlined word or phrase in each of the sentences below. Write it on the line. You may have to change the form of the word. The first one has been done for you.

_____survey_____ 1. Taking the time to <u>look over</u> all of the items on the test is one strategy good test-takers use.

_____ 2. The college advisor's <u>course of action</u> was to meet with each prospective student individually.

_____ 3. Researchers who are <u>authorities</u> in the field of test-taking have published numerous articles outlining effective study techniques.

_____ 4. He <u>clearly</u> decided to enroll in law school and follow his dream of becoming a lawyer.

_____ 5. <u>Setting aside</u> time to prepare for an exam should entail more than just blocking out the 24 hours before the exam to study; preparing for an exam is ongoing from the first day of the semester.

_____ 6. While nothing can <u>guarantee</u> you a passing grade on every exam you take, reviewing your lecture notes and anticipating possible exam questions are good habits to get into.

C. Read the sentences and determine whether each underlined word form is used correctly. If it is used correctly, put a *C* in the blank; if it is used incorrectly, put an *I* in the blank and correct the word form. If there are two underlined words, put both letters in the blank. The first one has been done for you.

_____|_____ 1. You might want to make notes in the margins of your textbook while

you read. Alternative, you might choose to outline the chapter in your
notebook.

_____ 2. Reading all of the assign chapters as presented in the course
syllabus will ensure you are always prepared for class.

_____ 3. My chemistry and math finals overlapped by an hour, so I had to
make special arrangements with my math professor to take the test
at another time.

_____ 4. I take a specifically approach when I have to study for an exam: I review
my notes, write down possible questions, and skim over the chapters.

_____ 5. My friend Josh believes he's an expertly test-taker. He says he's never
failed a test in his entire life!

Reading and Understanding Test Questions

Students spend hours and hours of their time reading chapters from their textbooks, studying journal articles on reserve in the library, and researching information in books and online. Yet when it comes to reading the directions on a test, many students don't bother, assuming they know how to answer true/false or multiple-choice questions. This approach has cost many students a good grade on an exam!

No matter what kind of test you take, it is important to read the directions in order to understand what you are expected to do. Thus, begin each type of test with a careful reading of the directions followed by a careful reading of the test items themselves.

True/False

Qualifiers: words that limit or restrict meaning

Not all true/false tests are the same. Some require you to simply identify which statements are true and which are false. Others might contain an additional task such as *correct any false answer to make it true*. It is only by reading the directions that you will know what to do.

As you read each statement in a true/false test, break the statement into parts and evaluate each. Each part has to be true for the entire statement to be true; that is, if one part of the statement is false, then the entire statement is false. As you read, underline any qualifiers in the statements. Statements with *all, always, never, no one, none, only,* or *everyone* usually tend to be false. Those with *generally, usually, probably, sometimes, often, most,* or *some* are oftentimes true.

Multiple Choice

This form of question tests your knowledge of facts. One type of question is in the form of an incomplete sentence; one of the choices given correctly completes the sentence. Another type might make a statement and ask a question. One of the choices answers the question. Generally, as you read each statement, try to answer or complete it before looking at the choices given. If one of the choices given matches your answer, select it.

Because directions for multiple-choice questions can vary widely, read the directions carefully before you begin reading the questions. The directions may ask you to *choose the answer that best completes the question*. In this case, you may find that more than one answer is correct. The best, most complete answer is the one that is true all of the time.

You might also be asked to *choose all answers that apply* or be given the choice *all of the above* or *none of the above*. In these situations, read each choice carefully. It sometimes helps to re-read the statement with each of the choices. Eliminate choices you know are incorrect. As with true/false questions, underline any qualifiers. Pay close attention to the use of negative words such as *not, never,* or *except* as used in expressions *which of the following is **not*** or *all of the following **except***. Failing to note the negative qualifiers will lead you to choose the opposite answer.

Matching

These questions require you to match an item in one column with another item in a second column. Read the directions to see whether an answer can be used more than once. Before you begin to match items, check to see if there are more answers than items; that is, determine if any answers will not be used. Begin by answering the easy items first and crossing out answers as you use them. This will let you know which answers are still available.

ACTIVITY 7

Did the Student Follow the Directions?

Below are the directions for questions on an objective test and one student's answers to them. Read both the test directions and the student's answers. Then decide whether the student followed the directions. The first one has been done for you.

A. Directions: Complete each statement by putting the number of the correct answer in the blank.

1. Multiple-choice questions test your knowledge of __facts__ .
   a. opinions   b. facts   c. ideas

2. Some multiple-choice questions contain qualifying words such as _____.
   a. always and never   b. a, an, the   c. verbs and nouns

3. As you read each statement in a multiple-choice question, you should __c__ before looking at the choices.
   a. not answer it   b. eliminate two answers   c. try to answer it

Your task: Decide whether each answer above follows the directions. Explain why it does or does not. *The first answer does not follow the directions because the student wrote the word in the blank instead of putting the number in the blank. The second answer does not follow the directions either because the student circled the answer instead of putting the number 1 in the blank. The third answer follows the directions because the student put the number 3 in the blank. The directions say to put the number in the blank.*

B. Directions: Read the following statements about study habits. If a statement is true, write *true* in the blank; if a statement is false, write *false* and then explain why it is false.

____T____ 1. Good students prepare for class by reading the assigned chapter and reviewing lecture notes.

__false__ 2. Every student who studies at least three hours for a test will pass it.

____F____ 3. Students who study only the night before a test will fail the test.

C is false because students who cram the night before a test often pass it. They just won't remember the information after the test is over because it is in their short-term memory.

Your task: Decide whether each answer above follows the directions. Explain why it does or does not. _____

_____

_____

   C. Directions: Read the statements about study habits. Then choose the best answer.

     1. An example of a good study habit is
       a. reviewing one's notes before class.
       b. reviewing one's notes after class.
       c. reviewing one's notes regularly.
     2. All of the following are examples of poor study habits except
       a. studying for a test at the last minute.
       b. not highlighting important details.
       c. not putting off doing one's homework.

Your task: Explain why each answer above is right or wrong. _____

_____

_____

   D. Directions: Match the phrases in Column A with the study habits or test-taking skills in Column B. Use all of the choices in Column B.

Column A	Column B
_b_ 1. studying for a test _e_ 2. during a test _a_ 3. after a test	a. study the answers you got wrong b. make a study schedule c. predict possible test questions d. skim the test before starting e. read the directions carefully

Your task: Decide whether the directions above were followed. Give reasons for your decision. _____

_____

_____

Other Types of Test Questions

While true/false, multiple choice, and matching are common test formats, they are not the only ones you will encounter in your classes. Test formats that require you to provide the answers rather than select an answer from those provided are also common. Fill-in-the-blank, short answer, and essay questions require you to demonstrate your knowledge of a particular topic.

Fill-in-the-blank

These types of questions are commonly found on language tests. Read the directions to find out if there is one word for each blank or if answers can contain multiple words. Is there a word bank, a list of words to choose from? Can words be used more than once? Read each sentence to get an idea of the topic and to determine the grammatical structure that will fit: noun, verb, adjective, or adverb, for example. As you fill in the blanks, write down all of the answers that will fit. Then go back and choose the one that seems to fit the best.

Short Answer

These questions are similar to fill-in-the-blank in that they require you to supply the answer and often ask you to *define, list,* or *identify* terms. Do the directions require you to provide a word or a phrase or a complete sentence? Underline any key words in the question to help you focus on the answer. It is important to give as much information in your answer as you can, but it is also important to convey the information clearly. Use grammatical clues from the question to help you. What do the verbs ask you to do? Do the questions contain *wh-* words: *who, what, where, when, why?*

Essay

Although essay tests contain fewer questions than objective tests, they often have the same total point value. Thus, it is important to read and follow the directions and understand the test questions in order to get the most points possible. Underline the key elements in the directions. Are you required to answer all of the questions, or do you have a selection to choose from? Pay attention to the point value for each question; this will tell you the overall importance of the question on the exam. Plan to spend more time on a question worth 20 points than on one worth 5 points.

Within each essay question there are a number of tasks to be completed. Your first task is to determine the topic of the question, the topic you will write about. Read the question and try to state the topic in one or two words or a short phrase. Your second task is to determine how many requirements the question has—that is, how many parts need to be addressed. The answer lies in the verb and the *wh-* question words used in the question. Examples of verbs commonly used in essay questions include *analyze, compare, define, list, outline, state,* and *summarize.* (See Appendix 6 on page 292 for a list of terms, meanings, and examples). Examples of *wh-* question words are *who, what, why, when, where, which,* and *how.* Underline the topic and any *wh-* words in the question. For the prompt *Describe the different rhetorical styles used in academic writing and explain how each is used,* you would identify the topic as *rhetorical styles* and address the two parts of the question, indicated by the verb *describe* and by the verb + *wh-* word *explain how.*

Once you have studied the question and determined how many parts your answer will have, make a short outline. This will ensure that you answer each part of the question and earn the most points possible. Begin your answer by restating the topic of the question and providing a clue to the organization of your answer. For example, a response to the prompt *Describe the different rhetorical styles used in academic writing and explain how each is used,* might begin "There are eight different rhetorical styles used in academic writing: narration, definition, classification, process, argument, cause/effect, compare/contrast, and reaction." Be sure to use details and examples in your response to show your instructor you are knowledgeable about the subject.

> **Key elements:** the important parts of the directions that tell you what to do

Prompt: the question you respond to and/or directions you follow on an essay test

Did the Student Follow the Directions?

Below are the directions for test questions that require the student to provide an answer rather than to select one. Read both the test directions and the student's answers. Then complete your stated task, which includes deciding whether the answers are acceptable or whether the student followed the directions. The first one has been done for you.

A. Directions: Read the statements below. Fill in the blank or complete the sentence with the correct word or words from the word bank. Do not use a word/phrase more than once.

objective	subjective	true/false
multiple choice	essay exams	short answer tests

1. A _____ test is an example of a(n) objective test. (true/false)
2. Tests that require you to supply a written answer are called _____. (short answer tests)

Your task: First, underline the clues in the sentence that help determine the answer. Next, try to find at least two possible answers for each sentence. Finally, read the student's answers, which are given in parentheses above, and determine if they are acceptable or not. Explain why.

1. A true/false test is an <u>example of an objective test.</u> /A multiple-choice test is an <u>example of an objective test.</u>

2. Tests that require you to <u>supply a written answer</u> are called essay exams./Tests that require you to <u>supply a written answer</u> are called short answer tests.

   The student's answers are acceptable because the student did not use the same word or phrase more than once.

B. Directions: Read the study advice below. Fill in the blank or complete the sentence with the correct word or words from the word bank. Words can be used more than once.

counselor	advisor	classmate
tutor	writing center	tutoring center
study	prepare	pass

1. Students who need extra help with a subject should visit a(n) _____ on campus. (a tutor)
2. Study groups are a good way to _____ for class lectures and discussions. (prepare)
3. A tutor can help you _____ for a test. (prepare)

Your task: First, underline the clues in the sentence that help determine the answer. Next, try to find at least two possible answers for each sentence. Finally, read the student's answers, which are given in parentheses above, and determine if they are acceptable or not. Explain why. _____

_____

_____

C. Directions: Read and complete each statement below. Use your own words.

  1. The keys to doing well on a test are _____. (very important for your grades)
  2. An example of an objective test is _____. (easier than a subjective test)
  3. A subjective exam is defined as _____. (the opposite of an objective exam)

Your task: First, underline the key elements in each statement. Next, read the student's answers, which are given in parentheses above, and determine if they are acceptable or not. Explain why. _____

_____

_____

D. Directions: Read and answer two of the three essay questions below.
  1. Compare the types of questions found on objective and subjective tests.
  2. Summarize the strategies good test-takers use.
  3. List some of the ways students can increase their test scores.

Your task: First, underline the key elements in each statement. Next, read the beginning of the student's responses, which are given below, to each of the test questions. Then decide whether the directions were followed. Give reasons for your decision.

  a. Compare the types of questions found on objective and subjective tests.

  Objective tests contain questions that provide information and require the student to make a choice among possible answers. For example, a true/false test is objective. Subjective tests, on the other hand, require students to write out the answer. A short answer or fill-in-the-blank test is an example of a subjective test.

  b. Summarize the strategies good test-takers use.

  Good test-takers use the following strategies: skim the test, read the directions, answer the easy questions first, don't spend too much time on one question, answer questions worth the most points first, and go over the test before handing it in.

  c. List some of the ways students can increase their test scores.

  Students can increase their test scores in many ways. It is important to get good test scores in order to pass the class. In addition, students need to prepare for class and hand in all required assignments on time. In class, students should ask questions and sit near the front of the class. This will force them to pay attention.

Identifying Text Structure—*Introduction to Outlining*

Text structure: the pattern or way the writer organizes and presents information

Preparing for class and studying for tests involve using a variety of techniques. Many students, as they read a textbook chapter for the first time, highlight or underline the main points of the reading. They may also make margin notes in which they summarize key points or ideas. Later, as they study for a test, they need only re-read the marked text. Outlining or summarizing the chapter is another technique students use to become familiar with the material in their textbook. No matter which technique you choose, understanding the text structure of the material will aid you in remembering and reviewing information.

Text structures are the patterns of organization writers use to present their ideas. Common text structures include *definition, narration, comparison/contrast, cause/effect, process, problem/solution,* and *argumentation.* Recognizing these patterns while you read not only improves your comprehension of the material, but also aids you in outlining the material.

Outlining is a method of organizing information so that it is easy to read. An outline contains the title of the chapter, the headings and subheadings of the sections, the main idea of the paragraphs, and important details that support the main idea. Compare the format and the partial outline for Reading 1 below.

General Outline Format	Reading 1

Chapter Title
I. Section heading
  A. Subheading
    1. Paragraph main idea
      a. Supporting detail
      b. Supporting detail
    2. Paragraph main idea
      a. Supporting detail
      b. Supporting detail
    3. Paragraph main idea
  B. Subheading
    1. Paragraph main idea
    2. Paragraph main idea
II. Section heading
  A. Subheading
    1. Paragraph main idea
    2. Paragraph main idea
  B. Subheading
    1. Paragraph main idea
    2. Paragraph main idea
  C. Subheading
    1. Paragraph main idea
    2. Paragraph main idea
	Success in College
	I. Taking Objective Tests
	  A. Overview of Exam
	    1. Skim each part
	      a. easy vs. difficult
	      b. note point values
	      c. overlapping answers
	  B. Plan Approach
	    1. Read directions for entire test
	      a. plan approach
	      b. allocate time for each part
	    2. Start anywhere
	      a. recommend high point questions first
	      b. easy questions, then hard ones
	    3. General strategies
	      a. never leave blank answers
	      b. never change answers
	      c. check test before handing it in
	  C. Specific Strategies
	    1. True/false questions
	    2. Multiple-choice questions
	    3. Matching questions

After outlining a chapter section, take some time to review it. Try to determine the pattern of organization the writer has used to present the information. In the passage above, the writer has explained the process for taking objective tests. The information is given in time order; that is, the writer explains what to do before, during, and after the test.

ACTIVITY 9

Text Structure and Outlining

A. Study the following partial outlines and circle the pattern of organization each outline suggests.

>   1. Objective vs. Subjective Tests
>   I. Similarities
>   A. Knowledge
>   1. Any course content
>   2. Assess various levels of learning
>   B. Length of time
>   1. Design for any time period
>   II. Differences
>   A. Correcting
>   1. Objective tests
>   a. easy to correct
>   b. quick to correct

      2. Subjective tests

        a. difficult to correct

        b. require time to read

    B. Test questions

      1. Objective – more items

        a. true/false

        b. matching

        c. multiple choice

      2. Subjective – fewer items

        a. short answer

        b. fill in the blank

        c. essay

Pattern of organization: Cause/Effect   Definition   Compare/Contrast

2. Outlines

  I. Description

    A. Method of organizing information

      1. Main ideas

      2. Important details

    B. Types

      1. Formal

      2. Informal

  II. Uses

    A. Reading

      1. Textbooks

        a. understand chapter information

        b. study for tests

      2. Research

        a. summarize information

        b. use for presentations, papers

    B. Writing

      1. Essays

        a. plan main ideas

        b. list details

        c. organize in logical order

Pattern of organization: Narration   Cause/Effect   Definition

3. My First College Exam

  I. Class

    A. Western Civilization

      1. Dates and important events

      2. Causes and effects of wars

    B. Least favorite class

      1. Instructor

      2. Topic

  II. Feelings

    A. Studying for test

      1. Procrastinated

        a. started studying the night before

        b. watched TV while studying

        2. Worried
            a. couldn't remember dates
            b. didn't know what to expect on test
    B. Taking test
        1. Tired
            a. stayed up all night
            b. drank too much coffee—felt sick
            c. eyes were red and blurry
        2. Scared
            a. couldn't answer any essay questions
            b. guessed at true/false
            c. knew only a few multiple choice

Pattern of organization: Narration   Compare/Contrast   Process

B. Outline the short reading passages below on a separate piece of paper and circle the pattern of organization each passage follows.

1. Studying for an exam is not a difficult process to follow. It actually begins the first day of the semester, in your first class. You need to follow the syllabus, the outline of the class for the entire semester, that the instructor gives you. Read each assigned chapter before class and highlight the key points in each section of the chapter. Take notes during the class, and ask the instructor questions if there are concepts you do not understand.

   After each class, review your notes, making sure you understand everything you have written down. Go back to the textbook and compare the text to your notes. Check to see if you have missed any main points. Make an outline or write notes in the margin of the text to help you remember the information. This will help you later.

   Begin reviewing for the actual test about a week before the exam. Review your notes and the highlighted parts of the chapter. Summarize each section of the chapter in your own words. If you cannot summarize a section, re-read it until you understand it. Study the vocabulary and questions at the end of the chapter. Try to anticipate the kinds of questions the instructor will ask and write the answers to them.

   Do a final review the night before the exam. Quickly review your notes and the highlighted areas of the chapter again. Quiz yourself and study anything you have trouble with. Then, get a good night's sleep. The next day, eat a good breakfast and head for school. Walk into the classroom feeling confident and knowing you are well prepared.

Pattern of organization: Narration   Process   Definition

2. A syllabus is an outline of a course of study. It contains a wealth of information for the student and should be kept at hand during the entire semester. Although instructors have their own individual formats, most course syllabi include the same kinds of information. The following is some basic information found in a typical course syllabus.

   The course syllabus provides basic information about the class to the student. This information includes such things as the course title, the meeting times and location of the course, the instructor's name and contact information, and the instructor's office hours. It usually contains the title of any required textbook for the course as well.

Many syllabi include a general overview of the course as well as specific goals and objectives for the course. This section of the syllabus might also include the kinds of activities students will participate in: individual, small group, and large group activities. The syllabus will also include the requirements of the course: assignments, essays, research projects, presentations, and fieldwork are all examples of possible requirements.

Along with the requirements of the course, the instructor will state the grading policy. This includes how the students will be graded and the weights of individual components. For example, students may be graded on homework assignments, essays, exams, attendance, and participation. An instructor may assign weights of 10 percent to homework, 30 percent to essays, 30 percent to exams, 20 percent to presentations, and 10 percent to attendance and participation.

The syllabus also offers a schedule for the course. It may be divided into weeks or into individual class meetings. The schedule includes the topics to be discussed and the chapters or readings that relate to the topics. Page numbers are usually given for the chapters in the textbook, and titles of outside readings are provided. Dates of exams are also usually listed on the course syllabus.

Pattern of organization: Narration   Process   Definition

READING 2 ● On Your Own

In the first section of this chapter, you read about taking objective tests, reading and understanding test questions, and following directions. You practiced the skills and strategies of surveying, predicting, and summarizing with Reading 1. In this section you will practice these same skills with a new reading. You will also practice using context to guess the meaning of unfamiliar words.

Get Ready to Read

My Test-taking Strategies

Read the following test-taking strategies and put an X in front of the ones that you use. Discuss your answers with a partner.

_____ 1. I look over the entire exam before I start answering questions.

_____ 2. I underline each part of the test question that is important.

_____ 3. I write a short outline for each question before I answer it.

_____ 4. I set aside a specific amount of time for answering each question or section.

_____ 5. I look over the entire test before I hand it in.

Survey and Predict

A. Using the following steps, survey Reading 2 and predict what information you will find.

    1. Read the title.

    2. Read the first paragraph.

    3. Read the headings.

    4. Look for any graphic or visual aids in the reading.

    5. Look for key terms in bold.

    6. Read the last paragraph.

B. Write your prediction here: _____

_____

C. Now read the passage to see if your prediction is correct. Try to read as quickly as you can. Do not stop to look up words in your dictionary.

Reading 2

Taking Subjective Tests

Subjective exams, which include **short answer** and **essay questions**, require you to write out an answer. If given a choice, many students would opt for objective over subjective exams. Students mistakenly believe that because "the answers are there," objective tests are easier. In fact, subjective tests—essay exams—offer you more opportunity to demonstrate to the instructor what you know rather than what you don't know. Because the number of essay questions an instructor can include on a test is limited, questions usually cover only the major aspects of the chapter or topic. This gives you the advantage of anticipating what will be included on the exam. As with objective exams, taking short answer or essay exams requires an organized approach, including understanding the types of questions commonly asked.

Overview of Exam

Once you have the exam, take time to review it. Read the directions carefully to determine whether you need to answer all of the essay questions or only a certain number (three out of five, for example). In the latter case, skim all of the questions and mark the ones you are confident about answering. If the test includes both short answer and essay questions, note the point values for each section, and focus on the questions that offer the most points.

Strategies

As you skim each question, underline the topic and the requirement(s) for each. A short answer question or prompt often requires only a definition and an example or a simple list of items. *Name three recurring themes/images in Salvador Dalí's paintings* is an example of a short answer prompt. In contrast, an essay question often has more than one requirement. Since each requirement contributes to the total points, it is crucial to address and answer all of the requirements. Consider the following essay prompt: *Artist Salvador Dalí is quoted as saying, "You have to systematically create confusion; it sets creativity free. Everything that is contradictory creates life." Explain what Dalí meant by this statement, and support your explanation with examples from at least two of the artist's works.* You are given two tasks: (1) explain Dalí's quote and (2) use examples from his art to support your explanation. Addressing only one of the tasks would result in the loss of half of the points for this question! A good strategy is to underline each task in the question, thus lessening your chance of responding to only a part of the question and receiving only partial points.

Plan Approach

Once you have familiarized yourself with the test and have chosen the questions you will answer, plan your approach. First, determine how much time you have for each question. Divide your time among the number of questions you must answer and tasks you must address; give yourself more time to answer the questions that have the most point values. In general, essay questions will require longer answers, so allow more time for essay questions than for short answer types.

Next, carefully read each question again to understand what information a complete answer requires. Be familiar with the key words generally used in essay questions. If, for example, you are asked to **analyze** a historical event or a character in a story, you are being asked to write about the individual parts of the event or character and to show how they relate to the entire event or character. If you are asked to **define** a subject or a term, you must offer a complete meaning and include an example of its use. If you are asked to trace the events that led up to something, you are expected to give a step-by-step explanation of the process that led to the event.

Outline Answers

Once you have understood the question and underlined the requirements, write a short outline for each question you will answer. Jot down the key words and main ideas that you will use in your response. This strategy will aid you in writing your response more quickly. In addition, if you run out of time, your instructor may award partial points for the information in your outline. Some test-takers **outline** the answer to every question on the test and then go back and write responses to the questions for which they have the most or the strongest information.

After you outline your responses, begin writing your answers. Follow your outline and write clear, complete sentences for each main point in the outline. Be sure your answers address the question. Include definitions that help demonstrate your knowledge of the subject. Write as much as you can to answer the question and to get the full point value. If you run out of the time you have allotted for the question or can't recall any more information, go on to the next question. You can always return to a question later. Do not **"pad"** your answers with useless information. In response to the Salvador Dalí question above, stating *Salvador Dalí was a very famous painter who is known for his many colorful and surreal paintings* is an example of "padding" an answer—adding information about the topic that is irrelevant to or does not answer the question.

Final Review

Once you have finished writing responses to all of the questions, review the exam. Make sure you have followed the directions and answered the required number of questions. Make sure you have responded to each requirement in the question. Re-read your answers: Do they answer the question? Proofread each answer and correct any grammatical, spelling, or punctuation errors. Turn in your exam and leave the room, knowing that you have taken the best approach to answering each essay or short answer question on the exam.

Key Concept Words

analyze – (v.) to show how the parts relate to the whole
define – (v.) to provide the meaning for
essay questions – (n.) questions that require the test-taker to respond with a written answer of several sentences or paragraphs
outline – (v.) to list the main points or main ideas
pad – (v.) to include unrelated or unnecessary information
short answer questions – (n.) questions that require the test-taker to respond with a written answer, often a definition or explanation and example and usually a few sentences in length

Glossed Words

latter – (adj.) last, later; **led** – (v.) preceded or went before, caused; **lessening** – (n.) reducing or diminishing; **opt** – (v.) to choose or select; **proofread** – (v.) to look for and correct mistakes; **quote** – (n.) a statement of someone's words; **recurring** – (adj.) happening regularly, again and again

Summarizing

Share What You Read

Use two or three sentences to tell your partner what you thought the reading was about. Then listen to your partner's sentences. If you disagree, go back and find support for your summary. Write your summary statement below.

Summary: _____

_____

Check Your Comprehension

Read each statement and circle *T* if it is *true* or *F* if it is *false*. Change a false statement to make it true.

T / F   1. Essay exams are examples of subjective tests.

T / F   2. A subjective test will have more questions than an objective test.

T / F   3. Subjective tests sometimes offer the test-taker a choice of questions to answer.

T / F   4. All subjective exams have multiple requirements or tasks for each question on the exam.

T / F   5. A good strategy is to divide your time among the number of questions and the number of tasks for each question.

T / F   6. Being familiar with key words used in essay questions will help improve your score.

T / F   7. Writing a short outline for each question will slow down your response time.

T / F   8. Grammar, spelling, and punctuation errors will never lower your score if your answer is correct.

T / F   9. To get the full point value for a question, write as much as you can to answer the question.

T / F   10. Review your exam before handing it in and check to see that you have followed directions.

Academic Word List

Scan and Define

A. Look at the ten words listed below. Scan the reading and underline the words from the list. Write the definitions for the words you know. Do not use a dictionary.

1. aid (v.) <u>to help or assist</u>

2. aspect _____

3. contradictory _____

4. contribute _____

5. crucial _____

6. error _____

7. irrelevant _____

8. respond _____

9. task _____

10. trace (v.) _____

B. Share your definitions with a partner and then with the rest of your classmates. As a group, try to complete the definitions for all ten words. Use a dictionary to check the definitions if you are unsure about them. Then complete the vocabulary activity.

Vocabulary Challenge

A. Circle the word that does not belong. The first one has been done for you. The words in bold are from the Academic Word List above.

1. **aspect**	feature	(appearance)	part
2. **contribute**	add	give	pay
3. **crucial**	important	decisive	difficult
4. **irrelevant**	unrelated	pertinent	extraneous
5. **tasks**	chores	assignments	hobbies
6. **trace**	explain	follow	track
7. **aid**	assist	favor	serve
8. **error**	problem	mistake	inaccuracy

B. Circle the word that is closest in meaning to the boldfaced word in the sentences below. The first one has been done for you.

1. Dalí stated, "You have to create confusion; it sets creativity free. Everything that is **contradictory** creates life."

   a. opposite   (b. contrary)   c. deniable

2. Make sure you have **responded** to each requirement in the question.
   a. answered   b. replied   c. reacted

3. Essay test questions usually cover only the major **aspects** of the chapter or topic.
   a. interpretations   b. viewpoints   c. features

4. Since each requirement in an essay question **contributes** to the total points, reading the question carefully is a basic, common-sense strategy to follow.
   a. gives   b. donates   c. provides

5. In addition, since each requirement in an essay question contributes to the total points, it is **crucial** to answer all of the requirements.
   a. severe   b. important   c. significant

6. You are given two **tasks:** (1) explain Dalí's quote and (2) use examples from his art to support your explanation.
   a. chores   b. jobs   c. assignments

Using Context to Guess Meaning—*Contrast*

When you read for comprehension, your goal is to understand the main idea and the major points of the passage. Sometimes, as you read, you come across words that are unfamiliar to you. When this happens, you can do one of three things: consult a dictionary, skip over the word, or guess its meaning.

Consulting the dictionary multiple times while you are reading takes time and disrupts your concentration. Skipping over an unfamiliar word usually will not affect your overall comprehension, but if the word is used several times in the reading, it is a key word, and you need to find out what it means. Guessing the meaning of a word from the context in which it is used is a third option. Although some meanings are easier to guess than others, there are strategies that you can learn to use. Using these strategies successfully will save you time and improve your language and reading skills.

Read the sentence and explanation below to see how a contrast clue helps define the word *crucial.*

The kind of pencil you use to take an exam is unimportant; on the other hand, following directions on an exam is <u>crucial</u>.

The sentence compares a pencil to following directions in the context of taking an exam. The phrase **on the other hand** signals a contrast between the two. Since the kind of pencil used is *unimportant,* following directions—in contrast—must be important. *Crucial,* then, means important.

 ACTIVITY 16   *Guess Meaning from Context*

Read the sentences below. Use the contrast clues to determine the meaning of the words in bold. On the line, write the definition of the word. Share your definition with a partner and explain how you guessed the meaning.

1. On my history exam, first I had to write a general explanation of the causes of World War I, but then later in the same exam, I had to **trace** the events that led up to World War II.

   trace = _____

2. At first, the student had a hard time answering the test question because all four of the answers seemed important. However, upon reading the question a second time, she found that three of the answers contained information that was, in fact, **irrelevant** to the question.

    irrelevant = _____

3. A research paper requires you to write a long, well-composed, detailed outline. Because exams have time limits, an outline for an essay test question, in contrast, requires you to just **jot** down key words and main ideas before you begin to write.

    jot = _____

4. The scheduled class period was three hours, yet the professor **allotted** students only one hour for the exam.

    allotted = _____

5. Unlike my roommate, who had **recurring** problems passing essay exams last semester, I only had a problem passing my essay exams once.

    recurring = _____

6. The test was so unfair! Although three of the essay questions each had one **task** and were worth 25 points each, another question had three **tasks** and was worth only 6 points. I had to write just as much to get only about a fourth of the points!

    task = _____

WRITING 1A ● Skills and Strategies

In this section, you will learn some skills and strategies associated with the writing process. It includes the grammar of conditional sentences, which is one of the grammatical structures used in the readings. In this section, you will also practice the different steps in responding to essay questions: outlining, revising, editing, and proofreading.

The Grammar of Conditionals

A conditional sentence expresses the relationship between two sets of circumstances: a condition and an outcome. While most conditionals begin with the *if*-clause, it is also possible to begin with the outcome. When the conditional sentence begins with the outcome, do not use a comma to separate the two clauses. Study the types of conditionals in the chart on the following page.

Type of Conditional	*If*-clause (condition)	Outcome
1. factual in the present or past	If I score 70 on a test,	I pass it.
	If I got good grades,	my parents rewarded me.
2. future plans or possibilities	If I score 90 on this exam,	I will celebrate!
	If I study for the test,	I should/might pass it.
3. present hypothetical (the condition is unlikely or almost impossible)	If I knew the answer,	I would tell you.
	If I were the teacher,	I would make the exam easy.
4. past hypothetical (the condition is definitely impossible)	If I had passed the test,	I would have passed the course.

Note the form of the verb in each conditional:

If-clause	Outcome
1. simple present	simple present
simple past	simple past
2. simple present	will + verb
simple present	should/may/might/can + verb
3. simple past*	would/could + verb
4. past perfect	would/could + have + past participle

*The situation remains in the present despite the use of a past tense form. Note that the form of the verb *to be* in this conditional uses *were. Were* is used for all persons: If I were, If you were, If he were, If it were, etc.

ACTIVITY *Recognize Conditionals*

A. Read the conditional sentences and underline the verb forms in each clause. Then use the charts above to help you identify which of the four conditionals the sentence represents. Discuss your answers with a partner.

   1. If different parts of the test cover the same material or address the same topic, you may find the answer to one question in another part of the test.

   2. If any part of the statement is false, then the answer is false.

   3. If you leave an answer blank, it will be wrong.

   4. If they had a choice, many students would opt for objective over subjective exams.

   5. If you follow the directions, you will do well.

B. Look back at Readings 1 and 2 and find three conditional sentences. Write them below.

   1. _____

   2. _____

   3. _____

Use Conditionals

A. Fill in the blanks with the correct form of the verb in parentheses to form conditional sentences. If you need extra help, the words in parentheses at the end of the sentence indicate the type of conditional it is (the number refers to the number in the first chart on the previous page) and the tense. Refer to the charts above for information on each type.

1. If you (be) _____ unsure of a term, (read) _____ the statement or definition first and then (try) _____ to define it with one of the terms. (1st / present)

2. If the question (say) _____ to trace the events that led up to something, I (give) _____ a step-by-step explanation of the process that led to the event. (1st / past)

3. If I (run, negative) _____ out of time, I (get) _____ a much better score than I did. (4th / past)

4. If he (misread) _____ the directions for the last section, he (fail) _____ the entire exam. (3rd / present)

5. If you (study) _____ for the exam and (follow) _____ the directions, your score (be) _____ more than enough to pass. (2nd / future)

B. Write four conditional sentences of your own. They can be about any topic.

1. _____

2. _____

3. _____

4. _____

Sentence Essentials

Dependent and Independent Clauses

Clause: a group of words containing a subject and a verb

All sentences are constructed from clauses: groups of words containing a subject and a verb. An independent clause contains a complete idea and can stand alone as a simple sentence. A dependent clause, however, does not contain a complete idea and must be attached to an independent clause.

Independent Clause	Dependent Clause
Specific strategies exist for taking tests.	which will help you get a good grade
You should look over the exam carefully.	once you receive it
Don't be in a hurry to leave the room!	when you finish the test

Identify Dependent and Independent Clauses

Read the following statements. If the statement is a complete sentence (an independent clause), put *I* in the blank. If the statement is an incomplete sentence or a dependent clause, put *D* in the blank.

_____ 1. Never leave a test answer blank.

_____ 2. First, read the directions for the entire test.

_____ 3. After you have skimmed the test.

_____ 4. If you are asked to analyze a historical event.

_____ 5. Carefully read each question on the exam.

_____ 6. What you know rather than what you don't know.

_____ 7. Subjective exams require you to write out an answer.

Simple Sentences and Compound Sentences

Simple sentences consist of one independent clause. For example:

<u>Subjective exams</u> <u>include</u> short answer and essay questions.

    Subject   Verb   (complement)

It is possible to have more than one independent clause in a sentence. Combining two or more independent clauses creates a compound sentence.

There are three ways to combine independent clauses to create a compound sentence.

1. Comma + Coordinating Conjunction

One way to build a compound sentence is to join the clauses with a comma and coordinating conjunction. The coordinating conjunctions are *for, and, nor, but, or, yet,* and *so.*

Note: An easy way to remember the coordinating conjunctions is with the acronym *fanboys: f* stands for *for; **a*** stands for *and; **n*** is for *nor; **b*** is for *but; **o*** is for *or; **y*** is for *yet; **s*** is for *so.*

Examples:

    Most students are intimidated by essay exams. There are strategies to become a better test-taker.

    Most students are intimidated by essay exams, but there are strategies to become a better test-taker.

    Some students do not read the directions carefully. They do not follow the directions.

    Some students do not read the directions carefully, nor do they follow them.

2. Semicolon + Conjunctive Adverb + Comma

Compound sentences can also be created using conjunctive adverbs. A semicolon (;) follows the first independent clause, and a comma follows the conjunctive adverb.

Example:

    Most students are intimidated by essay exams; however, there are strategies to become a better test-taker.

Coordinating conjunctions and conjunctive adverbs show the relationship between clauses. The following chart shows the coordinating conjunctions and conjunctive adverbs that share similar meanings.

Coordinating Conjunction	Use and Meaning	Conjunctive Adverb*
and	introduces another idea or more information	also, besides, furthermore, moreover
or	introduces an alternative	otherwise
so	introduces a result	accordingly, consequently, hence, therefore, thus
but *yet*	introduces contrast	however, instead, nevertheless, nonetheless, on the other hand
for	introduces reason	—
nor	introduces another negative idea	—

*Sometimes referred to as transitions or connectors.

3. Semicolon

Two independent clauses can also be joined by a semicolon (;) to make a compound sentence. The two clauses must be related in their topic and meaning.

Example:

> Divide your time among the number of questions you must answer; give yourself more time for questions with the most point values.

Identify Sentence Type

Read the following sentences. If the sentence is a simple sentence, put *S* in the blank. If the sentence is a compound sentence, put *C* in the blank. Then underline the subject(s) and circle the verb(s) in each sentence.

_____ 1. You may choose to start at the beginning and work your way straight through to the end.

_____ 2. Objective exams and subjective exams are commonly used to test content knowledge.

_____ 3. Some students prefer to take objective exams, but others prefer to take subjective exams.

_____ 4. You may find the answer to a question in another part of the test or another question in the same section.

_____ 5. You may decide to answer the easy questions first, or you may choose to answer the hard ones first.

_____ 6. Taking short answer or essay exams requires an organized approach.

_____ 7. You should read the directions for each section carefully, for the directions may change from one section to another.

Complete the Sentence

Read the beginning of each sentence. Then complete the sentence using the coordinating conjunction in parentheses and your own words. Be sure to use correct punctuation. The first one has been done for you.

1. Read each multiple-choice question (and) *Read each multiple-choice question, and try to answer it without looking at the choices given.*

2. Most students prefer to take objective tests (but) _____

_____

3. Some students study a lot for tests (yet) _____

_____

4. It's important to read and follow the directions (or) _____

_____

5. A few students never take notes in class (nor) _____

_____

6. I've studied for the test and feel confident (so) _____

_____

 ACTIVITY 22

Choose the Conjunction

Read the two sentences and fill in the correct coordinating conjunction. Sometimes more than one answer is possible. The first one has been done for you.

1. Your instructor may decide to give you objective exams, __*or*__ you may be given subjective exams.

2. Students often think objective exams are easier than subjective ones, _____ that is not always true.

3. Directions are not always the same, _____ you need to read them every time you take a test.

4. For essay tests, underline the topic of each question, _____ note the requirements for each question, too.

5. Plan your time well, _____ you want to be able to review your test before you hand it in.

6. The directions are an integral part of every test, _____ many students don't bother to read them.

7. You should not change answers on a test without a good reason, _____ should you leave a test answer blank unless there is a penalty for wrong answers.

ACTIVITY 23

Rewrite the Sentence

Read the compound sentences below and rewrite them using the coordinating conjunction, conjunctive adverb, and/or punctuation given. The first one has been done for you.

1. Objective exams include true/false and multiple-choice questions; subjective exams include short answer and essays.

   on the other hand <u>*Objective exams include true/false and multiple-choice questions;*</u>
   <u>*on the other hand, subjective exams include short answer and essays.*</u>

2. Read the directions for each part of the exam carefully, or you may end up losing points for not following directions.

   otherwise – _____

   _____

3. Underlining phrases in test questions helps you focus your attention, and it may also help you recall the correct answer.

   moreover – _____

   _____

   ; — _____

   _____

4. Handing in your test eliminates any opportunity to go back and review it; therefore, be sure you have answered every question and followed all the directions on the test.

   so – _____

   _____

   ; — _____

   _____

5. Most students believe they can score higher on objective tests than on subjective ones; subjective tests actually offer students more opportunity to demonstrate their knowledge.

   yet – _____

   _____

   nevertheless – _____

   _____

6. Essay questions will require relatively long answers; allow more time for essay questions than for short-answer questions.

   consequently – _____

   _____

   so – _____

   _____

Making the Connection

Reading and writing are connected in several ways. Both are active processes: reading requires you to interact with the text in order to understand the main idea and evaluate the supporting details; writing requires you to state your main idea clearly and to offer examples, facts, and other support for the main idea. Both skills improve with practice, and what you learn about one skill will also help you understand the other. The better your skills are, the better you will be able to meet everyday tasks which require you to read and write.

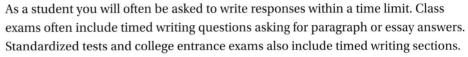

Get Ready to Write

Timed Writing

As a student you will often be asked to write responses within a time limit. Class exams often include timed writing questions asking for paragraph or essay answers. Standardized tests and college entrance exams also include timed writing sections.

Many students feel very intimidated by timed writing questions. There are, however, ways to improve your skills in timed writing. The five-step approach to answering timed-writing questions outlined below involves reading the question, managing your time, planning your writing, writing, and editing/proofreading.

Step 1: Read the Question

Read the question very carefully. Make sure you understand what the question requires you to do. Although this first step sounds obvious, misreading the question is the most common mistake made in timed writing. Look for key words in the questions that give you instructions on how to write your answer. Then underline those words. Examples of key words are *explain, discuss, analyze,* and *summarize.* (See Appendix 6 on page 292 for a list of terms, meanings, and examples.)

Define Key Words

Below are key words commonly found in exam questions. Work with a partner to match the key words with their uses. Write the letter of the correct description on the line.

Key Word—Understanding   **Description**

_____ 1. agree or disagree   a. another word for disagree

_____ 2. analyze   b. defend a point of view with proof (facts, examples)

_____ 3. argue   c. take one position and defend it throughout the essay; do not address both positions

_____ 4. challenge   d. place the ideas into categories

_____ 5. classify   e. look at different parts of an idea and discuss what it means or why it is important

Key Word—Relationships   **Description**

_____ 6. compare   a. write about the strengths and weaknesses of an argument

_____ 7. contrast   b. write about the similarities between two things or ideas

_____ 8. critique   c. explain what something means and give examples

_____ 9. debate   d. write about the differences between two things or ideas

_____ 10. define   e. take one position and defend it throughout the essay; address both positions of the argument/issue

Key Word—Interpret	Description
_____ 11. evaluate	a. point out an idea; discuss it and what it is called
_____ 12. identify	b. explain the arguments for and against a subject; state which arguments are stronger
_____ 13. justify	c. show how a theory or principle works in a specific situation
_____ 14. apply	d. write what the main points of the subject or topic
_____ 15. summarize	e. give reasons or examples that support a situation or event

The key words listed above can be divided into three categories of tasks that test-takers perform: prove understanding, show relationships, and interpret. Each category is explained below.

Prove Understanding

The most basic task in timed writing is to demonstrate that you have a solid understanding of the topics presented in course lectures and/or readings. Your answer relays information from your memory about the subject. With this type of task, you do not offer an opinion or argument in your answer unless specifically asked to do so. The sample questions below come from actual textbooks.

Name the five senses and rank them in descending order of their capacity to provide information about our environment.

What is the four-field approach to the discipline of anthropology?

Show Relationships

Some key words ask you to show how things are or are not connected. Again, these questions do not necessarily ask for an opinion. Your answers should be based on information presented in class and in class readings. The sample questions below require answers that show relationships.

How does the status of women in eighteenth-century South Carolina relate to that of mid-nineteenth-century America as described in the essay "Sarah Grimké Argues for Gender Equality"?

Compare and contrast the rational choice theory and the ecocultural theory.

Interpret

The last category of tasks asks you to express your own ideas about a subject. Your opinion must be supported by evidence such as examples or definitions from the course lectures, readings, or research. Interpretation questions are common on standardized tests. In a standardized test, the focus is on the test-taker's writing abilities rather than on a particular subject matter. The sample questions below might appear on a standardized test.

Evaluate the following statement by Martin Luther King, Jr.: "He who passively accepts evil is as much involved in it as he who helps to perpetuate it."

Some educators believe that high school should be extended to a fifth year to better prepare students for the increasing demands of colleges and employers. Other educators disagree, saying students would lose interest in school and drop out. Which view do you support and why?

Identify the Key Words

Read each statement carefully. Underline the key words that state the task the test-taker has to perform.

1. Briefly summarize the role of gravity in high and low tides.

2. Describe the concepts of Newton's Laws and provide examples that demonstrate how each law applies to an object and its resultant state of motion.

3. Using examples, explain the difference between a dialect and an accent.

4. Cultural universals are traits that all cultures have in common although they are not always obvious. List five cultural universals and offer an example that demonstrates a contrasting approach to the same cultural feature.

5. Define the political terms *conservatism* and *liberalism* and explain how their meanings have changed over the past century.

6. Describe the stages of cultural shock that people experience after moving to a new country or becoming part of an unfamiliar culture.

7. Identify the causes of the American counterculture movement of the 1960s.

8. Contrast the causes for the increase in the rate of diabetes among children with those for the increase in adults.

9. Analyze the problems developing countries experience as they use their natural resources to further their economic development.

10. Defend the use of wiretapping by agencies of state and federal governments.

Step 2: Manage Your Time

In timed writing, your time should be divided among the different stages of writing: planning, writing, and editing. For example, for a one-hour essay, spend the first fifteen to twenty minutes planning, the next thirty minutes writing, and the last ten to fifteen minutes proofreading your work. On a test with multiple writing questions, plan to spend more time on questions worth more points.

You can practice writing under a time limit by using questions in your textbook. At the end of each chapter, the author often provides questions for further thought or discussion. Select a question and set your watch alarm or other timer for ten or fifteen minutes; then answer the question. Publishers of standardized tests also publish preparation manuals that contain sample questions. Again, set a timer and practice planning, writing, and editing your answer within the allotted time.

Step 3: Plan Your Writing

After reading the question, do not immediately begin writing your answer. Just as it is important to plan assigned essays and paragraphs, it is also necessary to plan when writing under the pressure of time. Many students think skipping this step saves more time for actual writing. This is a mistake. Planning will actually help you write more effectively and finish faster. Choose the planning strategy that you are most comfortable with: outlining, clustering, or listing.

Outline

An outline provides the clearest structure. Based on the task the question presents, begin with a topic sentence for a paragraph, or a thesis statement for an essay answer. Then list the ideas that support your thesis. Under each of these ideas, list details and examples. Your outline can be as formal or informal as you choose.

Outline _the theories about the universe of Ptolemy, Copernicus, and Kepler._

Ptolemy
     Earth → center of the universe—geocentric
     Moon, Mercury Venus, the Sun, Mars, Saturn orbited around Earth
     Planet orbits were circular

Copernicus
     Sun → center of universe—heliocentric
     Mercury, Venus, Earth, Mars, Jupiter, Saturn orbited around Sun—Moon did not.
     Circular orbits
     Able to calculate the scale of the universe

Kepler
     Heliocentric
     Planets' orbits are elliptical, not circular
     Planets move at varying speeds
     Planets closest to Sun move the fastest

Cluster

With this method you can put the topic in the center of the page and then branch out with your supporting ideas and details.

Describe the classifications of vertebrates in the Animal Kingdom.

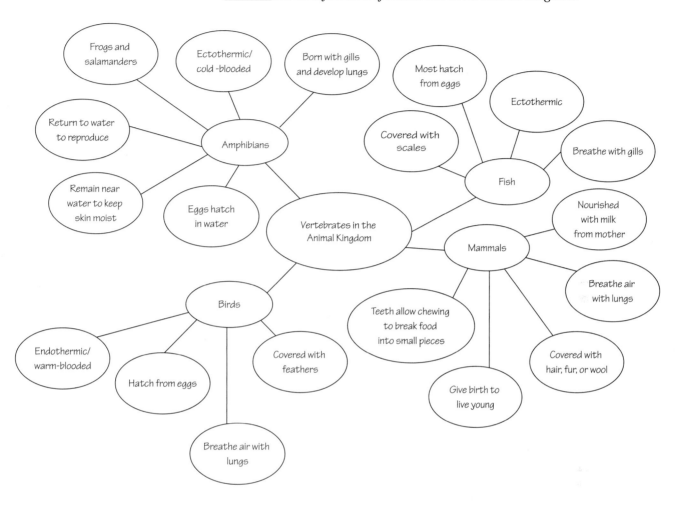

List

Lists have less structure than outlines but can still be helpful. The lists can be divided, for example, for a compare/contrast or cause/effect essay.

Contrast the characteristics of terrestrial and Jovian planets.

Terrestrial	Jovian
solid, rocky	gaseous
small diameter	large diameter
closer to the Sun	far from Sun
high-temperature environment	low-temperature environment
close together	widely separated

Plan Written Responses

Read each test question and underline the key words. Show how you would plan your answer using the outline, cluster, or list method on a separate piece of paper.

1. List and explain some examples of everyday uses of the standard measurements of length, mass, and time.

2. Describe a time when you were cheated by someone who sold you something. How did you feel about it then? How do you feel about it now?

3. Discuss the extent to which you agree or disagree with the following statement: *Competitive sports encourage students to do whatever is necessary to win, including cheating and risking their health.* Use reasons and examples from your experience and class readings to support your view.

4. There are Internet sites that offer students essays, research papers, or even doctoral dissertations for a fee. Do you think such businesses should be allowed to exist? What kind of impact, if any, would such businesses have on education? What, if anything, should happen to students who are found to have used such a service?

5. Some people think that a college education should be available to all citizens. Others think that only the best students should receive this opportunity. Which viewpoint do you agree with? Provide support your answer.

Step 4: Write Your Response

When writing under a time limit, your goal is to be clear and concise. Perfection is not expected. Professors and graders will not deduct points when they see words or sentences scratched out as long as the remaining writing is effective.

Remember the purpose of your exam: to demonstrate what you have learned. While in some classes the writing itself may not be graded, using good writing skills is important if you want to show your professor evidence of your knowledge about a topic. Professors will not overlook major gaps in information, so a poorly structured essay or paragraph will not help you prove you know the answer.

Standardized exam questions focus less on a student's knowledge of a particular topic and more on the test-taker's ability to write effectively under a time limit. Graders or raters want to see evidence of logical thinking and the basic elements of good writing.

Timed writings should have the same elements as other types of writing: an introduction with a topic sentence for a paragraph or thesis statement for an essay, a body containing supporting information, and a conclusion.

- **Introduction**—The introduction in a timed essay should be brief and direct. It should contain a topic sentence. Do not allow yourself to become stuck on an introduction. If necessary, skip to writing the essay body and go back to the introduction later to finish it.

- **Body**—The body of a short essay answer contains supporting sentences and details. In a longer essay answer, the body should contain one or more paragraphs that support your thesis. Each paragraph should include a topic sentence and supporting details such as facts or explanations.

- **Conclusion**—In timed writing, your conclusion can be less formal than in most essays. The conclusion can be a summary of the main points and a restatement of the thesis. If time permits, develop the conclusion further.

Step 5: Editing and Proofreading

Spend the last minutes of your time examining your work. Look for major errors in the content or structure first. Then look for spelling and grammatical errors. Finally, if there is still time, go back and improve the introduction and/or the conclusion. Do not recopy the entire essay.

How Did They Do That?

Although writers may take different approaches to the writing process, most writers follow a common sequence. They introduce their main idea or topic sentence first, offer details to support the main idea next, and end with a concluding statement.

Following a specific sequence is important in timed writing because you have a limited amount of time in which to demonstrate your ability to express yourself clearly and concisely. In addition, addressing a short answer or essay question on a class exam requires you to demonstrate your knowledge of a subject or support an opinion, again within a limited amount of time. Approaching timed writing as a series of steps in a process will help you approach timed writing with confidence and will improve your timed-writing responses.

Follow the Steps

Refer to the examples below as you follow the steps the writer took to complete a short answer question and an essay question.

Test Questions

Short answer: *Explain what a multiple-choice question is and outline an effective approach to answering such a question on an exam. (8 pts.)*

Essay: *Many students prefer to take objective tests. What are the advantages and disadvantages of taking objective tests? (20 pts.)*

Short Answer Question

Step 1. Read the question. Look for key words and underline them. Decide what I am being asked to do.

<u>Explain</u> *what a multiple-choice question is and* <u>outline</u> *an effective approach to answering such a question on an exam.*

Key words are *explain* and *outline*. I need to define what a multiple-choice question is and then list the steps to take to answer this kind of question. I am being asked to prove I understand how to answer multiple-choice questions.

Step 2. Manage my time. Plan, write, and edit.

Plan: 1–2 minutes

Write: 3–6 minutes

Edit: 1–2 minutes

Total: 5–10 minutes

Step 3. Plan. List my ideas.

Define multiple choice

- can be incomplete sentence and answer completes it (2)
- tests knowledge of facts (1)
- can be a statement and asks a question—the choice answers the question (3)

Approach

- try to answer the question before reading the choices; if one choice matches answer, pick that one (4)
- read directions carefully—sometimes choose one answer, sometimes choose all that apply, sometimes none of the above (1)
- best answer is one that is true all of the time (6)
- eliminate wrong answers (5)
- underline qualifiers: not, never, always, etc. (2)
- watch out for words like except, not (3)

Step 4. Write. Start with topic. Use logical order. (*The test-taker went back to the list in Step 3 and numbered ideas in order.*) End with a conclusion.

　　A multiple-choice question is one that tests a person's knowledge of facts. Multiple-choice questions can be an incomplete sentence, and the answer will complete it. It can also be a statement and asks a question. The choice answers the question. An effective approach to answering multiple-choice questions includes (1) reading the directions carefully to find out whether you need to choose one answer or all that apply; (2) underlining the qualifiers such as not, never, always, etc.; (3) watching out for words such as *except* or *not* in the question; (4) trying to answer the question before reading the choices and then picking the choice that matches your answer; (5) eliminating wrong answers; and (6) the best answer is one that is true all the time. This is the approach to take.

Step 5. Edit and proofread. Check for content and structure first. Check spelling and grammar second. (*The test-taker's ideas for changes are listed below.*)

- ☐ content—everything is okay; the answer tells what a multiple-choice question is and gives the steps in the approach
- ☐ structure—the steps in the approach are all in one sentence, which is too long. Break into six separate steps and use transitions. (first, second, next, finally)
- ☐ structure—the last sentence isn't a very good concluding sentence. Change it to "This is the best approach to taking a multiple-choice test."

☐ spelling—everything is okay

☐ grammar—everything looks okay. Maybe change *Multiple-choice questions* in the second sentence to *A multiple-choice question* because *an incomplete sentence* follows it and that's singular.

Essay Question

Step 1. Read the question. Look for key words and underline them. Decide what I am being asked to do.

Many students prefer to take objective tests. What are the <u>advantages and disadvantages</u> of taking <u>objective tests</u>?

Key words are advantages and disadvantages. I need to list the good and bad points of objective tests. I am being asked to prove that I understand what objective tests are (multiple choice, true/false, etc.). I am also being asked to interpret objective tests as good/bad by comparing their different points.

Step 2. Manage my time. Plan, write, and edit.

Plan: 3–4 minutes

Write: 10–13 minutes

Edit: 2–3 minutes

Total: 15–20 minutes

Step 3. Plan. List my ideas.

<u>Advantages</u>

- the answer is there for you (1)
- you can sometimes find clues to the answer in another question (4)
- in true/false, any part of the statement that is false makes whole thing false (3)
- can eliminate incorrect choices (5)
- don't have to worry about spelling and grammar (6)
- techniques for taking them (2)
- everyone has the same chance of passing—the instructor can't be biased (7)

<u>Disadvantages</u>

- can be really long (1)
- most often tests your knowledge of facts, so if you don't know, you have to guess (2)
- sometimes you can read a question different ways or overanalyze a question (4)
- it's either right or wrong—can't get extra points for what you know as in an essay exam (3)

Step 4. Write. Start with topic. Use logical order. (*The test-taker went back to the list in Step 3 and numbered ideas in order.*) End with a conclusion.

Exams are usually one of two types: subjective or objective. Subjective exams require the student to write either a short answer or a longer essay. Objective exams include multiple choice, true/false, and/or matching questions. In general, most students prefer to take objective tests because they feel objective tests offer more advantages than disadvantages.

One of the advantages of objective exams is that the answer is there, on the paper. This often makes students feel less anxious. Another advantage is that there are specific techniques students can use to take objective tests. For example, if any part of a true/false question is false, then the entire statement is false. Qualifying words such as *always* or *never* are also clues that a true/false question is false. Another advantage of objective tests is that sometimes the answer to a question is located in another part of the test. Related to this is the fact that the test-taker can eliminate incorrect choices and then choose the best answer that remains. Because objective tests provide the answers to choose from, students don't have to worry about their spelling or grammar or punctuation as they do in subjective tests. Finally, everyone who takes an objective test has the same chance of passing; the instructor can't show any bias by marking one answer higher than another.

Despite these advantages, however, objective tests do offer some disadvantages. For example, most objective tests are usually very long, so you have to work pretty fast to finish them in time. In addition, because objective tests most often test your knowledge of facts, you have to memorize a lot of information about the subject. If you don't know the answer to a question, you have to guess. If you guess correctly, it's not a problem. If you guess incorrectly, however, your score is lower. On objective tests, your answer is either right or wrong; students can't get extra points for what they know about a topic as they can in writing an essay on a subjective test. Finally, sometimes students spend too much time reading and analyzing a question, and they choose the wrong answer because they understand the question differently from what the instructor intended.

Depending on the student, he or she will favor subjective or objective exams. There are advantages and disadvantages for both kinds of tests. For objective tests, the advantages seem to outweigh the disadvantages.

Step 5. Edit and proofread. Check for content and structure first. Check spelling and grammar second. (*The test-taker's ideas for changes are listed below.*)
- ☐ content—everything is okay; focus is on objective tests and answer discusses both advantages and disadvantages
- ☐ structure—switch in person in third paragraph: change "you/your" to "students" so all paragraphs are consistent in person
- ☐ structure—change "related to this is the fact that" (too wordy) in the second paragraph to transition "in addition"
- ☐ structure—concluding sentence is weak; add transition "however" to point out contrast
- ☐ spelling—everything is okay
- ☐ grammar—replace contractions ("don't/can't" with "do not/cannot") so answer sounds more formal/academic

Timed Writing

Refer to the previous activity, *Follow the Steps,* before completing the next two activities: responding to a short answer question and an essay question.

Respond to Short Answer Questions

Re-read this chapter's sections on *Reading and Understanding Test Questions* and *Other Types of Test Questions* (pages 7 and 9), and then respond to two of the following questions. You will have 15 minutes to plan, write, and edit your responses. Write your responses on a separate piece of paper or on a computer. Each question is worth 5 points.

A. Define what a multiple-choice question is and list two strategies to use when answering this type of question.

B. List the steps in responding to an essay question.

C. Explain the difference between a short answer question and an essay question.

Respond to Essay Questions

Re-read this chapter's readings, "Taking Objective Tests" and "Taking Subjective Tests," (pages 3 and 17) and then respond to one of the following questions. You will have 30 minutes to plan, write, and edit your response. Write your response on a separate piece of paper or on a computer. Each question is worth 20 points.

A. Many students prefer to take objective exams, thinking that all the answers are there on the paper. Studies show, however, that students often have a better chance of passing a subjective exam than an objective one. Describe the approach a successful test-taker should follow when taking a subjective exam. Include examples in your answer.

B. Students who have good test-taking skills do better on tests than students who do not have those skills. Outline a good approach to taking an objective exam and discuss some specific test-taking strategies that students can use to reduce errors and score better on those kinds of tests. Include examples in your answer.

Final Check

Follow the Steps

A. Follow the steps outlined below to determine whether or not you completed the response in Activity 29 correctly.

1. Assignment
   - ☐ I responded to two short answer questions.
   - ☐ I responded to one essay question.

2. Read the question
   - ☐ I understood each question.
   - ☐ I underlined key words for each question.
   - ☐ I understood what I was being asked to do for each question.

3. Managed time
   - ☐ I determined how much time to allot each item in short answer questions.
   - ☐ I divided time into planning, writing, and editing/proofreading.
   - ☐ I did not run out of time.

4. Planned response
   - ☐ I divided time equally between both short answer questions.
   - ☐ I listed my ideas for each question.
   - ☐ I organized/numbered my ideas in logical order for each question.

5. Wrote response
   - ☐ I started with the topic.
   - ☐ I listed ideas in logical order.
   - ☐ I ended with a conclusion.

6. Edited and proofread
   - ☐ I checked content.
   - ☐ I checked structure.
   - ☐ I checked spelling.
   - ☐ I checked grammar.

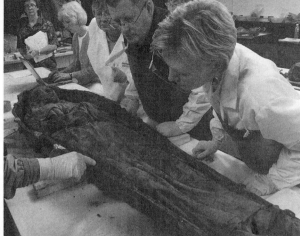

2 From the Social Sciences: Cultural Anthropology

Anthropology is the study of the origins and behavior of man. The field includes the study of how societies and their cultures developed over time. An understanding of different cultures and the different approaches used to solve the problems every culture encounters is required for those who want to succeed in today's global society.

Using your general knowledge and experience with different cultures, discuss the following questions with a partner or in a small group.

- How does studying different cultures help us understand our own?
- What are some ways anthropologists might collect data and information?
- What types of jobs would be available to people studying anthropology?

This chapter will help you understand some of the **key concepts** of anthropology such as

- the four fields of anthropology
- approaches anthropologists take to studying cultures
- methods used in ethnographic fieldwork
- cross-cultural comparisons and theory development

Get Ready to Read

True or False

Read the following statements and decide if they are true or false. Share your answers with a classmate.

1. Archaeologists study material objects of past cultures.   TRUE   FALSE

2. Anthropology takes a cross-cultural approach to studying   TRUE   FALSE
    humankind.

3. Linguists study humans as biological organisms.   TRUE   FALSE

4. Research conducted by anthropologists can help doctors.   TRUE   FALSE

5. Anthropologists both study and observe individuals.   TRUE   FALSE

Surveying and Predicting

Survey and Predict

A. Follow the steps below to survey Reading 1.

1. Read the title. Write it here. _____

2. Read the first paragraph. Write one or two words that tell the topic or what
    the paragraph is about. _____

3. Write the main idea, what the writer wants you to know about the topic, here.

    _____

4. Read the headings, the titles of the sections in the reading.

5. Look for any graphic or visual aids in the reading. Graphic aids are charts,
    graphs, pictures, maps, diagrams, etc.

6. Look for key (important) terms related to the topic. They are usually in bold.

7. Read the last paragraph. It is a summary of the entire reading.

B. Share your survey answers with a partner and discuss what you think the reading
will be about. Then circle the number of the statement below that matches your
prediction.

1. The passage will summarize the main points of the field of anthropology.

2. The passage will explain each of the four different fields of anthropology.

3. The passage will describe how anthropologists collect data.

C. Now read the passage to see if your prediction is correct. Try to read as quickly as
you can. Do not stop to look up words in your dictionary.

The Essence of Anthropology

Anthropology is the study of humankind everywhere, throughout time. Anthropology produces knowledge about what makes people different from one another and what they all share in common. Anthropologists work within four fields of the discipline. While **physical anthropologists** focus on humans as biological organisms (tracing evolutionary development and looking at biological variations), **cultural anthropologists** investigate the contrasting ways groups of humans think, feel, and behave. **Archaeologists** try to recover information about human cultures—usually from the past—by studying material objects, skeletal remains, and settlements. Meanwhile, **linguists** study languages—communication systems by which cultures are maintained and passed onto succeeding generations. Practitioners in all four fields are informed by one another's findings and united by a common anthropological perspective on the human condition.

Developing Theories

Anthropologists, like other scholars, are concerned with the description and explanation of reality. They formulate and test hypotheses—tentative explanations of observed phenomena—concerning humankind. Their aim is to develop reliable theories—interpretations or explanations supported by bodies of data—about our species. These data are usually collected through fieldwork—a particular kind of hands-on research that makes anthropologists so familiar with a situation that they can begin to recognize patterns, regularities, and exceptions. It is also through careful observation (combined with comparison) that anthropologists test their theories.

Compare All Humans

In studying humankind, early anthropologists came to the conclusion that to fully understand the complexities of human thought, feelings, behavior, and biology, it was necessary to study and compare all humans, wherever and whenever. More than any other feature, this unique **cross-cultural**, long-term perspective distinguishes anthropology from other social sciences. Anthropologists are not the only scholars who study people, but they are uniquely holistic in their approach, focusing on the interconnections and interdependence of all aspects of the human experience, past and present. It is this holistic and integrative perspective that equips anthropologists to grapple with an issue of overriding importance for all of us today: globalization.

Globalization

Doing research in all corners of the world, anthropologists are confronted with the impact of globalization on human communities wherever they are located. As **participant observers**, they describe and try to explain how individuals and organizations respond to the massive changes confronting them. Anthropologists may also find out how local responses sometimes change the global flows directed at them.

Since all of us now live in a global village, we can no longer afford the luxury of ignoring our neighbors, no matter how distant they may seem. In this age of globalization, anthropology may not only provide humanity with useful insights concerning diversity, but it may also assist us in avoiding or overcoming significant problems born of that diversity. In countless social arenas, from schools to businesses to hospitals to emergency centers, anthropologists have done cross-cultural research that makes it possible for educators, businesspeople, doctors, and humanitarians to do their work more effectively.

Key Concept Words

archaeologists – (n.) scientists who recover and analyze material and remains

cross-cultural – (adj.) comparing two or more cultures; between or across cultures

cultural anthropologists – (n.) scientists who study human cultures

linguists – (n.) scientists who study language and communication and their relationship to a culture or society

participant observers – (n.) scientists who learn about a culture by participating in and observing a society

physical anthropologists – (n.) scientists who study humans as biological organisms

Glossed Words

discipline – (n.) a field of study; **grapple** – (v.) to struggle with physically or mentally; **holistic** – (adj.) related to the whole or total context; **humankind** – (n.) human beings; **insight** – (n.) a look into or the true explanation of something; **luxury of ignoring** – (n.) dismissing something because it is thought to be unnecessary; **massive** – (adj.) large, huge, enormous; **overriding importance** – (n.) having more importance than anything else; **practitioners** – (n.) people who do skilled work; **skeletal remains** – (n.) the bones (skeleton) of a human being that are left after the body decomposes.

Summarizing

Share What You Read

Use two or three sentences to tell your partner what you thought the reading was about. Then listen to your partner's sentences. Next, read the following statements and circle the number of the statement that best summarizes the reading.

1. Anthropology provides us with knowledge and insights about people who lived hundreds and thousands of years ago.

2. Anthropology includes physical and cultural anthropology as well as archaeology and linguistics.

3. Anthropology involves four fields, all of which contribute our knowledge about what people around the world have and don't have in common.

Check Your Comprehension

A. Match the terms in Column A with their definitions in Column B to complete the sentences.

_____ 1. Archaeologists

_____ 2. Linguists

_____ 3. Cultural anthropologists

_____ 4. Physical anthropologists

_____ 5. Theories

_____ 6. Data

_____ 7. Social arenas

_____ 8. Hypotheses

a. include businesses, schools, hospitals, and emergency centers.

b. are tentative explanations of observed events involving people.

c. study languages and communication systems that cultures maintained and passed onto following generations.

d. include information collected through research, including observation and participation.

e. are interpretations or explanations supported by bodies of data.

f. investigate contrasting ways groups of humans think, feel, and behave.

g. recover information about human cultures by studying material objects, skeletal remains, and settlements.

h. focus on humans as biological organisms and trace evolutionary development.

Academic Word List

ACTIVITY **5**

Scan and Define

A. Look at the ten words listed below. Scan the reading and underline the words from the list. Write the definitions for the words you know. Do not use a dictionary. The first one has been done for you.

1. equip _to furnish or provide_ _____

2. feature (n.) _____

3. focus (v.) _____

4. formulate _____

5. impact (n.) _____

6. investigate _____

7. perspective _____

8. phenomena _____

9. reliable _____

10. unique _____

B. Share your definitions with a partner and then with the rest of your classmates. As a group, try to complete the definitions for all ten words. Use a dictionary to check the definitions if you are unsure about them. Then complete the vocabulary activity.

ACTIVITY **6**

Vocabulary Challenge

A. Using your dictionary, work with a partner to find the missing word forms and complete the chart. If no form exists, draw a line in the space. The first one has been done for you.

Noun	Verb	Adjective	Adverb
1. feature	feature	featured, featuring	---------
2. focus			
3. impact			
4.	investigate		
5. phenomena			
6.		reliable	
7.		unique	

B. Substitute one of the words from the Academic Word list for the underlined word or phrase. You may have to change the form of the word or add a word. The first one has been done for you.

1. Physical anthropologists <u>study and look at</u> humans as biological organisms while linguists study the communication systems by which cultures are maintained and passed on.
study and look at = *focus (on)*

2. Studying and comparing all humans, wherever they are, is the unique cross-cultural long-term <u>view</u> that distinguishes anthropology from other social sciences such as political science, linguistics, and psychology.
view = _____

3. Anthropologists <u>create</u> and test hypotheses concerning humankind in order to develop reliable theories.
create = _____

4. The goal of anthropologists is to develop <u>sound</u> theories about our species.
sound = _____

5. What is interesting about anthropologists is the fact that they are <u>singularly</u> holistic in their approach—that is, they consider all aspects of the human experience, past and present.
singularly = _____

6. It is their holistic perspective that <u>provides what is needed for</u> anthropologists to grapple with today's issue of globalization.
provides what is needed for = _____

7. Doing research in all corners of the world, anthropologists are confronted with the <u>effect</u> of globalization on human communities wherever they are located.
effect = _____

Stated Main Idea

> **Main idea:** the most important idea the writer wants the reader to know

The *main idea* of a passage is its general topic and includes what the author wants the reader to know about the topic. In a paragraph, the main idea is included in the topic sentence. In a longer passage, the main idea is included in the thesis statement, which often gives the reader a clue as to how the author will develop the main idea. The main idea of a passage, then, ties all of the paragraphs together. Main ideas can be stated or implied, but in academic works, the main idea is generally stated.

Locating the main idea in a reading can sometimes be challenging. Generally, the main idea of a reading passage is near the end of the introductory paragraph and is often the last sentence in the paragraph. The main idea of a supporting paragraph, however, is usually the first sentence in the paragraph. Use the title of the reading as well as headings for sections of the reading to help you determine the main idea.

ACTIVITY 7 — Find the Stated Main Idea

A. Below is an introductory paragraph on cultural anthropology. Underline the main idea.

What Is Anthropology?

Anthropologists travel to different parts of the world to study little-known cultures (cultural anthropologists) and languages (anthropological linguists), but they also study culturally distinct groups within their own cultures. Anthropologists also unearth fossil remains (physical anthropologists) and various artifacts (archaeologists). Even though these anthropological subspecialties engage in substantially different types of activities and generate different types of data, they are all directed toward a single purpose. That purpose is the scientific study of humans, both biologically and culturally, in whatever form, time period, or region of the world they might be found.

B. Below are partial paragraphs from the body of a passage on cultural anthropology. Underline the main idea in each paragraph.

1. The branch of anthropology that deals with the study of specific contemporary cultures (ethnography) and the more general underlying patterns of human culture derived through culture comparisons (ethnology) is called cultural anthropology. Before cultural anthropologists can examine cultural differences and similarities throughout the world, they must first describe the features of specific cultures in as much detail as possible. These detailed descriptions are the result of extensive field studies in which the anthropologist observes, talks to, and lives with the people he or she is studying.

2. Ethnology is the comparative study of contemporary cultures, wherever they may be found. Ethnologists seek to understand both why people today and in the recent past differ in terms of ideas and behavior patterns and what all cultures in the world have in common with one another. The primary objective of ethnology is to uncover general cultural principles, the "rules" that govern human behavior.

3. Ethnographers and ethnologists face a daunting task as they describe and compare the many peoples of the world today. A small number of cultural anthropologists must deal with enormous cultural diversity, numerous features of culture that could be compared, and a wide range of theoretical frameworks for comparing them. To describe even the least complex cultures requires many months of interviewing people and observing their behavior.

ACTIVITY 8 — Choose the Main Idea

A. Read the paragraphs and circle the letter of the main idea for each.

1. Activities such as taking courses about different cultures, participating in local internships with international organizations, living in the university's international dormitory, and participating in study abroad programs all combine to provide students with valuable skills that go beyond mastery of subject content. Although many educators have their own list of competencies, they can agree on a basic core of skills. These skills involve developing a broad perspective, appreciating other points of view, and operating comfortably in ambiguous situations.

a. Studying cultural anthropology is valuable because of the skills and competencies that it helps develop.

b. We now know that the study of cultural anthropology has relevance to our everyday lives.

c. Studying other cultures can help us better meet our professional goals and lead more satisfying lives.

2. This skill involves seeing the big picture and the interrelatedness of the parts. A basic anthropological strategy for understanding other cultures is to look at a cultural feature from within its original cultural context rather than looking at it from the perspective of one's own culture. In other words, the student of anthropology is continually being asked to analyze a part of a culture in relationship to the whole.

   a. The study of different cultures provides a much better understanding of one's own.

   b. Studying cultural anthropology makes us more aware of other cultures as well as our own.

   c. Studying cultural anthropology helps develop a broad perspective.

3. Being inquisitive, nonjudgmental, and open to new ways of thinking is vital if we are to adapt to ever-changing environments. This involves, essentially, willingness to learn and postpone making evaluations until more facts are known. Such a capacity also requires suppressing one's ego and letting go of old paradigms. It does not mean giving up one's cultural values in favor of others.

   a. Appreciating other perspectives is one of the skills studying cultural anthropology helps us develop.

   b. Studying cultural anthropology helps one see the positive and negative aspects of one's own culture.

   c. Studying one's own culture is one of the competencies needed for living in a multicultural society.

4. Success in the twenty-first century requires an emphasis on cultural awareness and cross-cultural teamwork, not just personal awareness and individual mastery. Both private and public institutions are becoming increasingly more global in focus. If young adults are to be successful at working within and leading these culturally complex organizations, they will need to know the underlying cultural assumptions of the diverse people on those multicultural teams.

   a. Understanding different cultures can contribute to the solution of pressing societal problems.

   b. The study of cultural anthropology helps develop competency by emphasizing global teamwork.

   c. Studying cultural anthropology will result in more job opportunities to work abroad.

Identifying Text Structure—*Summary*

Summary: a general overview of the main points of a text or passage

When writers first introduce a subject to their audience, they often begin with a general overview of the topic. They present the reader with the major topics related to the subject and offer important points about each topic. In Reading 1, the author introduces the topic of *anthropology* by providing a general definition. Following the definition, the author then lists the four fields of anthropology and describes what anthropologists in each field do. This information is all contained in the first paragraph.

The remainder of the reading explains, in general terms, what anthropologists do and how globalization influences their work. The writer concludes the passage by referencing the fact that anthropologists have, through their work, provided valuable insights to society through their cross-cultural research. The writer offers no specific examples.

These characteristics are common to the text structure of *summary*. While the writer may include some supporting information for the main idea and major topics, minor details are generally omitted. The reader is given only a general look at a subject.

Summaries are commonly used in textbooks, both to begin and end chapters. The beginning of a chapter introduces the key points that will be developed in more detail in the chapter. The chapter often concludes with a final summary of the key points that have been addressed. In addition to textbooks, reviews of books, short stories, plays, and films commonly include summaries. News and academic articles, as well as essays, often employ summary writing.

Key Words—*Summary*

Readers who recognize key words associated with different text structures can increase their reading speed and improve their comprehension. However, because summary focuses on the general concepts of a topic, key words and phrases also tend to be general. Some of the key words associated with the text structure of summary include the following.

all/all in all	commonly	overall	some
based on	generally	overview	typically
basically	in general	many	usually

Recognize Key Words

Read the sentences below and underline the key words associated with the pattern of summary.

1. Anthropological data are usually collected through fieldwork—a particular kind of hands-on research that makes anthropologists so familiar with a situation that they can begin to recognize patterns, regularities, and exceptions.

2. Anthropologists generally work in one of four fields: cultural, linguistic, physical, or archaeological anthropology.

3. What all anthropologists have in common is their aim to develop reliable theories about our species.

4. Anthropologists typically act as participant observers, describing and trying to explain how individuals and organizations respond to changes brought on by globalization.

5. Overall, anthropologists contribute to our understanding of each other as part of the global community.

ACTIVITY 10

Use Key Words

Summarize the main ideas in the following sentences. Include the key word in parentheses in your sentence. The first one has been done for you.

1. Cultural anthropology is the study of customary patterns in human behavior, thought, and feelings. It focuses on humans as culture-producing and culture-reproducing creatures. (typically) *Cultural anthropology, the study of customary* *patterns in human behavior, thought, and feelings, typically focuses on humans as* *culture-producing and culture-reproducing creatures.*

2. Physical anthropologists study humans as biological organisms. Physical anthropologists are experts in the anatomy of human bones and tissues. (generally)
   _____
   _____

3. Ethnographers use participant observation to understand a particular way of life. This involves eating a people's food, sleeping under their roof, learning how to speak and behave acceptably, and personally experiencing their habits and customs. (commonly) _____
   _____

4. Most archaeologists concentrate on the human past and find clues to human behavior that go back thousands of years. Archaeologists who do not concentrate on the past instead study material objects in contemporary settings. (some) _____
   _____

5. Linguists may deal with the description of a language, the history of languages, or language in relation to social and cultural contexts. The three approaches yield valuable information about how people communicate and how they understand the world around them. (all) _____
   _____
   _____

6. Linguistic anthropology is practiced in a number of applied settings. It may help preserve or revive languages. It may help create written forms of some languages. (overall) _____
   _____

ACTIVITY 11

Summarize Main Ideas

Summarize the main ideas or key points from each paragraph in Reading 1. First, list the key points in the paragraph. Then formulate a sentence incorporating those points. Use the headings in the reading to help you focus on the key points. Include key words in your summaries.

1. Paragraph 1
   Key points: _____
   Summary: _____

2. Paragraph 2
   Key points: _____
   Summary: _____

3. Paragraph 3

   Key points: _____

   Summary: _____

4. Paragraph 4

   Key points: _____

   Summary: _____

5. Paragraph 5

   Key points: _____

   Summary: _____

READING 2 ● On Your Own

In the first section of this chapter, you learned about stated main ideas and summaries. You practiced the skills and strategies of surveying, predicting, and summarizing with Reading 1. In this section you will practice these same skills with a new reading. You will also practice using context to guess the meaning of unfamiliar words.

Get Ready to Read

Agree or Disagree

Read the following statements and decide whether you agree or disagree. Circle your choice. Discuss your answers and your reasons for them with a partner.

1. The cultures of people pursuing traditional ways of life are primitive. AGREE DISAGREE

2. Observing and participating in a community is one way to learn its rules and standards. AGREE DISAGREE

3. Pressuring traditional cultures to change their ways is necessary and beneficial. AGREE DISAGREE

4. Theories about culture help us understand others' ideas and actions. AGREE DISAGREE

5. Theories about a specific culture can change if new information is found. AGREE DISAGREE

ACTIVITY 13

Survey and Predict

A. Using the following steps, survey Reading 2 and predict what the reading will be about.

1. Read the title.

2. Read the first paragraph and identify the main idea.

3. Read the headings.

4. Look for any graphic or visual aids in the reading.

5. Look for key terms in bold.

6. Read the last paragraph.

B. Write your prediction here: _____

_____

C. Now read the passage to see if your prediction is correct. Try to read as quickly as you can. Do not stop to look up words in your dictionary.

Reading 2

Ethnographic Research: Its History, Methods, and Theories

History

Cultural anthropology emerged as a formal discipline during the heyday of colonialism (1870s–1950s) when many European anthropologists focused on the study of traditional peoples and their cultures in the colonies overseas. For instance, French anthropologists did most of their research in North and West Africa and Southeast Asia; British anthropologists in southern and East Africa; Dutch anthropologists in what has become Indonesia, Western New Guinea, and Suriname; and Belgian anthropologists in the Congo of Africa. Meanwhile, anthropologists in Canada and the United States focused primarily on their own countries' American Indian and Eskimo communities—usually residing on tracts of land known as reservations, or in remote Arctic villages.

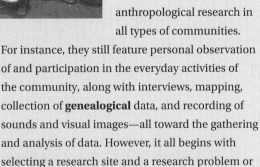

At one time it was common practice to compare people still pursuing traditional lifeways, based on hunting, fishing, gathering, and/or small-scale farming or herding, with the ancient prehistoric ancestors of Europeans and to categorize the cultures of these traditional peoples as "**primitive**." Although anthropologists have long abandoned such **ethnocentric** terminology, many others continue to think and speak of these traditional cultures in terms of being "underdeveloped" or even "undeveloped." This misconception helped state societies, commercial enterprises, and other powerful outside groups justify expanding their activities and even invading the lands belonging to these peoples, often exerting overwhelming pressure on them to change their ancestral ways.

Methods

Every culture comprises underlying rules or standards that are rarely obvious. A major challenge to the anthropologist is to identify and analyze those rules. Fundamental to the effort is **ethnographic fieldwork**—extended on-location research to gather detailed and in-depth information on a society's customary ideas, values, and practices through participation in its collective social life.

While it is true that early anthropologists worked primarily in small-scale societies and that the scope of social-cultural anthropology has since expanded to include urban life in complex industrial and postindustrial societies, ethnographic fieldwork methods developed in the early state of the discipline continue to be central to anthropological research in all types of communities. For instance, they still feature personal observation of and participation in the everyday activities of the community, along with interviews, mapping, collection of **genealogical** data, and recording of sounds and visual images—all toward the gathering and analysis of data. However, it all begins with selecting a research site and a research problem or question.

Theories

Largely descriptive in nature, ethnography provides the basic data needed for *ethnology*—the branch of cultural anthropology that makes cross-cultural comparisons and develops theories that explain why certain important differences or similarities occur between groups. The end product of anthropological research, if properly carried out, is a theory or coherent statement about culture or human nature that provides an explanatory framework for understanding the ideas and actions of the people who have been studied. In short, a **theory** is an explanation or interpretation supported by a reliable body of data.

Anthropologists do not claim any theory about culture to be the only and final word or absolute truth. Rather they judge or measure a theory's validity and soundness by varying degrees of probability; what is considered to be "true" is what is most probable. But while anthropologists are reluctant about making absolute statements about complex issues such as exactly how cultures function or change, they can and do provide fact-based evidence about whether assumptions have support or are unfounded and thus not true. Thus, a theory, contrary to widespread misuse of the term, is much more than mere speculation; it is a critically examined explanation of observed reality.

So it is that, as our cross-cultural knowledge expands, the odds favor some anthropological theories over others; old explanations or interpretations must sometimes be discarded as new theories based on better or more complete evidence are shown to be more effective or probable.

Key Concept Words

cultural anthropology – (n.) the study of human cultures

ethnocentric – (adj.) believing that one's own culture is the only "proper" one

ethnographic fieldwork – (n.) collecting information about a culture by participating in the culture's society

ethnology – (n.) the study of cultures from a comparative view to explain differences and similarities

genealogical – (adj.) relating to the history of a family; ancestral information

primitive – (adj.) unsophisticated, in an early stage of development

theory – (n.) an explanation that is supported by data

Glossed Words

absolute – (adj.) certain or definite; **coherent** – (adj.) logical, clear; **discarded** – (v.) gotten rid of, thrown out; **framework** – (n.) structure or set of ideas; **heyday** – (n.) time or period of success, the best time; **mere speculation** – (n.) a simple guess; based on nothing more than a guess; **peoples** – (n.) a group of persons sharing a common language, culture, religion, or lifestyle; **reluctant** – (adj.) hesitant, unwilling; **small-scale** – (adj.) not large; limited; **tracts of land** – (n.) areas or pieces/plots of land; **unfounded** – (adj.) not based on fact, untrue; **urban** – (adj.) related to the city; **varying** – (adj.) changing, differing

Summarizing

Share What You Read

Use two or three sentences to tell your partner what you thought the reading was about. Then listen to your partner's sentences. If you disagree, go back and find support for your summary. Write your summary statement below.

Summary: _____

_____

ACTIVITY 15

Check Your Comprehension

Circle the word(s) that best complete(s) the sentence.

1. Anthropologists in Canada and the United States focused on the American Indian and Eskimo communities living on *reservations / islands*.

2. An example of an ethnocentric term is describing a culture as *traditional / undeveloped*.

3. Early anthropologists worked primarily in *industrial / small-scale* societies.

4. *Selecting a research site / Identifying underlying cultural rules* is the first step in the anthropological method.

5. Every culture has underlying rules or standards that are *very / seldom* obvious.

6. Recording sounds and visual images of a community *is / is not* part of ethnographic fieldwork.

7. The branch of anthropology that deals with making cross-cultural comparisons and developing theories is called *ethnology / ethnocentricity*.

8. Old anthropological theories are replaced by new ones when there is evidence to show the new theories are *less / more* effective or probable.

9. Anthropologists are *reluctant / eager* to make definite statements about complex cultural issues.

10. An anthropological theory is one that offers explanations for understanding the ideas and actions of the people who *have been / will be* studied.

Academic Word List

ACTIVITY 16

Scan and Define

A. Look at the ten words listed below. Scan the reading and underline the words from the list. Write the definitions for the words you know. Do not use a dictionary. The first one has been done for you.

1. challenge (n.) *a difficult or hard job*

2. comprise _____

3. emerge _____

4. justify _____

5. obvious _____

6. odds _____

7. primarily _____

8. scope (n.) _____

9. underlying _____

10. widespread _____

B. Share your definitions with a partner and then with the rest of your classmates. As a group, try to complete the definitions for all ten words. Use a dictionary to check the definitions if you are unsure about them. Then complete the vocabulary activity.

Vocabulary Challenge

A. Read the words in Column A. Identify the words in Columns B–E as either synonyms (S) or antonyms (A) of the words in Column A. Put *S* or *A* in the blank.

Column A	Column B	Column C	Column D	Column E
1. emerge	_____ disappear	_____ rise from	_____ become evident	_____ come to exist
2. obvious	_____ apparent	_____ unnoticed	_____ hidden	_____ visible
3. underlying	_____ fundamental	_____ present	_____ open	_____ explicit
4. widespread	_____ concentrated	_____ limited	_____ far-reaching	_____ global

B. Decide whether the following statements are true or false based on the meaning of the underlined word. If a statement is true, put a *T* in the blank; if it is false, put an *F* in the blank. Share your answers with a partner and explain the reasons for your false answers.

_____ 1. If the <u>odds</u> favor some anthropological theories over others as our cross-cultural knowledge continues to expand, the new theories are more complete or more probable.

_____ 2. If a culture <u>comprises</u> rules or standards that are rarely obvious, those rules and standards are excluded from that culture.

_____ 3. Identifying and analyzing a society's ideas and values is a <u>challenge</u> to the anthropologist. This means that it is fairly easy for the anthropologist to gather information and draw conclusions.

_____ 4. If a particular custom is <u>widespread</u>, it means that all of the people in the same culture practice it.

_____ 5. All of the rules or standards of a culture are included in the anthropologist's research. Thus, the <u>scope</u> of the anthropologist's research study is quite large.

_____ 6. In the past, commercial enterprises and powerful outside groups <u>justified</u> the pressure they exerted on what they called "undeveloped" or "underdeveloped" cultures to change their ancestral ways. This means that the enterprises and outside groups provided reasons or explanations for their actions.

Using Context to Guess Meaning—*Definition*

Academic textbooks are filled with field- or subject-specific terms and phrases. As writers introduce these terms and phrases in the text, they also include their definitions. These definitions often follow the verbs *is, are, refers to,* and *means.* Definitions may also be set off by punctuation: commas, colons, dashes, or parentheses. Recognizing definition clues will speed your reading and help you understand unfamiliar words.

Study the examples below.

1. *Anthropology **is** the study of humankind everywhere, throughout time.*
   The verb ***is*** introduces the definition of the word *anthropology*.

2. *Fieldwork **refers to** a particular kind of hands-on research that makes anthropologists so familiar with a situation that they can begin to recognize patterns, regularities, and exceptions.*
   The verb ***refers to*** introduces the definition of the word *fieldwork*.

3. *Fundamental to the effort is ethnographic fieldwork—extended on-location research to gather detailed and in-depth information on a society's customary ideas, values, and practices through participation in its collective social life.*
   The dash (—) introduces the definition of the phrase *ethnographic fieldwork*.

4. *Anthropologists formulate and test hypotheses, tentative explanations of observed phenomena, concerning mankind.*
   The commas (**, . . . ,**) set off the definition of the term *hypotheses*.

Guess Meaning from Context

Read the sentences below. Use the verbs and/or the punctuation to determine the meaning of the word or phrases in bold. On the line, write the definition of the word. Share your definitions with a partner and explain how you guessed the meaning.

1. It was common practice to compare people still pursuing **traditional lifeways**—hunting, fishing, gathering, and/or small-scale farming or herding—with the ancient prehistoric ancestors of Europeans.
   traditional lifeways = _____

2. Ethnography provides the basic data needed for **ethnology,** the branch of cultural anthropology that makes cross-cultural comparisons and develops theories that explain why certain important differences or similarities occur between groups.
   ethnology = _____

3. **Cultural anthropology** refers to the investigation of the contrasting ways groups of humans think, feel, and behave.
   cultural anthropology = _____

4. Every culture comprises underlying **rules** (standards) that are rarely obvious.
   rules = _____

5. The end product of anthropological research, if properly carried out, is a theory. A **theory** is a coherent statement about culture or human nature that provides an explanatory framework for understanding the ideas and actions of the people who have been studied.
   theory = _____

6. Anthropologists measure a theory's validity by varying degrees of probability. By **validity**, anthropologists mean what is considered to be "true" is what is most probable.
   validity = _____

In this section, you will learn some skills and strategies associated with the writing process. It includes the grammar of noun clauses, which is one of the grammatical structures used in the readings. In this section, you will practice the different steps in the writing process and will write a paragraph of summary.

The Grammar of Noun Clauses

A noun clause is a group of words that contains a subject and a verb and that functions as a noun. A noun clause can be the subject of a sentence, the object of a verb, or the object of a preposition. Noun clauses begin with a relative pronoun or adverb including *who, what, why, when, how, where, which, that, whether,* and *if.* Study the noun clauses in the chart below.

Subject	Verb	Object/Complement
What anthropologists have in common	is	their study of humankind everywhere, throughout time.
Anthropologists	try to explain	**how individuals and organizations respond to the massive changes confronting them.**
Their findings	were	**that many cultures share similar beliefs and values.**
The linguistic anthropologists	focused	on **why some languages were not passed on to succeeding generations.**

 Recognize Noun Clauses

Read the following sentences and underline the noun clauses. Identify the clauses as subjects or objects by putting an *S* or *O* in the blank.

_____ 1. Anthropologists concluded that it was necessary to study and compare all humans, wherever and whenever.

_____ 2. Why cross-cultural differences between groups exists is the focus of anthropological research.

_____ 3. It is not important how distant our neighbors may be; we are all members of a global village.

_____ 4. Where anthropologists conduct their studies doesn't really matter in this age of industrial and postindustrial society.

_____ 5. Researchers are interested in who the rule-makers of a society are.

 Use Noun Clauses

Match the phrases or clauses in Column A with the noun clauses in Column B to make sentences. Share your sentences with a partner. Add appropriate punctuation to each sentence.

Column A
_____ 1. I would like to know
_____ 2. He is interested in
_____ 3. People in any country in the world are
_____ 4. Did you know
_____ 5. Can you tell me

Column B
a. who anthropologists live with and study
b. how people decide to study this field
c. that there were four fields of anthropology
d. what a physical anthropologist does
e. if anthropologists earn a good living

Sentence Essentials

Complex Sentences

Complex sentences are formed by joining a dependent clause to an independent clause. There are three kinds of dependent clauses: adjective clauses, adverb clauses, and noun clauses. (See The Grammar of Adjective Clauses in Chapter 5, The Grammar of Adverb Clauses in Chapter 6, and The Grammar of Noun Clauses in this chapter for more information on each type of clause.)

Dependent Clause Type	Complex Sentence (*dependent clause* + independent clause)
adjective clause	Anthropologists *who recover information about human culture* are called archaeologists.
adverb clause	*After they formulate and test hypotheses,* anthropologists develop theories.
noun clause	*What anthropologists discover* is shared with educators and businesspeople.

Identify Dependent Clauses

Read the complex sentences and underline the dependent clause in each sentence. The first one has been done for you.

Adjective Clauses

1. Every culture has rules or standards <u>that are not always obvious to newcomers.</u>

2. Anthropological research results in statements about the culture of the people who have been studied.

3. Linguists study the languages that cultures maintain and pass on to succeeding generations.

Adverb Clauses

4. Since all of us now live in a global village, we can no longer ignore our world neighbors.

5. Anthropologists no longer use the term "primitive" to describe cultures of traditional peoples although many people continue to refer to those cultures as "undeveloped" or "underdeveloped."

6. Before they share their theories, anthropologists test them through careful observation combined with comparison.

Noun Clauses

7. Anthropologists try to describe how individuals and organizations respond to massive changes.

8. Ethnology is a branch of cultural anthropology and explains why certain important differences or similarities occur between groups of people.

9. That anthropologists continue to develop new theories about culture makes anthropology an exciting career choice.

Joining Clauses with Subordinators

Depending on the type of clause, specific subordinators are used to join dependent and independent clauses. The chart below contains some of the most commonly used subordinators. See Appendix 3 on page 283 for a more comprehensive list.

Clause	Subordinator	Examples
adjective	relative pronoun/relative adverb	who, that, which, whose, when, where
adverb	subordinating conjunction	although, even though, if, as, because, since, in order that, after, as soon as, before, once, while
noun	*wh-* word/that	who, what, that, how, why, when

Joining Clauses with Punctuation

When an adverb (dependent) clause comes before an independent clause in a sentence, the adverb clause is followed by a comma. When the adverb clause follows an independent clause, no comma is needed except when using *while/whereas* to show contrast or opposition.

Although anthropologists may work in one of four different disciplines, they are united in their perspective of the human condition.

Anthropologists are united in their perspective of the human condition *although they may work in one of four different disciplines.*

Physical anthropologists focus on humans as biological organisms, *whereas cultural anthropologists investigate the ways groups of humans think, feel, and behave.*

ACTIVITY **22**

Combine Clauses and Punctuate the Sentences

Combine the clauses to create complex sentences. Include correct punctuation. The first one has been done for you.

1. archaeologists study the cultures of people/lived hundreds and thousands of years ago / who <u>Archaeologists study the cultures of people who lived hundreds and thousands of years ago.</u>

2. sociolinguists concern themselves with language as it is used in social contexts/ ethnolinguists study the relationship between language and culture/while _____

   _____

   _____

3. globalization has led to a natural sharing of cultures/separate cultures are unlikely to evolve into one world culture/even though _____

   _____

4. it is easy to understand/people are drawn to the field of anthropology and its many branches/why _____

   _____

5. some anthropologists study paleoanthropology/is the study of human evolution/ which _____

   _____

6. television viewers are beginning to understand/the role of forensic anthropology is in crime investigation/what _____

   _____

Create Complex Sentences

Create complex sentences of your own by combining dependent and independent clauses. The sentences can be about any topic.

1. _____
2. _____
3. _____
4. _____

Compound-Complex Sentences

A compound-complex sentence is exactly what it sounds like: a sentence made up of two (or more) independent clauses and at least one dependent clause. It is possible to have different combinations of dependent and independent clauses.

| independent clauses |
| dependent clause |

Two independent clauses + one dependent clause:
Anthropologists work within four fields of the discipline; because they are holistic in their approach, they focus on the interconnections and interdependence of all aspects of the human experience.

| independent clauses |
| dependent clauses |

Two independent clauses + two dependent clauses:
Anthropologists study what humans think and how humans feel, but they do not judge humans.

 ACTIVITY **24**

Identify the Parts of a Compound-Complex Sentence

Read each of the compound-complex sentences below. Underline the independent clauses. Circle the dependent clauses.

1. Anthropologists who conduct research in all corners of the world are confronted with the impact of globalization on human communities wherever they are located, and they share this information with each other and with us.

2. Anthropology produces knowledge about what makes people different from one another and what they all share in common; this knowledge helps us learn about our global neighbors.

3. What cultural anthropologists do is investigate the different ways groups of humans think, feel, and behave; this fieldwork, which is a particular kind of hands-on research, helps anthropologists begin to recognize patterns, regularities, and exceptions.

4. Because their research deals with the past, archaeologists, who travel around the world to collect their material, sometimes have to make inferences about a specific culture; studying material objects, skeletal remains, and settlements is the focus of their work.

5. We have learned from anthropological linguists how to teach English as a second language; after studying and describing the structure of a language, linguists are able to develop strategies that help learners acquire English.

Joining Clauses with Conjunctive Adverbs

The clauses in compound-complex sentences may be joined by the same subordinators listed in the previous chart or with connectors called *conjunctive adverbs,* sometimes also referred to as *transitional words.* The chart below contains some of the most commonly used conjunctive adverbs. See Appendix 3 on page 283 for a more comprehensive list.

Conjunctive Adverbs/ Transitional Words	Use and Meaning
also, furthermore, moreover, besides	introduces another idea or more information
otherwise	introduces a condition
as a result, consequently, therefore, thus	introduces a result
however, nevertheless, nonetheless	introduces contrast that is unexpected
however, on the contrary, on the other hand	introduces direct contrast
then, meanwhile, afterward	introduces a sequence

ACTIVITY 25

Use Conjunctive Adverbs

Read the sentences and fill in the blank with the correct conjunctive adverb. Sometimes more than one answer is possible.

1. Anthropology produces knowledge about what makes people different from one another; _____, it produces knowledge about what they all share in common.

2. Physical anthropologists focus on humans as biological organisms; _____, cultural anthropologists investigate the contrasting ways groups of humans think, feel, and behave.

3. Anthropologists are not the only scholars who study people; _____, they are uniquely holistic in their approach.

4. Anthropologists have done extensive cross-cultural research; _____, educators, businesspeople, doctors, and humanitarians can do their work more effectively.

5. Every culture comprises underlying rules or standards that are rarely obvious; _____, it is a major challenge for anthropologists to identify and analyze those rules.

6. Fieldwork, personal observation of and participation in the everyday activities of the community continue to be central to anthropological research; _____, there would be no data to catalogue and analyze.

Punctuation

For the compound part of the sentence, follow the rules for punctuating compound sentences:

1. Comma + Coordinating Conjunction (*fanboys: for, and, nor, but, or, yet, so*)
   Anthropologists study what humans think and how humans feel, *but* they do not judge humans.

2. Semicolon + Conjunctive Adverb + Comma

   Anthropologists study what humans think and how humans feel; *however,* they do not judge humans.

3. Semicolon

   Anthropologists study what humans think and how humans feel; they do not judge humans.

For the complex part of the sentence, follow the rule for punctuating complex sentences:

Adverb Clause + Comma + Independent Clause

Although anthropologists study what humans think and how humans feel, they do not judge humans.

Punctuate Compound-Complex Sentences

Punctuate the sentences below. The first one has been done for you.

1. People who study cultural anthropology have a variety of careers to choose from ___;___ they can work in international business ___,___ or they can work with immigrant and refugees, for example.

2. Archaeologists reconstruct cultures from what they unearth _____ they are able to analyze some of the remains they find in a laboratory _____ however _____ some of the objects they find must be left at the site.

3. Anthropological linguists are scholars who study both modern and ancient languages _____ they may study the grammar and phonology of a language _____ or they may focus on the origin of a language.

4. Both culture and environment influence how humans evolve over time _____ physical anthropologists study the evolution of humans _____ in addition _____ they study the variation that exists among humans throughout the world.

5. Medical anthropologists study the factors that affect the health of particular members of the community _____ they are trained anthropologists _____ but they also have backgrounds in nursing, psychiatry, or social work, for example.

6. Although urban anthropologists were studying urban life during the 1950s _____ the field did not expand rapidly until the 1960s _____ people began to move from rural to urban areas in large numbers _____ and anthropologists turned their attention to the relationship between cities and society as a whole.

Combine and Punctuate the Sentences

Combine the sentences below to make compound-complex sentences. Include correct punctuation. The first one has been done for you.

1. how humans have evolved over time and why humans from different parts of the world vary from one another direct the research of physical anthropologists/the focus of their study is the effect of culture on human development/in addition they consider the effect of environmental factors on human development

   How humans have evolved over time and why humans from different parts of the world vary from one another direct the research of physical anthropologists; the focus of their study is the effect of culture on human development; in addition, they consider the effect of environmental factors on human development.

2. Franz Boas, who is often referred to as the Father of American Anthropology, trained many now-famous anthropologists/his approach was to collect data through extensive fieldwork/from the data, he then developed general theories _____

_____

_____

3. Edward Sapir is best known for the Sapir-Whorf hypothesis, which states there is a connection between people's view of the world and the language they speak/Sapir was a famous linguistic anthropologist/and he was also one of Franz Boas's students _____

_____

_____

4. Margaret Mead was a cultural anthropologist who became famous for her study *Coming of Age in Samoa*/her research focused on Samoan adolescents and their transition to adulthood/but it also made a cross-cultural comparison with adolescents in the United States and caused much controversy there. _____

_____

_____

_____

5. In the 1981 adventure film *Raiders of the Lost Ark,* Dr. Indiana Jones is an archaeologist who searches for lost treasures in various parts of the world/the character of Indiana Jones was played by Harrison Ford/and the Oscar-winning film was the joint project of George Lucas and Steven Spielberg _____

_____

_____

Anthropologist Margaret Mead

 ACTIVITY **28**

Create Compound-Complex Sentences

Create compound-complex sentences of your own. They can be about any topic.

1. _____

_____

2. _____

_____

3. _____

_____

4. _____

_____

Making the Connection

In most textbooks, a chapter begins with an overview of the topic and introduces the key points that will be developed in the chapter. The chapter often concludes with a final summary of the key points that have been addressed. Readers can use these summaries to activate their background knowledge about the topic before they read and to test their comprehension after they have finished reading. Writers compose summaries as they conduct research, write reaction or response papers, and formulate conclusions to their essays.

Get Ready to Write

Structure of a Paragraph

A paragraph is a group of sentences about a single topic. All of the sentences in a paragraph must be related to the topic; they must also be in a logical order. The ability to write a paragraph is needed to write an essay. Because an essay comprises several paragraphs, writers who can organize and express their ideas in a well-written paragaraph generally have no trouble writing essays.

Although writers may take different approaches to the writing process, most writers follow a common sequence when writing a paragraph. They begin their paragraph by introducing the main idea or topic sentence. The body of the paragraph contains the details that support the main idea. The paragraph then ends with a concluding sentence. The chart below illustrates the structure of a paragraph using the first paragraph of Reading 1.

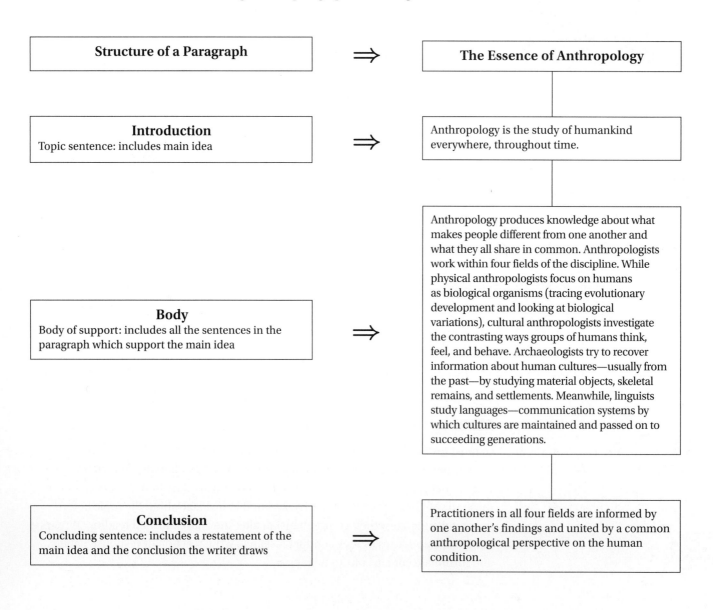

| Structure of a Paragraph | ⇒ | The Essence of Anthropology |

Introduction
Topic sentence: includes main idea

⇒

Anthropology is the study of humankind everywhere, throughout time.

Body
Body of support: includes all the sentences in the paragraph which support the main idea

⇒

Anthropology produces knowledge about what makes people different from one another and what they all share in common. Anthropologists work within four fields of the discipline. While physical anthropologists focus on humans as biological organisms (tracing evolutionary development and looking at biological variations), cultural anthropologists investigate the contrasting ways groups of humans think, feel, and behave. Archaeologists try to recover information about human cultures—usually from the past—by studying material objects, skeletal remains, and settlements. Meanwhile, linguists study languages—communication systems by which cultures are maintained and passed on to succeeding generations.

Conclusion
Concluding sentence: includes a restatement of the main idea and the conclusion the writer draws

⇒

Practitioners in all four fields are informed by one another's findings and united by a common anthropological perspective on the human condition.

ACTIVITY 29

Identify the Parts of a Paragraph

Identify the parts of each remaining paragraph in Reading 1. Underline the topic sentence in each paragraph. Enclose the body sentences in brackets: [ ]. Circle the concluding sentence.

Characteristics of Paragraph Elements

Every paragraph comprises basic elements: a topic sentence, body sentences, and a concluding sentence. Study the characteristics of each below.

The topic sentence

- is often the first sentence of a paragraph
- contains the main idea—the topic or subject of the paragraph
- often gives the reader a clue to the specific information the paragraph will contain; it is more specific than the main idea

Example: *People study anthropology for several reasons.*

Body sentences

- relate to the topic sentence
- support the main idea in the topic sentence
- may include examples, facts, or statistics
- flow smoothly from one to the next
- follow a logical order (general → specific or least important → most important, for example)

Examples: *One reason is that they may be interested in learning about how humans have evolved over time. Another reason is that they may have an interest in languages and want to study how languages have developed. Some people study anthropology because they are interested in culture and want to know how people around the world are similar and different.*

The concluding sentence

- signals the end of the paragraph
- may restate the topic sentence in different words
- may summarize the main points in the paragraph
- may offer a final comment, suggestion, opinion

Example: *Anthropology offers such a variety of career opportunities that it is easy to see why it is a popular field.*

ACTIVITY 30

Organize the Paragraph

Read the sentences. Put a *1* in front of the topic sentence. Number the body sentences *2, 3, 4,* and *5*. Put a *6* in front of the concluding sentence.

A. Cultural Anthropology

_____ a. An example of a cultural universal is marriage.

_____ b. This field focuses on the cultural similarities and differences among people.

_____ c. Cultural anthropology is one of the four fields of anthropology.

_____ d. Examining these similarities and differences is the work of the cultural anthropologist.

(continued on page 66)

_____ e. Cultural features that are similar around the world are called cultural universals.

_____ f. Cultural differences that people experience sometimes lead to culture shock.

B. Culture Shock

_____ a. The feeling of isolation may lead to withdrawal.

_____ b. Culture shock is a feeling of stress that comes from trying to function in a new culture.

_____ c. A person who experiences culture shock may feel alone, isolated from the new society.

_____ d. Staying at home and not interacting with others is an example of withdrawal.

_____ e. In time, most people eventually adjust to the new culture, and their culture shock disappears.

_____ f. People who are new to a culture often go through culture shock.

C. Archaeology

_____ a. With a Bachelor's or Master's degree, you have a wide range of employment possibilities.

_____ b. Archaeologists can choose from a variety of job opportunities in this country.

_____ c. One job opportunity for archaeologists is to work in a museum.

_____ d. Another opportunity is to work for the state or federal government.

_____ e. Museum responsibilities could include overseeing the museum collection and organizing displays.

_____ f. Such work might involve overseeing an archaeological site in a state or federal park, for example.

Paraphrasing and Summarizing

Paraphrasing: using your own words to explain a quote, passage or text

Good writers support the topic sentence of a paragraph or the thesis statement of an essay with examples, facts, statistics, and even personal experiences. Writers sometimes quote specific information directly in their writing; other times they paraphrase or summarize the information.

Paraphrasing and summarizing are useful tools for academic writing. For example, you may need to paraphrase an essay or summarize a chapter as a class assignment. You may have to present or discuss general ideas or well-known concepts from the textbook and/or outside sources. When you paraphrase or summarize, you *do not* copy the information directly out of the text. Instead, you use your own words and do not include your own opinions. However, it is acceptable to use technical or concept words that are related to the subject of the text.

By paraphrasing and summarizing correctly, you avoid plagiarizing another writer's work. Avoiding plagiarism requires you to change the words as well as the structure of the original work. Substituting synonyms but following the same grammatical structure is still considered plagiarism. See the example below.

Original text: *People study anthropology for several reasons.*

Plagiarized: *People take classes in anthropology for many reasons.*

Paraphrased: *Many factors draw people to the field of anthropology.*

Paraphrasing Text

Paraphrasing means using your own words to explain what the passage or text is about. When you paraphrase a passage or section of a text, you paraphrase all of the information in the text. As a result, a paraphrase of a section will be almost as long as the original passage.

In order to paraphrase a text you are reading, follow these steps:

1. Be sure you understand the section you have read. Look up any words that are unfamiliar or that you do not understand.

2. List, in your own words, the ideas and details presented in the section.

3. Convert the ideas and details into sentences.

4. Read your paraphrase to make sure there has been no change in meaning.

5. If you write your paraphrase in a notebook, identify the source of the paraphrase.

 ACTIVITY 31

Paraphrase Quotes

Read each of the following quotes. Then, paraphrase the quote using your own words. The first one has been done for you.

1. "An eye for an eye leaves the whole world blind." Mahatma Gandhi (political/spiritual leader) <u>Responding to violence with violence does not work; the violence only continues to spread.</u>

2. "The best of prophets of the future is the past." Lord Byron (English poet) _____

_____

3. "It's not what you find; it's what you find out." David Hurst-Thomas (archaeologist) _____

_____

4. "Those who know nothing of foreign languages know nothing of their own." Johann Wolfgang von Goethe (author) _____

_____

5. "I do not want my house to be walled in on all sides and my windows to be stuffed. I want the cultures of all the lands to be blown about my house as freely as possible. But I refuse to be blown off my feet by any." Mahatma Gandhi

_____

_____

6. "Every time we liberate a woman, we liberate a man." Margaret Mead (cultural anthropologist) _____

_____

7. "One generation plants the trees; another gets the shade." Proverb _____
_____

8. "We did not inherit the land from our forefathers—we are borrowing it from our children." Unknown _____

9. "Never believe that a few caring people can't change the world. For indeed, that's all who ever have." Margaret Mead _____
_____

Paraphrase Paragraphs

Read each paragraph carefully. With a partner, follow the steps above to paraphrase the paragraphs on a separate sheet of paper. The first one has been done for you. Notice that it is similar in length to the original.

1. Anthropology is the study of people—their origins, their development, and contemporary variations, wherever and whenever they have been found. Of all disciplines that study humans, anthropology is by far the broadest in scope. The subject matter of anthropology includes fossilized human remains of early humans, artifacts and other materials from prehistoric and historic archaeological sites, and all of the contemporary and historical cultures of the world. The task that anthropology has set for itself is an enormous one. Anthropologists strive for an understanding of the biological and cultural origins and evolutionary development of the species. They are concerned with all humans, both past and present, as well as their behavior patterns, thought systems, and material possessions. In short, anthropology aims to describe, in the broadest sense, what it means to be human. *Anthropology can be defined as the study of human beings and everything about them from both the present and past. Anthropology covers a wider range of study than many other fields do. For example, anthropologists study the present and past cultures of people. They study the physical objects that are found during archaeological excavations, including any skeletal remains they may find. The goal of anthropologists is to understand how human beings have developed, both physically and culturally, since the beginning of their existence. They do this by studying the way people think and act and by examining objects that people use and own. Its goal is to explain the essence of a human being.*

2. The study of humans from a biological perspective is called physical anthropology. Essentially, physical anthropologists are concerned with two areas of investigation. First, they are interested in reconstructing the evolutionary record of the human species; that is, they ask questions about the emergence of humans and how humans have evolved up to the present time. This area of physical anthropology is known as paleoanthropology. The second area of concern to physical anthropologists deals with how and why physical traits of contemporary human populations vary throughout the world. This area of investigation is called human variation. Physical anthropologists study how culture and environment have influenced these two areas of biological evolution and contemporary variation.

3. Historical linguistics deals with the emergence of language in general, and how specific languages have diverged over time. Some of the earliest anthropological interest in language focused on the historical connections between languages. For example, nineteenth-century linguists working with

European languages demonstrated similarities in the sound systems between a particular language and an earlier parent language from which the language was derived. In other words, by comparing contemporary languages, linguists have been able to identify language families. Through techniques such as glottochronology, linguists can now approximate when two languages began to diverge from each other.

4. Experts in the field of archaeology study the lifeways of people from the past by excavating and analyzing the material culture they have left behind. The purpose of archaeology is not to fill up museums by collecting relics from prehistoric societies. It is to understand cultural adaptations of ancient peoples by at least partially reconstructing their cultures. Because archaeologists concentrate on societies of the past, they are limited to working with material culture. From these material remains, however, archaeologists are able to infer many nonmaterial ideas and behavior patterns held by people thousands of years ago.

Summarizing

Summarizing: using your own words to give a brief overview of a text or lecture

Summarizing means using your own words to give a brief overview of a text, lecture, or other form of communication. Unlike paraphrasing, which includes all of the information of a text, summarizing includes only the main ideas and important details in the text. As a result, a summary will be much shorter than the original passage.

In order to summarize a text you are reading, follow these steps:

1. Be sure you understand the section you have read. Look up any words that are unfamiliar or that you do not understand.

2. Identify the main ideas and most important points in the section.

3. List, in your own words, the ideas and important points in the section.

4. Convert the ideas and important points into sentences.

5. Read your summary to make sure there has been no change in meaning.

6. If you write your summary in a notebook, identify the source of the summary.

ACTIVITY 33

Summarize Paragraphs

Re-read each paragraph in Activity 32 and follow the steps listed above to summarize the paragraphs on a separate sheet of paper. The first one has been done for you. The underlined words and phrases are the main ideas and most important points in the selection.

1. Anthropology is the study of people—their origins, their development, and contemporary variations, wherever and whenever they have been found. Of all disciplines that study humans, anthropology is by far the broadest in scope. The subject matter of anthropology includes fossilized human remains of early humans, artifacts, and other materials from prehistoric and historic archaeological sites, and all of the contemporary and historical cultures of the world. The task that anthropology has set for itself is an enormous one. Anthropologists strive for an understanding of the biological and cultural origins and evolutionary development of the species. They are concerned with all humans, both past and present, as well as their behavior patterns, thought

systems, and material possessions. In short, anthropology aims to describe, in the broadest sense, what it means to be human.

Anthropology—

the study of humans, ancient to present

wider range than any other human study field

origin of cultures

evolution

behavior, beliefs, material objects

Summary—Anthropology is the study of human beings, from ancient times to today. Having the widest range of any field studying humans, anthropology examines not only biological and evolutionary evidence, but also the origins of culture and beliefs.

Synthesizing

Synthesizing: combining information from two or more sources to form a new, separate document

Along with paraphrasing and summarizing, synthesizing is a skill you will use during your academic studies. To prepare for one of your classes, you might first study the chapter from the textbook and then read an online article; later, you take notes during a class lecture. Combining the information from the three sources gives you the "complete" picture of the subject.

Similarly, to write an essay or research paper, you might consult several sources for information related to your topic. Combining the information from multiple sources requires you to synthesize the material—to put all of the parts together to make a complete, coherent document. Synthesizing, thus, means integrating or blending information from multiple sources.

Steps in Synthesizing

1. Read the original source documents.
2. Choose the information that you want to include. Note the source.
3. Put information with similar ideas together.
4. Paraphrase or summarize the information.
5. Organize the information in a logical order.
6. Rewrite the information as a paragraph, combining it with your own ideas.
7. Add transitions and make other changes as necessary.

Read the two paragraphs below and then follow the steps to see how information from each was selected and then synthesized to form a new paragraph.

Steps 1 and 2: Read the original source documents and choose the information to include.

Paragraph 1: The Nuclear Family

The term "nuclear family" refers to a family that consists of a husband, wife, and children. It is formed by marriage and is considered the basic family structure. Although the nuclear family may still be connected to the larger family of the spouses' parents, brothers, and sisters, it is essentially independent. This allows the family to move to a new location when a job or occupation requires it. (Source 1)

Paragraph 2: The Changing Family Structure
As <u>today's family structures have changed</u>, so, too, have the terms that define them. Take, for example, the term "nuclear family." The typical nuclear family is no longer defined as a husband, wife, and their offspring. Instead, the <u>nuclear family is now one or two parents and children</u>. Within this definition, <u>stepparents and stepchildren</u> are also included. (Source 2)

Steps 3, 4, and 5: Put similar ideas together, paraphrase/summarize them, and put them in logical order.

- "nuclear family" refers to a family that consists of a husband, wife, and children + nuclear family is now one or two parents and children + stepparents and stepchildren
- formed by marriage
- connected to the larger family but still independent
- basic family structure + today's family structures have changed

One family type is called the "nuclear family." The traditional nuclear family is a household that includes a married couple and their children. The nuclear family today includes either one or two parents and can include a stepmother or stepfather. The children in today's nuclear family include stepchildren. The traditional nuclear family formed as a result of marriage between partners, was considered the basic family structure, and was not reliant on its larger, extended family. The family structure of contemporary society has changed.

Steps 6 and 7: Rewrite the information, add original ideas, and make necessary changes.
original ideas: women are marrying at a later age or not getting married/single-parent households are increasing/couples get divorced and one person takes custody of the children.

Change in the Nuclear Family
There are numerous family types. One type is called the "nuclear family." The traditional nuclear family is defined as a household that includes a married couple and their children. The nuclear family today, however, includes either one or two parents and can also include a stepmother or stepfather. The children in today's nuclear family include stepchildren as well. In the past, the nuclear family formed as a result of marriage between partners, was considered the basic family structure, and was not reliant on its larger, extended family. Today, women are marrying at a later age or are deciding not to marry at all. In addition, the number of single-parent households is increasing as couples get divorced and one spouse takes custody of the children. Thus, as the family structure of contemporary society has changed, the definitions have changed, too.

Practice Synthesizing

Follow the steps listed above to synthesize the information in the two paragraphs below on a separate sheet of paper.

Paragraph 1: The Extended Family
The extended family consists of a nuclear family (husband, wife, children) plus close relatives. These close relatives often extend or expand the family by adding another generation. That is, the expanded family often includes the parents of one of the spouses. The extended family is not as common in large countries today as it was in the past when large families were needed to work on the farms. The change of a country from agrarian to industrial is the reason for the change.

Paragraph 2: Reasons for Increase in Extended Families

The number of extended families is starting to rise as elderly parents leave their homes to move in with and be taken care of by their grown, adult children. The extended family, common in Hispanic and Asian countries, is defined as two or more nuclear families that are related. This family structure is also common among immigrants because this type of arrangement has economic benefits, including affordable housing. In addition, generations of farm families often live together in order to provide the labor needed to care for the land and animals.

How Did They Do That?

This section of the chapter focuses on paragraph writing and presents the step-by-step development of a summary paragraph. A summary paragraph is often used when writers include information from outside sources in their writing.

Writing a Summary Paragraph

Writing a summary paragraph differs from other types of paragraph writing. It does not require brainstorming a topic and details, for example. The purpose of a summary paragraph is to present another writer's main ideas and major support details. Because many of the minor details are excluded, a summary is much shorter than the original passage.

Summaries are used in different ways. A presentation, essay, or research paper might require you to consult multiple sources; you will want to summarize each of your sources as you gather information. A class assignment to watch and critique a news program or political debate will require you to summarize what you heard. Responding or reacting to a literary work—a poem or short story—will also require you to write a summary.

Follow the Steps

Below is a summary of Reading 1, "The Essence of Anthropology." Follow the steps to see how the writer summarized multiple paragraphs of text.

The Essence of Anthropology

Anthropology is the study of humans throughout the world from the beginning of their existence. There are four fields: physical, cultural, archaeological, and linguistic. Anthropologists create theories based on hypotheses they have formulated and tested. By living among the people they study, they are able to collect the data to test their hypotheses. Because their research is conducted while living among the people they study, anthropologists are generally also able to observe characteristics of the people and to recognize which habits or traits are common and which are uncommon. Because anthropologists basically compare all humans, they take a cross-cultural perspective. Their overall approach is both holistic and integrative. For example, globalization and its impact on societies is one thing that can be described and explained by the anthropologists. They look at how individuals respond to the changes caused by globalization and learn how those responses also influence globalization. Anthropologists also provide explanations related to diversity. Educators, businesspeople, doctors, and humanitarians are just some of the people who are able to work more effectively because of the research conducted by anthropologists.

1. **Be sure you understand the section you have read. Look up any words that are unfamiliar or that you do not understand.**

The writer wrote definitions of words not understood. Find the words in the original text and circle them.

fieldwork—working among the people they study; cross-cultural, long-term perspective— studying/comparing all humans from past to present; holistic—emphasis on the whole, not just the parts; the parts are all interdependent

2. **Identify the main ideas and most important points in the section.**

The writer underlined main ideas and important points in the text, and wrote notes in the margins. For each sentence in the summary paragraph, find its related idea in the original text and highlight or underline it.

3. **List, in your own words, the ideas and important points in the section.**

The following outline contains the writer's own words for important ideas and details in the reading. Put a check mark (✓) next to each idea in the outline that the writer included in the summary paragraph.

Outline for Reading 1

The Essence of Anthropology
  I. Anthropology
      A. Study of humans throughout the world from beginning of time
      B. Four areas
          1. Physical
          2. Cultural
          3. Archaeological
          4. Linguistic
  II. Create Theories
      A. Aim of anthropology
          1. Create/test hypotheses
          2. Collect data to test hypotheses
              a. live among people they study
              b. recognize characteristics, common/uncommon habits or traits
              c. observe
  III. Compare All Humans
      A. Cross-cultural perspective
      B. Holistic approach
      C. Integrative approach
  IV. Globalization
      A. Impacts societies
          1. describe/explain how individuals respond to changes
          2. discover how responses influence globalization

B. Anthropologists provide explanations about diversity
  1. Research helps others do work more effectively
     a. educators
     b. businesspeople
     c. doctors
     d. humanitarians

4. Convert the ideas and important points into sentences.

Compare the phrases in the outline with the completed paragraph. You will notice that the writer made the phrases into complete sentences. Choose one of the outline sections. On a separate piece of paper, convert the ideas into sentences. Then compare your sentences with the writer's summary sentences.

5. Read your summary to make sure there has been no change in meaning.

The sample paragraph does not contain any information that is not in the original reading. There are no opinions added, even though the paragraph is in the writer's own words.

6. Identify the source of the summary.

You will need to know the original source for the information if you include it in a presentation, essay, research paper, or other work.

Source: Haviland, W., Prins, H.E.L., Walrath, D., & McBride, B. (2008). *Cultural Anthropology: The Human Challenge* 12th ed. Belmont, CA: Wadsworth Thomson Learning. 3, 19.

WRITING 2 • **On Your Own**

Paragraph of Summary

Write Your Paragraph

Following the steps listed below, write a summary paragraph of Reading 2, "Ethnographic Research: Its History, Methods, and Theories."

1. Be sure you understand what you have read. Look up any words that are unfamiliar or that you do not understand.

2. Identify the main ideas and most important points in the section. (Highlight or underline them.)

3. List, in your own words, the ideas and important points in the section. (Make an outline.)

4. Convert the ideas and important points into sentences. (Put in paragraph format.)

5. Read your summary to make sure there has been no change in meaning.

6. Identify the source of the summary. (Note: Same source as Reading 1 above but change pages 3 and 19 to page 62.)

ACTIVITY **37**

Revising
Follow the Steps

A. Follow the steps outlined below to revise the paragraph of summary.

Revising Checklist

1. Assignment

   ☐ follows the assignment to write a paragraph of summary for Reading 2

   ☐ follows the six steps listed in the assignment

   ☐ includes the source of the summary

   ☐ uses the writer's own words

2. Topic sentence

   ☐ states the main idea of Reading 2

   ☐ is a complete sentence

3. Body of details

   ☐ includes the topic sentence of each paragraph of Reading 2

   ☐ includes the main points of each body paragraph of Reading 2

   ☐ includes major supporting details of Reading 2

   ☐ omits minor details of Reading 2

   ☐ omits examples unless needed for understanding

   ☐ omits personal ideas or opinions not in Reading 2

   ☐ uses complete sentences

4. Concluding sentence

   ☐ restates the topic sentence or summarizes main points

   ☐ makes a final comment

B. Share your summary with a classmate. Ask your classmate to use the Revising Checklist to check your paragraph and give you some feedback. Make any changes to your paragraph that you feel are necessary. The changes you make should improve your paragraph.

Editing and Proofreading: looking for and correcting errors in grammar, spelling, punctuation, and formatting

Editing and Proofreading
The Final Steps

A. Follow the steps outlined below to edit and proofread the paragraph of summary you wrote.

Editing and Proofreading Checklist

1. Grammar
   - ☐ Verb tenses are correct.
   - ☐ Each subject agrees with its verb (singular/plural).
   - ☐ Prepositions are correct.
   - ☐ Pronouns are correct (agree in number/gender).
   - ☐ No articles are missing (*a, an, the*).

2. Spelling
   - ☐ All the words are spelled correctly.
   - ☐ Abbreviations, if any, are used correctly.
   - ☐ First word of each sentence begins with a capital letter.

3. Punctuation
   - ☐ All sentences end with a punctuation mark.
   - ☐ Periods are after statements and question marks are after questions.
   - ☐ Commas, colons, and dashes are used correctly to define terms.

4. Sentences
   - ☐ All sentences are complete.
   - ☐ Each sentence has a subject and a verb.
   - ☐ There are no fragments.

5. Format
   - ☐ Paragraph has a title.
   - ☐ All sentences are in paragraph format (not listed or numbered).
   - ☐ Writer's name is on the paper.
   - ☐ Paper is neat, clean, and legible (easily read).

B. Share your paragraph with a classmate. Ask your classmate to use the Editing and Proofreading Checklist to check your paragraph and mark any errors in grammar, spelling, punctuation, sentences, or paragraph format.

C. Fix any mistakes your paragraph contained. Proofread your paragraph one more time. Turn in your final draft to your instructor.

3. From Business: Business Ethics

Business is a popular major in many colleges and universities, and common in today's business curriculum are courses in business ethics. Because a company's image influences consumers and investors alike, many corporations have created specific behavioral guidelines for their employees to follow. Companies or organizations that engage in or condone unfair business practices or whose company managers and executives are found breaking the law may pay the price with jail time or large fines.

Look at the drawing on this page and discuss the following questions with a partner or in a small group.

- Why do some high-level company executives engage in unethical behavior?
- How should people who defraud a company or who falsify company records be punished?
- What action can companies take to prevent similar kinds of wrongdoing from occurring again?

This chapter will help you understand some of the **key concepts** in business ethics such as

- codes of ethics
- ethics training
- corporate values
- ethical dilemmas

Get Ready to Read

Agree or Disagree

Read the following statements and decide whether you agree or disagree. Circle your choice. Discuss your answers and your reasons for them with a partner.

1. A personal code of ethics is no different from a business code of ethics. AGREE DISAGREE

2. Teaching employees about ethical standards is good business practice. AGREE DISAGREE

3. Employees who violate company ethics guidelines should be fired. AGREE DISAGREE

4. Codes of ethics are used just to give the company a positive image. AGREE DISAGREE

5. Ethics questions can be legal, regulatory, or policy-related in nature. AGREE DISAGREE

Surveying and Predicting

Survey and Predict

A. Follow the steps below to survey Reading 1 below.

1. Read the title. Write it here. _____

2. Read the first paragraph. Write one or two words that tell the topic or what the paragraph is about. _____

3. Write the main idea here. _____

4. Read the headings, the titles of the sections in the reading.

5. Look for any graphic or visual aids in the reading. Graphic aids are charts, graphs, pictures, maps, diagrams, etc.

6. Look for key (important) terms related to the topic. They are usually in bold.

7. Read the last paragraph. It is a summary of the entire reading.

B. Share your survey answers with a partner and discuss what you think the reading will be about. Then circle the number of the statement below that matches your prediction.

1. The passage will explain ways to affect employees' ethical conduct.

2. The passage will describe particular examples of unethical behavior of employees.

3. The passage will show how codes of ethics have little effect on managers and executives.

C. Now read the passage to see if your prediction is correct. Try to read as quickly as you can. Do not stop to look up words in your dictionary.

Organizations Can Influence Employees' Ethical Conduct

People choose between right and wrong based on their personal code of ethics. They are also influenced by the ethical environment created by their employers. Consider the following newspaper headlines:

- James Beard Foundation™ president forced to resign after spending hundreds of thousands of dollars on excessive salaries and meals
- Dennis Kozlowski, former top executive of Tyco, International™, convicted of **grand larceny**, conspiracy, securities fraud, and falsifying business records
- Bernie Ebbers, ex-WorldCom™ chief executive, sentenced to 25 years in prison for his role in **corporate fraud**

As these actual headlines illustrate, poor business ethics can contribute to a very **negative image** for a company, can be expensive for the firm and/or the executives involved, and can result in bankruptcy and jail time for the offenders. Organizations can, however, reduce the potential for these types of liability claims. Educating their employees about ethical standards, leading through example, and providing various informal and formal programs are all ways to have an effect on the ethical conduct of an organization's employees.

Establishing a Formal Code of Ethics

Most large companies and thousands of smaller ones have created, printed, and distributed codes of ethics. In general, having a **code of ethics** results in employees' knowing what their firm expects in terms of their responsibilities and behavior toward fellow employees, customers, and suppliers. Some ethical codes offer a lengthy and detailed set of guidelines for employees. Others are not really codes at all but rather summary statements of goals, policies, and priorities. Some companies have their codes framed and hung on office walls or printed on cards to be carried at all times by executives.

Leading by Example

Employees often follow the examples set by their managers. That is, leaders and managers establish patterns of behavior that determine what's acceptable and what's not within the organization. While Ben Cohen was president of Ben & Jerry's™ ice cream, he followed a policy that no one could earn a salary more than seven times the lowest-paid worker. He wanted all employees to feel that they were equal. At the time he resigned, company sales were $140 million and the lowest-paid worker earned $19,000 per year. Ben Cohen's salary was $133,000 based on the "seven times" rule. A typical top executive of a $140 million company might have earned 10 times Cohen's salary. Ben Cohen's actions helped shape the **ethical values** of Ben & Jerry's.

Offering Ethics Training Programs

In addition to providing a system to resolve ethical dilemmas, organizations also provide formal training in order to develop an awareness of questionable business activities and practice appropriate responses. Many American companies have some type of ethics training program. The ones that are most effective, like those created by Levi Strauss™, American Express™, and Campbell Soup Company, begin with techniques for solving **ethical dilemmas**. Next, employees are presented with a series of situations and asked to come up with the "best" ethical solution. Some companies have tried to add a bit of excitement and fun to their ethics-training programs by presenting them in the form of games. Citigroup™, for example, has created The Work Ethic, a board game in which participants strive to correctly answer legal, regulatory, policy-related, and judgment ethics questions.

Do codes of ethics make employees behave in a more ethical manner? Some people believe that they do. Others think that they are little more than public relations gimmicks. If **senior management** abides by the code of ethics and regularly emphasizes the code to employees, then it will likely have a positive influence on behavior.

Key Concept Words

code of ethics – (n.) guidelines for employees on moral/correct behavior

corporate fraud – (n.) a company's attempt to deceive or trick

ethical dilemmas – (n.) situations requiring a moral/correct decision

ethical values – (n.) moral beliefs or standards

grand larceny – (n.) the crime of taking a significant or large amount of property belonging to another

negative image – (n.) negative public opinion

senior management – (n.) high-level managers and executives of a company

Glossed Words

abide – (v.) to follow or obey; **convicted** – (v.) found guilty; **gimmicks** – (n.) tricks used to get someone to believe something; **liability claims** – (n.) accusations of unethical business practices; **questionable business activities** – (n.) actions that may have been morally wrong; **regulatory ethics questions**– (n.) accusations of not following the rules/regulations; **resign** – (v.) to quit or leave one's position or job; **sentenced** – (v.) to be given a punishment by the court

Summarizing

Share What You Read

Use two or three sentences to tell your partner what you thought the reading was about. Then listen to your partner's sentences. Next, read the following statements and circle the number of the statement that best summarizes the reading.

1. Companies and organizations create different codes of ethics for their employees.

2. Companies and organizations can have an effect on employees' business ethics.

3. Companies and organizations can eliminate the cause of poor business ethics among employees.

Check Your Comprehension

Read the following statements. Circle the letter of the answer that best completes the statement.

1. Publicity about a company executive who is accused of poor business ethics will most likely not result in
   a. a negative image for the company.
   b. jail time for the offender.
   c. increased profits.

2. A code of ethics provides employees with guidelines for behavior toward
   a. fellow employees, customers, and friends.
   b. fellow employees, customers, and suppliers.
   c. fellow employees, customers, and competitors.

3. Some codes of ethics are
   a. long and detailed sets of guidelines.
   b. printed in the local newspapers.
   c. distributed with the company's products.

4. The "seven times" rule at Ben & Jerry's ice cream company meant
   a. employees were allowed to eat ice cream seven times a week before they had to pay for it.
   b. no employees were allowed to be off more than seven days a month for illness.
   c. no employees were allowed to earn a salary more than seven times the lowest-paid worker.

5. An example of formal ethics training of employees is
   a. Campbell Soup Company's "soup and a sandwich" day.
   b. Levi Strauss' handing out printed codes of ethics.
   c. Citigroup's use of its board game, The Work Ethic.

6. Some people believe that codes of ethics
   a. are public relations gimmicks.
   b. do a lot to influence behavior.
   c. do not work outside the country.

● **Academic Word List**

Scan and Define

A. Look at the ten words listed below. Scan the reading and underline the words from the list. Write the definitions for the words you know. Do not use a dictionary. The first one has been done for you.

1. appropriate (adj.) *proper or fitting* _____

2. code (n.) _____

3. establish _____

4. ethics _____

5. illustrate _____

6. legal _____

7. potential (n.) _____

8. resolve (v.) _____

9. role _____

10. summary (adj.) _____

B. Share your definitions with a partner and then with the rest of your classmates. As a group, try to complete the definitions for all ten words. Use a dictionary to check the definitions if you are unsure about them. Then complete the vocabulary activity.

Vocabulary Challenge

A. Circle the word that does not belong. The words in bold are from the Academic Word List. The first one has been done for you.

1. **appropriate**	proper	(unsuitable)	fitting
2. **illustrate**	glow	depict	portray
3. **resolve**	settle	decide	argue
4. **summary**	condensed	concise	lengthy
5. **code**	collection	set	secret
6. **establish**	dissolve	institute	found
7. **potential**	possibility	reality	likelihood
8. **ethics**	morals	principles	dishonesty

B. Read the definition of the words below. Then decide which meaning is the one used in the sentence. Put the definition number next to the sentence. The first one has been done for you.

1. **role** *noun* **1.** the character an actor plays; **2.** the function a person performs in a group

   __2__ The role of the manager is to serve as an example to employees.

2. **summary** *adjective* **1.** concise, brief; **2.** quickly and without formal planning

   _____ In order to finish the meeting on time, the department heads offered summary statements on the status of their current projects.

3. **establish** *verb* **1.** to demonstrate or provide evidence for; **2.** to create or form

   _____ Today's corporations, with an eye on employee welfare, are establishing in-house gyms, day cares, and cafeterias.

4. **code** *noun* **1.** a set of principles or rules of conduct; **2.** a set of signals representing letters or numbers

   _____ Although dress codes have been relaxed in many companies, an employee still needs to dress appropriately for work: no flip-flops or tank tops, please!

5. **resolve** *verb* **1.** to make a decision to act; **2.** to solve a problem or situation

   _____ Grievance procedures need to be in place in order to resolve employee complaints efficiently and effectively.

6. **legal** *adjective* **1.** allowed by law; **2.** related to law

   _____ The court determined it was legal for the union members to go on strike for better working conditions.

7. **potential** *noun* **1.** the possibility of happening or occurring; **2.** a skill or ability that is not yet fully developed

   _____ With the popularity of the Internet, the potential for expanding our company's product line is almost limitless.

> **Implied main idea:** central idea suggested, not stated directly, by the topic and details

Implied Main Idea

In Chapter 2, you learned that the *main idea* of a passage is its general topic and includes what the author wants the reader to know about the topic. You also learned that the main idea can be stated or implied, and that in academic works, the main idea is generally stated.

Implied or unstated main ideas are commonly used in literature, but you may also find them in news articles, essays, and reviews. In the same way you use the title and/ or the headings of a reading passage to help you locate the stated main idea, you can determine the implied main idea of a passage by focusing on the topic and studying the details. Using your own words, combine the topic with what the details say about the topic in one sentence. That sentence is the (implied) main idea of the passage.

Example:

Social Responsibility

To slow the erosion of the world's resources, many companies are becoming more environmentally responsible. Toyota™ is now using "renewable" energy sources to power its facilities, making it the largest single user of clean power in the world. Toyota's first step in the United States was to turn to renewable sources such as solar, wind, geothermal, and water power for the electricity at its headquarters in Torrance and Irving, California.

American Express is a major supporter of the American Red Cross™. The organization relies almost entirely on charitable gifts to carry out its programs and services, which include disaster relief, armed-forces emergency relief, blood and tissues services, and health and safety services. The funds provided by American Express have enabled the Red Cross to deliver humanitarian relief to victims of numerous disasters around the world.

1. What is the topic? _social responsibility_____

2. What do the details say about the topic? _Toyota is trying to protect the_____ _environment. American Express contributes to charity to help victims of disasters._

3. What is the implied main idea? _Businesses are responsible for helping society in_ _any way they can._____

 ACTIVITY 7

Identify the Implied Main Idea

A. Read the paragraphs below. Circle the letter of the sentence that best expresses the main idea of the paragraph.

1.

Online Pharmaceuticals

There is increasing recognition of the Internet as a legitimate and important vehicle for drug sales. The disabled or otherwise homebound, for whom a trip to the pharmacy can be difficult, now have access to drugs. Consumers have the convenience of shopping 24 hours a day. There is an almost unlimited number of products available for customers. In addition, buying prescription drugs online offers privacy for those who don't want to discuss their medical condition in a public place.

   a. Prescription drug sales on the Internet can provide tremendous benefits to consumers.

   b. The Internet allows people to purchase prescriptions from the safety and comfort of their home.

   c. There are many benefits to consumers who have a computer at home.

2.

Online Pharmacies

There has been an increase in the number of online or Internet pharmacies. Patients who purchase drugs from illegitimate sites face the risk of potential side effects from inappropriately prescribed medications. Other risks include dangerous drug interactions or contaminated drugs. Related to that is the chance for possible ill effects of impure or unknown ingredients found in drugs that are manufactured under substandard conditions. Further risk to patients is posed by their inability to know what they are really getting when they buy some of these drugs. Although some patients may be purchasing genuine products, some may unknowingly be buying counterfeit copies that contain inert ingredients or outdated legitimate drugs that have been diverted to illegitimate resellers.

    a. Online or Internet pharmacies pose a serious threat to the health and safety of customers.

    b. Some Internet sites sell legitimate prescription drugs, but others dispense drugs illegally.

    c. Patients who buy prescription drugs from an illegitimate site are at risk for suffering negative effects.

3.

Fighting Spam

In 2003, it was estimated that 40 percent of all e-mail was spam—unsolicited commercial e-mail—two-thirds of which was false or misleading in some way. In 2003 the cost to business of spam was estimated at $10 billion annually. According to one Internet marketing research, some 206 billion spam items would be sent to American consumers by the year 2006—a figure that means every Internet user will receive 1,400 spam e-mails, twice as many as were received in 2003. Spam clogs ISP networks, undercuts the legitimacy of genuine online marketers, and burdens ordinary consumers with their staggering volume and their creepy content.

    a. There is no solution for stopping spam, and spam will likely continue to increase in volume.

    b. Stopping spam from bothering business and consumers is the responsibility of the government.

    c. Spam needs to be eliminated because of its cost to businesses and burden to consumers.

B. Read the paragraphs below. For each, circle the word or phrase that best expresses the topic of the paragraph. Determine what each detail says about or contributes to the topic. Then write a sentence that expresses the implied main idea.

    1.

The Remaking of the American University

For the new majority of students, higher education is not as central to their lives as it was for previous generations of students. . . . As a consequence, older, part-time, and working students, especially those with children, often said in a national study that I conducted that they wanted a very different type of relationship with their college than students have historically had. They preferred relationships like those they already had with their bank, the electric company, and the grocery. . . . They are looking for just four things from their college—convenience, service, quality, and low cost. . . . They are prime candidates for institutions like the University of Phoenix, now the largest private university in the U.S. They are also excellent candidates for distance learning programs that are available in their home or at the office at any hour.

Implied main idea: _____

_____

2.

Romantic and Electronic Stalking

Both men and women, but seemingly more men, are entering cyberspace in search of electronic courtship, more popularly referred to as "virtual love," as evidenced by the large number of online discussion forums devoted to meeting a mate. But online romance can be accompanied by or lead to online stalking. Indeed, the Internet is proving itself to be a hostile place for women, where female abuse can be found everywhere, including e-mail messages, chat rooms, and Usenet newsgroups. Technology has brought the emergence of electronic stalking, which differs from conventional stalking only in that the former is more sophisticated in its execution.

Implied main idea: _____

_____

3.

Regulation of the Internet

Piracy of music through peer-to-peer networks is now a major problem for some artists and corporations. The Justice Department has seized computers and software in raids on homes and businesses. These actions have targeted the illegal distribution of copyright-protected movies, software, games, and music. The government has also become concerned over losing control over telecommunications services (and resultant revenue) because of VOIP (voice over Internet protocol). The Internet environment is extremely dynamic, so what, if any, taxation and further regulation of VOIP occurs remains to be seen.

Implied main idea: _____

_____

Identifying Text Structure—*Cause/Effect*

Writers sometimes present a topic by offering the reasons for and/or the results of specific actions. In Reading 1, the author cites three newspaper headlines, all of which describe the results of the unethical conduct of three U.S. business executives: resignation, conviction, and prison sentence. The remainder of the reading describes actions that companies can take to influence the ethical conduct of their employees. This approach follows the text structure of *cause and effect*.

There is more than one way to use cause/effect to develop ideas. Commonly used methods include (1) one cause resulting in multiple effects, (2) multiple causes resulting in one effect, (3) multiple causes resulting in multiple effects, and (4) a chain of individual causes and effects. In Reading 1, the writer uses the second method and states that establishing a formal code of ethics, leading by example, and offering ethics training programs are all ways (causes) to influence ethical conduct (effect).

As a reader, recognizing the cause/effect method the writer uses will improve your understanding of the material. Recognizing the method allows you to anticipate the way the writer will present the support for the main idea.

Key Words—*Cause/Effect*

Good readers recognize the key words that are used with different text structures. Recognizing key words speeds your reading and improves your comprehension of the material. Some commonly used key words associated with the pattern of cause/effect include the following.

because/because of	result/as a result of	therefore
cause	reason	due to
for	thus	effect
since	consequence	as

Recognize Key Words

Read the sentences and circle the key words that show cause or effect. Then draw one line under the cause and two lines under the effect in each sentence.

1. A number of top business executives were forced to resign as a result of unethical business practices.

2. The bank teller was fired due to the fact that he knowingly cashed forged checks for his friends.

3. Money was missing from the cash register at the end of the day. Thus, the cashier's pay was docked for the same amount.

4. The company president lied to the judge under oath. This resulted in the president's being fined and sent to jail for 90 days.

5. The scientist alerted city officials to the contaminated city water supply. For coming forward, the scientist was given the city's "Good Citizen" award.

6. The same scientist lost her job the next day as a consequence of "blowing the whistle" on her employer, B. Greene, Inc.

Use Key Words

Read the sentences and fill in the blanks with one of the key words from the chart. Sometimes more than one answer is possible.

1. People choose to do right or wrong _____ their personal code of ethics.

2. Employees often follow the examples set by their managers. _____, if managers act ethically, employees can be expected to act ethically as well.

3. One of the _____ of ethics training programs is an increase in awareness of ethical dilemmas and what constitute appropriate responses.

4. The employee's gambling addiction _____ her to steal laptops from her employer and resell them online.

5. Ben Cohen instituted a salary limit policy at Ben & Jerry's to make all employees feel equal. _____ he himself followed the policy, no one complained that the policy was unfair.

6. People seem to learn information more easily and retain it longer when they're having fun. _____, Citigroup created The Work Ethic, a board game used for ethics training of its employees.

7. One of the _____ companies are investing in ethical training programs is to send a message to shareholders that social responsibility is as important as profits are to the company.

8. _____ he found a company that better suited his needs and personal values, he turned in his resignation last Friday.

READING 2 ● **On Your Own**

In the first section of this chapter, you learned about implied main ideas and cause/effect. You practiced the skills and strategies of surveying, predicting, and summarizing with Reading 1. In this section you will practice these same skills with a new reading. You will also practice using context to guess the meaning of unfamiliar words.

Get Ready to Read

Socially Responsible Activities

Read the following activities and put an X in front of the ones that you believe are "socially responsible." Discuss your answers with a partner.

_____ 1. not investing money in a company that makes tobacco products

_____ 2. cleaning up the water, land, or air that the company has polluted

_____ 3. negotiating a new contract with the employees' union representatives

_____ 4. using products that can be recycled

_____ 5. telling the stockholders the truth about the company's financial situation

Survey and Predict

A. Using the following steps, survey Reading 2 and predict what the reading will be about.

1. Read the title.

2. Read the first paragraph and identify the main idea.

3. Read the headings.

4. Look for any graphic or visual aids in the reading.

5. Look for key terms in bold.

6. Read the last paragraph.

B. Write your prediction here: _____

_____

C. Now read the passage to see if your prediction is correct. Try to read as quickly as you can. Do not stop to look up words in your dictionary.

Reading 2

Managing a Socially Responsible Business

Acting in an ethical manner is one of the components of the pyramid of corporate social responsibility. **Social responsibility** is the concern of businesses for the welfare of society as a whole. It consists of obligations beyond those required by law or union contract. This definition makes two important points. First, social responsibility is voluntary. Beneficial action required by law, such as cleaning up factories that are polluting air and water, is not voluntary. Second, the obligations of social responsibility are broad. Not only do they extend to and affect workers, suppliers, consumers, and communities, but also the investors in the company.

Aspects of Social Responsibility

Although a company's responsibility to make a profit might seem to be its main obligation to its **shareholders**, some investors increasingly are putting more emphasis on other aspects of social responsibility. Some investors are limiting their investments to **securities** that fit within their beliefs about ethical and social responsibility. This is called **social investing.** For example, a social investment fund might eliminate from consideration the securities of all companies that make tobacco products or liquor, manufacture weapons, or have a history of polluting.

Failure to Meet Responsibilities

This decade has been among the worst ever, in modern times, of companies failing to meet responsibilities to investors. Scandals at WorldCom, Krispy Kreme™, HealthSouth™, Enron™, and others so disturbed the investment community that they had a negative impact on the stock market. Investigators found companies claiming huge **assets** that never existed; falsified financial statements; huge loans by companies that could not be justified (or paid back); executives selling massive amounts of **stock** at high prices, then announcing several months later that the earnings were being restated at a much lower level, thus sending the stock crashing; and analysts making "buy" recommendations to the public while sending internal e-mails to coworkers stating that the stock was worthless. These scandals and their resultant effect on the stock market led some companies to take action.

Citigroup Takes Action

One company that decided to quickly alter the way it did business around the globe was Citigroup. Citigroup, the world's largest financial firm, earns about $47 million in **net profits** every day! The former Chief Executive Office (CEO), Sandy Weill, has now stepped up to chairman of the board, and Chuck Prince is the new CEO.*

Chuck Prince says he has found his purpose. He wants to be the chief executive officer who brings a new culture of ethics to Citigroup. This may seem odd for a man who was a close adviser to Sandy Weill, who built Citigroup's financial empire with a ruthless focus on cost-cutting, deal-making, and financial performance. He didn't spend much time talking about "values," "ethics," or "shared responsibilities." Now, those have become Mr. Prince's watchwords. He predicts his campaign will consume at least half of his executive time and energy in the next few years.

---

*2005 earnings; CEO 2003–2007

Communicating Values and Ethics

The company, under both Mr. Weill and Mr. Prince, has been caught misbehaving multiple times, on multiple continents. Mr. Prince says Citigroup isn't a company out of control. Instead, he argues that Citigroup's leaders—himself included—have failed to make their own values and ethics part of the fabric of the corporation. "We emphasized the **short-term performance** side of the equation exclusively," he said. "We didn't think we had to say: 'And by the way, don't violate the law.' There were unspoken assumptions that needed to be spoken."

The first sign Mr. Prince was serious about all this came when he fired three senior executives for failing to manage a problem in Japan. Citigroup's private bank there spent three years flouting the directives of regulators. The firing got the attention of everyone at the company, including some top executives who thought he had overreacted. Since then, he's been quietly constructing a plan to remake the company culture.

The result is a massive campaign that has begun at Citigroup. Many of the company's 300,000 employees gathered to watch a movie that traced the company's history and called on employees to make Citigroup "the most respected global financial-services company." Citigroup's top executives have been told to expect a host of changes that include annual ethics training for all employees, expanded training for top managers, anonymous appraisal of managers by their employees, a 30 percent increase in resources for **compliance** and **audit**, and changes in the way management compensation is calculated. In addition, Mr. Prince plans a global tour each year to reinforce the effort.

Key Concept Words

assets – (n.) property, cash, stock, inventory of a company

audit – (n.) checking to make sure the laws have been followed

compliance - (n.) following or obeying the laws

net profits – (n.) money a company has after paying all its expenses

securities – (n.) documents such as stocks or bonds which show ownership

shareholders – (n.) those who have invested money in the company

short-term performance – (n.) a focus on profits without considering the long-range effects

social investing – (n.) choosing a company to invest in based on the investor's beliefs or values

social responsibility – (n.) concern for the welfare of society as a whole

stock – (n.) a part ownership in a company; a share

Glossed Words

broad – (adj.) general, wide, not specific; **called on employees** – (v.) asked the workers to do something; **decade** – (n.) a period of ten years; **disturbed the investment community** – (v.) upset those who purchase stock or shares in companies; **eliminate from consideration** – (v.) to remove or exclude as a choice; **falsified** – (v.) misrepresented or provided untrue information; **flouting the directives of regulators** – (v.) paying no attention to or ignoring the orders or instructions of the people in charge of regulations (laws, rules); **overreact** – (v.) to react with a force or emotion that is stronger than necessary; **restated (earnings)** – (v.) changed the originally stated amount of the profits or investment gains of a business; **ruthless** – (adj.) merciless, without any thought to another's feelings or situation; **watchwords** – (n.) expressions used to generate enthusiasm or excitement; **worthless** – (adj.) useless, of little or no value.

Summarizing

Share What You Read

Use two or three sentences to tell your partner what you thought the reading was about. Then listen to your partner's sentences. If you disagree, go back and find support for your summary. Write your summary statement below.

Summary: _____

_____

_____

Check Your Comprehension

Read each statement and circle *T* if the statement is true and *F* if it is false. Change a false statement to make it true.

T / F   1. Social responsibility means businesses have concern for their workers, suppliers, customers, communities, and shareholders.

T / F   2. Some shareholders are more concerned with a company's ethical standards than with its earning a profit.

T / F   3. Scandals at some the largest companies, including WorldCom, Enron, and Krispy Kreme, have disturbed the investment community but have not affected the stock market.

T / F   4. Citigroup is one company that has not changed its approach to its culture of ethics.

T / F   5. Citigroup fired three senior executives at its private bank in Japan because of the executives' unethical behavior.

T / F   6. Ethics training is one way to incorporate a company's values into the corporation.

T / F   7. Acting in an ethical manner is just one part of corporate social responsibility.

T / F   8. Citigroup is a company out of control because its leaders have failed to be ethical.

T / F   9. One way to ensure that the company's values are carried out by its workers is by checking to make sure laws have been followed.

T / F   10. Changing the way company managers are paid is one way Citigroup plans to emphasize the company's new culture of ethics.

ACTIVITY 14

Academic Word List

Scan and Define

A. Look at the ten words listed below. Scan the reading and underline the words from the list. Write the definitions for the words you know. Do not use a dictionary.

1. alter *to change or modify* _____

2. beneficial _____

3. components _____

4. consist _____

5. consume _____

6. internal _____

7. investors _____

8. odd _____

9. reinforce _____

10. welfare _____

B. Share your definitions with a partner and then with the rest of your classmates. As a group, try to complete the definitions for all ten words. Use a dictionary to check the definitions if you are unsure about them. Then complete the vocabulary activity.

ACTIVITY 15

Vocabulary Challenge

A. Substitute one of the words from the Academic Word List for the underlined word or phrase. You may have to change the form of the word. The first one has been done for you.

1. Concern for employees is just one of the <u>parts</u> of a corporation's plan to be socially responsible.

   parts = *components* _____

2. Actions which a corporation takes, and which are <u>advantageous</u> for the workers, are by definition voluntary.

   advantageous = _____

3. Social responsibility on the part of businesses, large and small, is so common these days that it seems <u>strange</u> when companies are caught participating in illegal acts or behaviors.

   strange = _____

4. Gone are the days when companies had to look out for the <u>prosperity</u> of only their stockholders and employees.

   prosperity = _____

5. Social responsibility <u>is made up</u> of obligations beyond those required by law and include, for example, sponsoring a literacy program in the community, using renewable energy sources to power a company's facilities, and supporting employees' efforts to volunteer in the community.

   is made up (of) = _____

6. <u>Changing</u> the company's focus from one based solely on financial performance to one that includes a culture of ethics was the goal of Citigroup's CEO Chuck Prince.

changing = _____

B. Read the statements and then circle the correct answer or answers. Sometimes more than one answer is possible. The first one has been done for you.

1. Business executives attend meetings that consume large amounts of their time. Which of the following can also <u>consume</u> time?

   a. employee training   b. employee benefits   c. employee bonuses

2. Companies nowadays commonly have internal e-mail systems for communication with and among employees. Which of the following would not be considered part of a company's <u>internal</u> systems or workings?

   a. dental care   b. profit-sharing   c. promotions

3. Investors are people who contribute money to a company in return for part ownership of the company. Who could be an <u>investor</u> in a publicly traded company such as Microsoft™ or Coca-Cola™?

   a. employees   b. managers   c. nonemployees

4. Citigroup has in place a plan to reinforce its global effort on remaking the company culture. Which of the following can also be <u>reinforced</u>?

   a. vocabulary   b. behavior   c. people

5. Citigroup altered the way it did business around the world. Which of the following can also be <u>altered</u>?

   a. a person's beliefs   b. a person's intelligence   c. a person's behavior

6. One of the components of the pyramid of social responsibility is acting in an ethical manner. Which of the following can also be a <u>component</u> of social responsibility?

   a. following the law   b. contributing to charitable causes
   c. contributing to global warming

7. It may seem odd that the CEO of a large corporation, previously focused only on making a profit, wants to introduce a culture of ethics to the company. Which of the following may also be described as <u>odd</u>?

   a. treating all employees of a company as equals
   b. providing employee training on how to handle ethical dilemmas
   c. limiting the salary of the CEO and other executives

Using Context to Guess Meaning—*Synonyms/Antonyms*

Synonym: a word that means the same as another word

Antonym: a word that means the opposite of another word

Writers often use synonyms and antonyms to add variety to their writing and to clarify meanings. Their use of synonyms and antonyms can serve as context clues to help you understand unfamiliar words. Synonyms are similar to the definition clues you learned about in the previous chapter. They may follow the verbs *be, refer,* or *mean,* or they may be set off by punctuation. Antonyms are similar to the contrast clues you learned about in Chapter 1 and may be used with the words *but, however, unlike,* etc. Read the following sentences to see how synonyms and antonyms help define the words in bold.

1. *The Chief Executive Officer (CEO) of the company was fired for **unethical behavior**. He acted improperly when he gave money and tickets to sports events to city politicians.*

   The phrase *unethical behavior* in the first sentence is followed by the phrase *acted improperly* in the second. Behavior is the way a person acts, so these two words mean the same; *unethical*, then, must mean the same as *improper*. *Improper* is a synonym for *unethical*.

2. *Some companies have developed **formal codes of ethics** for their employees. Other companies, however, have put together summary statements of goals and policies.*

   The phrase *formal codes of ethics* is contrasted with *summary statements of goals and policies*. The word *however* indicates that a formal code is the opposite of or is not the same as summary statements. Thus, the reader can interpret *summary statements* to be informal statements (for proper behavior).

ACTIVITY 16

Guess Meaning from Context

Read the sentences below. Use the synonym or antonym in each sentence as a context clue to determine the meaning of the words in bold. Underline the synonym or antonym. Share your answers with a partner and explain how you guessed the meanings.

1. One of the components of the pyramid of **corporate** social responsibility is acting in an ethical manner. The social responsibility of businesses extends to their workers, suppliers, consumers, and communities as well as to their investors.

   corporate = _____

2. A social investment fund might eliminate from consideration the **securities** of all companies that make tobacco products, manufacture weapons, or have a history of polluting the environment. Instead the fund might buy stocks in companies that donate some of their profits to helping preserve the environment they rely on or the community in which they are located.

   securities = _____

3. Investigators found companies claiming huge **assets** that never existed. In fact, these companies had enormous liabilities: buildings for which rent or mortgages had not been paid in months, equipment that had been repossessed for nonpayment, and little or no cash in the bank.

   assets = _____

4. We didn't think we had to tell our overseas employees not to **violate** the law. We had always assumed our company managers and leaders would follow the law of the country they were in. We thought they were obeying it, and we were shocked to discover they were not.

   violate = _____

5. Citigroup's private bank in Japan spent three years **flouting** the directives of regulators. For their open opposition to Japan's bank regulators, Citigroup fired three of its senior executives working in Japan.

   flouting = _____

6. As CEO of Citigroup, Chuck Prince stated that the company's leaders had **failed** to make their own values and ethics a part of the fabric of the corporation. On the other hand, he insisted that they had succeeded in turning things around by initiating ethics training for all employees.

   failed = _____

7. During ethics training sessions, employees are **called on** to make the company "the most respected global-financial services company" in the world. By asking its employees, as representatives of the company, to act ethically, it hopes to gain back the respect it has lost.

   called on = _____

8. Citigroup has created an ethics training board game in which participants **strive** to correctly answer legal, regulatory, and judgment ethics questions. These questions are not your everyday, simple-to-answer ones; they require critical thinking and serious consideration.

   strive = _____

WRITING 1A • # Skills and Strategies

In this section, you will learn some skills and strategies associated with the writing process. It includes the grammar of parallel structures, which is one of the grammatical structures used in the readings. In this section, you will practice the different steps in the writing process and will write an essay of cause and effect.

The Grammar of Parallelism

Parallelism means balancing the grammatical structures you use in your writing. You balance grammatical structures when you keep similar parts of speech or structures together: nouns with nouns, verbs with verbs, and prepositional phrases with prepositional phrases, for example. Study the sample sentences below.

*Poor business ethics **can create** a negative image, **can be** expensive for the firm, and **can result** in bankruptcy.*

*Most large companies have **created, printed,** and **distributed** codes of ethics to their employees.*

*Leaders and managers establish patterns of behavior that determine **what is acceptable** and **what is not** within the organization.*

In the first example, the writer lists three results of poor business ethics. Each result begins with the modal verb *can* + verb. The verbs are then followed by objects or complements. In the second example, the writer follows the auxiliary *have* with three past participles: *created, printed, distributed.* In the third example, the writer follows the verb with two noun clauses: *what is acceptable* and *what is not.* Now look at some examples of writing that lacks parallelism.

*The CEO of the company was convicted of **larceny, fraud,** and **conspired** to deceive the shareholders.*

*The organization had trouble **financially, legally,** and **ethics problems**.*

*Training employees and **to lead** by example are two things management should do to promote ethics.*

In the first example, the writer lists three crimes: two are nouns and one is in verb form. *Conspired* needs to be changed to *conspiracy* (a noun) to make the list parallel. In the second example, the writer uses two adjectives and a noun phrase. Changing *ethics problems* to *ethically* will make the sentence elements parallel. In the third example, the subject consists of the gerund *training* and the infinitive *to lead*. Changing *to lead* to *leading* makes the sentence parallel.

 ACTIVITY **17**

Recognize Parallelism

A. Read the sentences below. If the sentence has parallelism, put *P* in the blank. If it lacks parallelism, put *NP* in the blank and correct the sentence to make it parallel.

_____ 1. Employees need to know what their firm expects in terms of their behavior toward fellow employees, customers, and suppliers.

_____ 2. Organizations provide formal training to develop an awareness of questionable business activities and to practice appropriate responses.

_____ 3. Some ethical codes are really summary statements of goals, policies, and what is a priority.

_____ 4. People might not invest in companies that make tobacco products, manufacture weapons, or if they pollute the environment.

_____ 5. The company has been caught misbehaving multiple times, on multiple continents.

_____ 6. Changes include annual ethics training for all employees, expanded training for top managers, and they will increase resources for compliance and audit.

_____ 7. People choose between what is right and doing wrong based on their personal codes of ethics.

_____ 8. Some companies have tried to add fun and be exciting to their ethics-training programs by presenting them in the form of games.

_____ 9. Some people believe that ethics training makes employees behave in a more ethical manner, and others believe it does not.

_____ 10. If senior management follows a code of ethics and emphasis is put on the code to employees, it will have a positive influence on behavior.

B. Write sentences of your own that contain parallel structures. Underline the parallel structures. Your sentences can be about any topic.

1. _____

   _____

2. _____

   _____

3. _____

   _____

4. _____

   _____

Sentence Essentials

Clause Relationships

In previous Sentence Essentials sections, you used dependent and independent clauses to form different sentence types: simple, compound, complex, and compound-complex. In this section, you will look more closely at the relationship between clauses.

Related Ideas

Writers often choose to join two independent clauses when the ideas in each are related. Ideas that are unrelated should be kept in separate clauses. Look at the examples below.

Related: *Some employees steal from their employers. These employees believe their low wages entitle them to take office supplies home or to copy company software programs for personal use.*

These two clauses are related because the second clause explains the reason for the statement in the first clause. The relationship between the two clauses can be expressed with the subordinating conjunction *because:* Some employees steal from their employers **because** they believe their low wages entitle them to take office supplies home or to copy company software programs for personal use.

Unrelated: *Some employees steal from their employers. Analysts estimate the cost of employee theft to be billions of dollars every year.*

Although the two clauses both mention employee theft, the connection between them is weak. The focus of the first clause is that some employees steal. The second clause addresses the total annual cost of all employee theft. The first clause refers to a smaller, subgroup of employees, while the second one refers to the cost of all employee theft. The relationship between the two clauses is unclear and difficult to express.

Related: *Employee theft is a big problem. Analysts estimate the cost of employee theft to be billions of dollars every year.*

The two clauses are related because each addresses the cost of employee theft. The first clause introduces a general statement, and the second clause offers a specific fact to support it. The relationship between the two can be expressed with the coordinating conjunction *and:* Employee theft is a big problem, **and** analysts estimate the cost of employee theft to be billions of dollars every year. The two clauses could also be joined with the subordinating conjunction *such* + noun + *that:* Employee theft is **such a big problem that** analysts estimate the cost to be billions of dollars every year.

 ACTIVITY 18

Are the Ideas Related?

Read the clauses. If the ideas in each clause are related, put *R* in the blank. If they are not related, put *NR* in the blank. Share your answers with a partner and explain the reason for your choice.

_____ 1. Poor business ethics can contribute to a negative image for a company. Ben Cohen followed a policy that no one could earn a salary more than seven times the lowest-paid worker.

_____ 2. Many American companies have ethics training programs for their employees. Companies need to provide a system to resolve ethical dilemmas.

_____ 3. Effective ethics training programs begin with techniques for solving ethical dilemmas. Employees are presented with a series of situations and have to come with the "best" ethical solution.

_____ 4. Today's corporations are establishing in-house gyms, day cares, and cafeterias. These companies are concerned about their employees' well-being.

_____ 5. The role of managers is to serve as an example to their employees. Leaders and managers establish patterns of behavior that determine what is and is not acceptable.

_____ 6. Employees need to follow the company's dress code and dress appropriately for work. Employees should receive a company handbook when they start working.

Equally Important Ideas

Writers may choose to join two independent clauses when the ideas in each clause are related and are equally important. Independent clauses are joined with coordinating conjunctions, conjunctive adverbs, or semicolons. Which method to use in joining the clauses is the writer's choice. Look at the examples below.

Business is a popular major in many colleges and universities, **and** *courses in business ethics are common in today's business curriculum.*

Business is a popular major in many colleges and universities; **in addition,** *courses in business ethics are common in today's business curriculum.*

Business is a popular major in many colleges and universities; courses in business ethics are common in today's business curriculum.

Ideas That Are Not Equally Important

When the ideas in two clauses are related but are not equally important, writers usually combine the ideas and form a complex sentence using an adjective, adverb, or noun clause. Look at the examples below; the important ideas are in bold.

Original ideas: Some employees violate their company's ethics guidelines. Those employees should be fired.

Employees who violate their company's ethics guidelines **should be fired**. (contains adjective clause)

If employees violate their company's ethics guidelines, **they should be fired**. (contains adverb clause)

Companies should fire *whoever violates their ethics guidelines.* (contains noun clause)

ACTIVITY 19

Are the Ideas Equal in Importance?

Read the sentences. If the ideas in each sentence are equal in importance, put *E* in the blank. If the ideas are not equal in importance, put *NE*.

_____ 1. People choose between right and wrong based on their personal code of ethics, and the decisions they make are further influenced by the ethical environment their employers have created.

_____ 2. Some ethical codes offer employees a long, detailed set of guidelines, but others are summary statements of goals, policies, and priorities.

_____ 3. In addition to providing a system to resolve ethical dilemmas, organizations also provide formal training to their employees.

_____ 4. If senior management abides by the code of ethics and regularly emphasizes it to employees, it will likely have a positive influence on behavior.

_____ 5. Although a company's responsibility to make a profit might seem to be its main obligation to its shareholders, some investors are putting more emphasis on other aspects of social responsibility.

_____ 6. Citigroup's top executives have been told to expect a host of changes; in addition, Mr. Prince plans a global tour each year to reinforce the effort.

Determining Whether/How to Combine Clauses

The important idea is in the independent or main clause while the less important idea is in the dependent or subordinate clause. In order to determine whether to combine ideas and what kind of sentence type to write, follow the steps in the chart below.

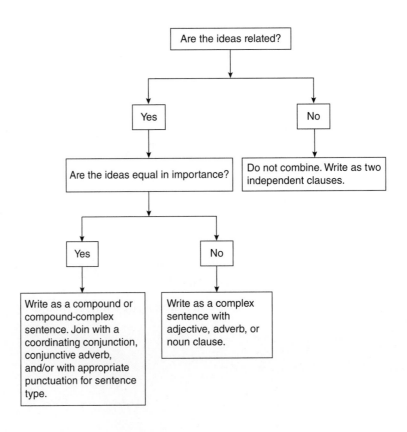

ACTIVITY 20 *Join Ideas Equal in Importance*

Connect the clauses to show that the ideas in each are equally important. There is more than one way to connect the clauses.

1. Some companies frame their code of ethics and hang it on office walls. Other companies print their code of ethics on cards to be carried by their executives.
    _____
    _____

2. Dennis Kozlowski of Tyco, International was convicted of grand larceny and falsifying business records. Bernie Ebbers of WorldCom was sentenced to 25 years in prison for his role in corporate fraud. _____
    _____
    _____

3. Some people believe that codes of ethics make employees behave in a more ethical manner. Others think that they are little more than public relations gimmicks. _____
    _____

4. Scandals at WorldCom, Krispy Kreme, and Enron had a negative impact on the stock market. Some companies decided to take action to change the way they did business. _____
    _____

 ACTIVITY 21 *Join Ideas Unequal in Importance*

Connect the clauses to show that the idea in one clause is more important than the idea in the other clause. As the writer, you will choose which idea receives emphasis. You may have to add, delete, or change some words. The first one has been done for you.

1. Mr. Prince was serious about communicating company values and ethics. Mr. Prince fired three senior executives for failing to manage a problem in Japan.
    Because Mr. Prince was serious about communicating company values and ethics, he
    fired three senior executives for failing to manage a problem in Japan.

2. He turned in his letter of resignation. He found a job at a company that was more in line with his work ethics. _____
    _____

3. The company accountant had been creating phony business accounts. She was fired and then charged with a criminal offense. _____
    _____

4. Social responsibility is a voluntary action taken by a company. It is not required by law or union contract. _____
    _____

5. It is well known. Employees who "blow the whistle" on their employers are often fired. _____
    _____

Making Sentences Parallel

Clauses that are connected show how ideas are related or equal in importance. Parallelism shows a similar relationship, but the balance is grammatical. In The Grammar of Parallelism in this chapter, you practiced recognizing parallel structures in sentences. In this section, you will practice writing sentences that contain parallel structures.

Parallelism means that the grammatical structures in a sentence are balanced: words with words, phrases with phrases, and clauses with clauses. Look at the examples below.

Sentence with Parallel Structure	Sentence Lacking Parallel Structure
Some ethical codes are really summary statements of **goals, policies,** and **priorities.**	Some ethical codes are really summary statements of **goals, policies,** and **what is a priority.**
Many businesses sell goods **in stores, over the Internet,** and **via catalogues.**	Many businesses sell goods **in stores, online,** and **catalogues.**
Employees need to know **what behavior is acceptable** and **what behavior is not.**	Employees need to know **what behavior is acceptable** and **how not to behave.**

In each of the example sentences above, the elements of the parallel structure were connected with *and.* It is possible to use other connectors including *or, either/or, neither/nor, both/and, not/but, not only/but also.* In the examples below, the underlined elements are parallel.

Ethics questions can be <u>legal</u>, <u>regulatory</u>, **or** <u>policy-related</u> in nature.

Companies need **either** <u>to provide training in ethics</u> **or** <u>to provide a system to solve ethical dilemmas.</u>

Neither <u>WorldCom</u> **nor** <u>Enron</u> could defend its unethical behavior towards its employees and stockholders.

Both <u>American Express</u> **and** <u>Levi Strauss</u> begin ethics training with solving ethical dilemmas.

The top executive of that company was charged **not** <u>with one crime</u> **but** <u>with two</u>.

Some companies **not only** <u>failed to meet their responsibilities to their investors</u> **but also** <u>had executives who were charged with corporate fraud.</u>

ACTIVITY **22**

Make Sentence Elements Parallel

Each sentence below has an error in parallelism. Rewrite each sentence, correcting the error. There may be more than one way to correct the error. The first one has been done for you.

1. Corporations have a social responsibility to their employees, shareholders, and the people who buy their products. *Corporations have a social responsibility to their employees, shareholders, and customers.*

2. Both air pollution and polluting the water cause harm to the communities in which businesses operate. _____

3. Employees either need to follow a company's code of ethics or to be fired for violating it. _____

_____

4. In the boardroom, an office, or on the factory floor—no matter where the employee works, he or she must behave in an ethical manner. _____

_____

_____

5. Some companies try not only to make ethics training fun but also they add excitement to it. _____

_____

6. Neither top executives nor people who are managers should put their company in a bad light by acting or to behave unethically. (contains two errors) _____

_____

Making the Connection

Good readers take advantage of the fact that the introduction to a passage contains the author's thesis statement (the main idea and what the author wants the reader to know about it). Finding this information in the introduction prepares the reader for the rest of the passage and improves the reader's overall comprehension of the passage. Good writers know they must capture the reader's attention in the first paragraph. Once they have done this, they need to let the reader know how the subject of the passage is going to be developed. For both the reader and the writer, the introduction and thesis statement are key elements in a passage.

WRITING 1B ● **The Process**

Get Ready to Write

Structure of an Essay

An essay is a group of paragraphs about a single topic. All of the paragraphs in an essay must be related to the topic; they must also be in a logical order. In order to write an essay, writers must be able to organize and express their ideas in paragraphs, the building blocks of an essay.

Writers may take different approaches to the writing process, but most writers follow a basic essay format. They begin their essay with a paragraph that introduces the thesis statement (the main idea and controlling idea). The body of the essay contains the details that support the thesis statement. Each body paragraph begins with a topic sentence that supports the thesis of the essay. The essay then ends with a concluding paragraph. The following chart illustrates the structure of an essay.

Structure of an Essay

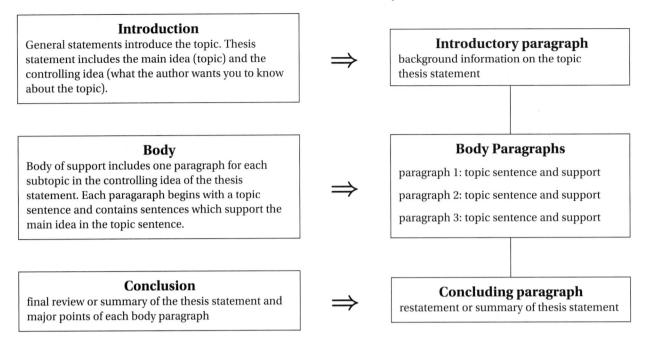

Introduction
General statements introduce the topic. Thesis statement includes the main idea (topic) and the controlling idea (what the author wants you to know about the topic).

⇒

Introductory paragraph
background information on the topic
thesis statement

Body
Body of support includes one paragraph for each subtopic in the controlling idea of the thesis statement. Each paragraph begins with a topic sentence and contains sentences which support the main idea in the topic sentence.

⇒

Body Paragraphs
paragraph 1: topic sentence and support
paragraph 2: topic sentence and support
paragraph 3: topic sentence and support

Conclusion
final review or summary of the thesis statement and major points of each body paragraph

⇒

Concluding paragraph
restatement or summary of thesis statement

Study the parts of the essay below. The thesis statement in the introduction and the topic sentence for each body paragraph have been underlined.

The Social Responsibility of Business

Introductory paragraph:

For years, the general pursuit of most, if not all, businesses was to make a profit and beat out the competition. Over the years, that view has changed. Companies, large and small, are beginning to view their responsibility to people other than the shareholders. <u>Companies have a social responsibility to their employees and to the community in which they operate, as well.</u>

Body paragraphs:

<u>Employees need and want more than just a paycheck from their employer, and businesses are beginning to recognize that their employees' welfare is part of their responsibility.</u> Businesses are finding ways to make work more personally satisfying for their employees. They offer their workers advanced training courses, provide opportunities for advancement within the company, and solicit input from employees on company policies and practices. Many corporations offer in-house day care, car or van pools, employee cafeterias, and on-site fitness centers. Employees are key to a company's success.

    <u>Businesses are also giving back to the communities in which they do business.</u> In addition to supporting community organizations and schools through donations of supplies and money, companies are also encouraging their employees to volunteer in the community. To show their support, businesses allow employees to volunteer during their work hours while still receiving compensation. This "release time" sends a positive message to both the community and the employee. Finally, businesses are aware of the need to be environmentally friendly. They are making an effort to use energy more efficiently and are reducing pollution through the use of antipollution and pollution control devices.

Concluding paragraph:

Although not all companies have jumped on the social responsibilty "bandwagon," it is only a matter of time before environmentally conscious consumers—through their pocketbooks—send messages to those companies without social consciences. In time, stockholders, too, will make more investment decisions based on a company's attitude toward the environment rather than just on its profit-making ability.

Identify the Parts of an Essay

Identify the parts of the essay in Reading 2. Underline the thesis statement and topic sentences in each body paragraph.

Characteristics of Essay Elements

Every essay comprises basic elements: an introduction, body, and conclusion. Study the characteristics of each below.

The introduction

- usually begins with a "hook" to get the reader's attention
- provides general background information about the topic
- leads to the thesis statement, which includes the topic and the controlling idea of the essay
- gives the reader an idea how the topic will be developed

The body

- contains one paragraph for each subtopic in the controlling idea
- each paragraph begins with a topic sentence
- each paragraph supports the main idea in the topic sentence
- each paragraph may include examples, facts, or statistics
- presents ideas in logical order (most important ⟶ least important, for example)

The conclusion

- signals the end of the essay
- may include a restatement, in different words, of the thesis statement
- may summarize the main points of the essay
- may offer a suggestion or make a prediction
- may offer a final comment about the topic
- does not introduce a new idea or topic

Introduction

The introductory paragraph of an essay accomplishes two things: it gets the reader's attention, and it offers the reader some background information on the topic. The introduction usually ends with the writer's thesis statement.

There are different techniques for beginning an introduction:

- ask a question
- provide statistics or facts
- describe an event or tell a story
- make a general statement followed by increasingly more specific statements
- use a quotation

The technique you use depends on your topic. It is also possible to use a combination of different techniques. Do not begin every essay with a question. In the examples below, the underlined thesis is the same, yet the techniques vary.

Question

Why do some businesses succeed and others fail? If the answer were obvious, more of us would feel comfortable starting up our own companies, knowing we were taking on very little risk. Although the success or failure of a particular business also depends on factors related to the business and to its owner, there are some characteristics successful businesses share. <u>Those characteristics include excellent customer service, quality goods, and happy employees.</u>

Statistics/Facts

Research shows that 50 percent of businesses close within five years of their start-up. Businesses fail for many reasons—poor market research, unrealistic product pricing, and ineffective advertising are just three. On the other hand, 50 percent of businesses are still open within five years of their start-up. <u>They are doing something right: paying attention to the customer, the product, and the employees are all factors in the success of a business.</u>

Event/Story

Fifty years ago, my great-grandfather came to this country from Europe. He couldn't speak English when he first arrived, but that didn't keep him from working. He opened up a small grocery store in the Italian neighborhood where he and my great-grandmother settled. Little by little, the store and its reputation grew. Eventually, my grandfather and then my father took over the store. <u>There are three reasons why this family business succeeded: outstanding customer service, quality products, and happy employees.</u>

General → Specific Statements

For many people, owning their own business is a dream. Some people work two or three jobs in order to save enough money to open a store with their name on the sign. Owning one's own business means taking a risk and putting in long hours, all in order to build the business. <u>In order to succeed, business owners also need to offer good customer service, sell quality products, and keep their employees happy.</u>

Quotation

"Success seems to be connected with action. Successful people keep moving. They make mistakes, but they don't quit." This quote from Conrad Hilton, founder of the Hilton Hotels™ chain, applies to nearly all successful businesses, be they large or small. <u>The action that is connected with success includes treating the customers right, offering the customers quality service, and keeping your employees happy.</u>

Organize the Introduction

Read the sentences. Put a *1* in front of the hook or opening sentence. Number the succeeding sentences *2, 3,* and *4.* Put a *5* in front of the thesis statement.

A.

The Business of Education

_____ 1. The cost of tuition and books and parking seems to rise every semester.

_____ 2. Many schools, however, are not putting the money they collect back into the campus.

_____ 3. Are we in the education business or the business of education?

_____ 4. At the same time, financial aid is hardly enough to cover the basic costs of school.

_____ 5. Colleges and universities need to put students first and profits second.

B.

Green Businesses

_____ 1. Cutting costs makes more economic sense than raising prices.

_____ 2. Being more energy-efficient helps business as well as the environment.

_____ 3. With rising energy costs, businesses either have to increase prices or cut costs.

_____ 4. Research shows that nearly 75 percent of U.S. businesses are making efforts to be energy efficient.

_____ 5. There are several steps that businesses can take both to cut energy costs and protect the environment.

C.

Conflicitng Business Cultures

_____ 1. They must decide how to deal with conflicting business cultures.

_____ 2. There are a number of ways business can deal with this international issue.

_____ 3. "When in Rome, do as the Romans do."

_____ 4. While tourists, however, go home, businesses cannot simply pack up and leave.

_____ 5. This saying applies to tourists and businesses alike as they encounter cultural differences.

ACTIVITY 25

Write an Introduction

On a separate sheet of paper, write short introductions of three to five sentences that lead to the thesis statements below. Begin the introduction with the technique indicated, and end with the thesis statement. You may change the wording of the thesis statement to fit your introduction.

A. Thesis Statement: Majoring in business can lead to a career in private companies, government agencies, or nonprofit organizations.

　　1. Question

　　2. General → Specific

B. Thesis Statement: Working in jobs they do not like affects people both psychologically and physically.

    1. Facts (or statistics)

    2. Quotation

C. Thesis Statement: A good employer is one who offers interesting work, job security, and good pay.

    1. Event (or story)

    2. General → Specific

Thesis statement

> **Thesis statement:** contains the topic and controlling idea for the essay

The thesis statement is the most important sentence in the introduction. It contains the topic and what you want the reader to know about it, sometimes referred to as the *controlling idea*. The controlling idea provides a focus for the topic and may be divided into subtopics. The thesis statement may also indicate how the essay will be developed; that is, it may refer to the steps in a process, to the similarities and differences between two things, or to the classification of similar objects.

Study the information contained in the example thesis statements below.

1. The characteristics of a **successful business** include **excellent customer service, quality goods**, and **happy employees**.
   - topic
   - controlling idea: three subtopics

2. **Business cultures** in the **United States and China** have both **similarities and differences**.
   - topic
   - controlling idea
   - essay development
   - essay development: compare/contrast

3. There are **several steps** that **businesses** can take both to **cut energy costs and protect the environment**.
   - topic
   - controlling idea: two subtopics

4. The pressure of **owning your own business** can **result** in increased **psychological and physical stress**.
   - essay development: cause/effect
   - topic
   - controlling idea: two subtopics

Forming the Thesis Statement

In order to write an effective thesis statement, you must know your topic and what you want to say about it. Because it is the most important sentence in the introduction and will lead the reader to the rest of your essay, your thesis statement must not be too general, nor should it be too specific. The statements below are examples of poor thesis statements.

1. *Studying business is interesting.* This thesis statement is too general. The writer needs to add a controlling idea to the topic *studying business*. Adding the phrase *for several reasons* is an improvement and tells the reader to expect three or four reasons why studying business is interesting.

2. *Shaking hands with a woman is common in the business culture of the United States.* This thesis statement is too specific. There is nothing left for the writer to say. The statement is actually a detail and could support a thesis statement about differences in business cultures between two countries or between genders, for example.

3. *Businesses should practice social responsibility.* This thesis statement expresses the writer's opinon but does not provide any further information. Adding reasons to the statement will make it a stronger thesis statement: *Businesses should practice social responsibility because their decisions and practices directly affect society and the environment.*

Evaluate Thesis Statements

Read the following thesis statements. Put a *G* on the line if the thesis statement is too general; put an *S* on the line if it is too specific. Make the general thesis statements stronger by adding information.

_____ 1. Women and men manage their businesses differently.

_____ 2. Starting up your own business is complicated.

_____ 3. Approximately a quarter of all businesses in the United States are owned by women.

_____ 4. Small business owners are very similar.

_____ 5. Opening your own business is exciting.

_____ 6. Male-owned businesses have more employees than female-owned businesses.

Develop Thesis Statements

Read the topics below. Create a thesis statement for each topic. Share your answers with a partner.

1. making your employees happy _____
   _____

2. how to get a good job _____
   _____

3. it's hard to be a salesperson _____
   _____

4. doing business in different cultures _____
   _____

5. owning my own business _____
   _____

How Did They Do That?

This section of the chapter focuses on essay writing and begins with an overview of the writing process. The characteristics of an essay of cause/effect follow the overview, and the section ends with a step-by-step look at how the writer used cause/effect to develop Reading 1, "Organizations Can Influence Employees' Ethical Conduct."

Overview of the Writing Process

Writers may take different approaches to the writing process. They follow the steps listed below but might complete them in a different order. Nevertheless, good writers plan before they begin to write. Planning means completing the steps outlined below. As you will see, writing an essay includes many of the same steps used to write a paragraph.

The first four steps in the essay-writing process—brainstorming the topic, narrowing the topic, brainstorming and narrowing details, and choosing the text structure—are the same whether you are writing a paragraph or an essay.

Brainstorming

Brainstorming is a method writers use to generate ideas for writing. When writers brainstorm a topic, they write down every idea they can think of that is related to the topic. No idea is excluded when brainstorming, so it makes no difference if the idea is good or bad, general or specific, broad or narrow. The goal is to list as many ideas as possible within a short period of time.

Before brainstorming, writers usually have an idea of who the audience or reader will be. They also have in mind the purpose of their writing: a letter for college admission, a research paper for a professor, a class project, or the answer to a question on an essay exam.

After brainstorming, writers go through their ideas and evaluate each one based on the appropriateness for the audience and purpose. They reject some ideas right away. They evaluate each idea on the list until have narrowed the list down to one topic. (See Appendix 2 on page 277 for examples of brainstorming methods.)

Narrowing the Topic

After brainstorming possible topics and choosing one, writers often need to narrow the topic if it is too general or too broad. Narrowing the topic means limiting the focus to a specific topic that can be covered completely in one paragraph or in one essay.

Brainstorming and Narrowing Details

Sometimes, during the initial brainstorming of a topic, writers generate ideas that can be included in the body of the paragraph or essay. Other times, writers have to brainstorm a second time in order to produce possible details to support the topic. Details may include facts, statistics, personal experiences, opinions, examples, or reasons. The writer chooses the ones that will best support the main idea of the paragraph or essay.

Choosing Text Structure

Once the writer decides which details to include to support the main idea, a logical text structure or pattern of organization often becomes clear. Common text structures include analysis, classification, cause/effect, compare/contrast, definition, exemplification, persuasion, process, and problem/solution. Although writers may combine text structures, they usually use one main pattern of organization.

At times, you will decide the structure or pattern of organization to use in your writing. Other times an assignment will determine or dictate the text structure for you. For example, an essay exam prompt might ask you to "classify the different fields of anthropology and explain each" or "discuss the causes and effects of cultural misunderstandings, providing specific examples." It is important to choose the text structure that best fits your main idea and details.

Writing the Thesis Statement

The thesis statement is the most important sentence in the essay and is often the last sentence in the introductory paragraph. It contains the topic and, through the controlling idea, the focus of the essay. It may also indicate how the essay will be developed.

Writing Topic Sentences

The topic sentence is the most important sentence in a paragraph and is often, but not always, the first sentence in the paragraph. It informs the reader what information the paragraph will contain and limits what the writer can include. In an essay, each element in the controlling idea of the thesis statement forms a topic sentence for one of the body paragraphs in the essay. You will practice writing topic sentences for the body paragraphs of an essay in the next chapter.

There are several important points to remember about topic sentences:

- A topic sentence is a complete sentence. It must have a subject, verb, and, in most instances, a complement.

- A topic sentence should be specific. It should let the reader know what to expect in the paragraph. *Business is a popular subject in college* is not a good topic sentence because it is too general. *Business is a diverse field of study comprising several sectors* is a good topic sentence because it is specific.

- A topic sentence should not be too specific, or the writer will have nothing more to add. *The American Cancer Society is a not-for-profit organization* is too limiting to be a good topic sentence.

- A topic sentence should not be a universally known fact. *Exports are goods and services which are sold outside of the home country of the business* is not a good topic sentence.

- A topic sentence should have a controlling idea that limits or restricts the focus or content in a paragraph. Look at the following examples:
  1. *Business serves several important functions in society.*
  2. *The cultural rules of a society influence the way people conduct business.*
  3. *There are three common types of business ownership.*

Each of the topic sentences above shares the topic of *business* but has different controlling ideas that let the reader know what the focus of the paragraph will be. Each paragraph would be unique because of the controlling idea.

Organizing the Essay

Once writers have completed the pre-writing steps and have chosen their thesis statement and topic sentences, they organize all their ideas before writing the first draft of an essay. Organizing ideas often takes the form of an outline, which may be formal or informal. An outline shows the writer whether the essay has sufficient support for each idea presented and whether ideas are presented in logical order. An outline also helps keep the writer focused on the thesis statement. Below is a sample outline for an essay.

Title of Essay

I. Introduction
   A. Hook and background information
   B. Thesis statement (main idea + controlling idea)

```
        II. Body
             A. Topic sentence (controlling idea 1) for body paragraph 1
                   1. Support
                         a. Detail
                         b. Detail
                   2. Support
                         a. Detail
                         b. Detail
             B. Topic sentence (controlling idea 2) for body paragraph 2
                   1. Support
                         a. Detail
                         b. Detail
                   2. Support
             C. Topic sentence (controlling idea 3) for body paragraph 3
                   1. Support
                   2. Support
                         a. Detail
                         b. Detail
       III. Conclusion
             A. Summary of main points or restatement of thesis
             B. Writer's final thoughts and comments on topic
```

Writing the Introduction

As noted in the previous section, the introductory paragraph of an essay gets the
reader's attention and offers the reader some background information on the topic.
The introductory paragraph of an essay usually ends with the thesis statement.

Writing the Body

The body paragraphs of an essay address the topic contained in the thesis
statement. Each paragraph focuses on one controlling idea in the thesis statement
and develops it through general and specific support. Each paragraph in an essay
typically begins with a topic sentence followed by general and specific support
in the form of explanations, facts, statistics, examples, and experiences. You
will practice writing different types of support sentences for body paragraphs in
Chapters 4–6.

Writing the Conclusion

The concluding paragraph of an essay serves the same purpose as a concluding
sentence in a paragraph: it marks the end of the essay and leaves the reader with
the writer's final thoughts about the topic. While the conclusion of an essay often
restates the thesis or summarizes the main points of the essay, it may also make a
prediction or pose a question. You will practice writing conclusions in Chapter 6.

Revising, Editing, and Proofreading

> **Revising:** rewriting an essay to improve its content, structure, and flow of ideas

The first draft of an essay is often called a *rough draft.* It is the first attempt at getting all of the ideas and support for the essay down on paper. Most writers focus on the content and organization of their essay during the writing of their first draft. Afterwards, as they re-read their essay, they check to see whether it has unity and coherence. Does each paragraph address one aspect of the thesis statement? Are the sentences and paragraphs in logical order? Writers revise or rewrite their essay as many times as necessary to ensure their ideas and support are presented clearly and logically. They may add or delete details, rearrange the order of sentences or paragraphs, and add transitions to make their ideas flow more smoothly.

After revising the essay for content and organization, writers turn their attention to the *mechanics* of writing. They edit their essay, looking for and correcting errors in grammar, punctuation, and spelling. They check for fragments and run-on sentences, incorrect use of articles and prepositions, and inconsistent verb tense. They look for errors in subject-verb agreement, singular and plural nouns, and word form. Once writers have edited their essay and made corrections, they write their final draft. They proofread the final draft of their essay, looking for errors they might have missed while editing and for new errors they might have made during the revision or editing process.

Essays of Cause/Effect

Essays of cause/effect

- explain the reason and/or result of some action, event, or situation
- can be used to inform or persuade the reader
- develop ideas in one of four ways:
  1. one cause resulting in one effect
  2. one cause resulting in multiple effects
  3. multiple causes resulting in one effect—Reading 1
  4. a chain of individual causes and effects
- can focus on the cause or the effect or both, but usually emphasize one more than the other
- use key words such as *cause, effect, reason, result, because, since, as, for, due to, thus, therefore, consequently,* and *so.*
- often begin with a general introduction to the topic
- contain a thesis statement that refers to both the cause and effect but makes clear what the essay will focus on

Follow the Writer's Steps

Refer to Reading 1, "Organizations Can Influence Employees' Ethical Conduct," as you follow the writer's steps in the essay-writing process.

1. Brainstorming

   Look at some of the writer's brainstorming ideas for the essay "Organizations Can Influence Employees' Ethical Conduct." In the following list, circle the idea the writer chose for the essay. Circle it in the reading as well.

ethics
what *ethics* means
ethical conduct
right vs. wrong
personal ethics
rules and laws
universal ethics

2. Narrowing the topic

    After choosing the very general topic *ethical conduct*, the writer narrowed it.
    Look at the writer's ideas for the topic. In the list below, circle the narrowed
    topic the writer chose. Underline it in the reading as well.

    ethical conduct
    cultural differences related to ethical conduct
    writing guidelines for ethical conduct
    ethical vs. unethical conduct
    influencing people's ethical conduct
    religious aspect of ethical conduct
    political aspect of ethical conduct

3. Brainstorming and narrowing details

    Look at the writer's list of possible details to support the topic *influencing
    people's ethical conduct*. Circle the details the writer chose to include in the
    essay. Draw two lines under the details in the essay as well.

    influencing people's ethical conduct

Reason for a person's conduct	Result of employee misconduct
personal ethics fear of going to jail greed due to low wages influenced by employer	negative image for company expensive for company to fix stockholders sell shares bankruptcy for company prison for company executives/employees customers stop buying products lawsuits
Reasons employees change behavior	**Result of addressing company ethics**
employers educate them about ethics employees sign agreements when hired employees see unethical people getting fired managers/executives set a good example managers threaten employees with being fired employees want to get promoted companies have ethics training programs	employees are more ethical good public relations companies save money positive effect on employees

4. Choosing the text structure

    Look at the categories the writer used for brainstorming and narrowing details
    in the previous activity. Listing the reasons and results for employee conduct/
    misconduct and reasons and results of employees' change in behavior suggests
    a cause-and-effect text structure. Find and number at least three sentences in
    the essay that explain the reasons employees change their behavior.

5. Writing the thesis statement

Look at the writer's thesis statement below. Does it contain the topic? Does it contain a controlling idea, what the writer wants the reader to know about the topic? Does it suggest a text structure of cause/effect? Label the three parts of the thesis statement: topic, controlling idea (what the writer wants the reader to know), and the clue to the text structure.

Thesis statement: *Educating their employees about ethical standards, leading through example, and providing various informal and formal programs are all ways to have an effect on the ethical conduct of an organization's employees.*

6. Writing the topic sentences for the body paragraphs

Locate the writer's thesis statement in the essay. Does the controlling idea contain the subtopics that will be discussed in the essay? Underline the subtopics in the controlling idea.

Look at the essay. Is there a body paragraph that addresses each subtopic? Is there a topic sentence for each paragraph? Find the topic sentences in the essay that address the subtopics and underline each one.

7. Organizing the essay

A. Look at the outline below for the essay "Organizations Can Influence Employees' Ethical Conduct." Compare the organization of the outline with the organization of the essay. Notice how the writer used the outline to arrange the details in a logical order using the text structure of cause/effect. Refer to the essay to fill in any missing information.

Organizations Can Influence Employees' Ethical Conduct

Thesis statement: *Educating their employees about ethical standards, leading through example, and providing various informal and formal programs are all ways to have an effect on the ethical conduct of an organization's employees.*

I. Choosing between right and wrong

  A. Personal code of ethics

  B. Ethical environment created by employers

  C. Consequences for business

    1. negative image

    2. expensive

    3. _____

    4. _____

  D. Reducing potential/causing change in behavior

    1. educate employees

    2. lead through example

    3. formal/informal training programs

II. _____

    A. Knowledge of what a firm expects

        1. responsibilities and behavior

        2. affects coworkers, customers, suppliers

    B. Types

        1. lengthy and detailed guidelines

        2. summary statements of goals, policies, priorities

III. _____

    A. Leaders and managers

        1. _____

        2. determine acceptable/unacceptable behavior

           a. Ben & Jerry's salary rule

IV. Organizations' offerings

    A. System to resolve dilemmas

    B. Formal training

        1. develop awareness

        2. practice appropriate responses

    C. Effective programs

        1. teach techniques for solving ethical dilemmas

           a. Levi Strauss
           b. _____
           c. _____

        2. _____
           a. Citigroup—board game

V. Effectiveness

    A. _____

    B. Others believe public relations gimmick

    C. _____

B. Using your own words and the outline in Part A, write one of the body paragraphs for the essay on a separate piece of paper. Choose section II, III, or IV in the outline. Do not change the order of the details, and do not copy the original paragraph.

C. Share your paragraph with a classmate who chose the same section in the outline. Look for similarities and differences in your paragraphs and discuss how two writers with the same information (details) can produce two different paragraphs. Share your answers with the class.

8. Writing the introduction

   Read the introductory paragraph. Identify the hook—how the writer captures the reader's attention. Following the hook, the writer makes some general statements about the topic. Enclose the general statements in parentheses. How does the writer end the introduction?

9. Writing the body

   Look at the outline the writer used to organize the essay (step 7 above). How many paragraphs are in the body of the essay? Explain how the number of paragraphs in the body relates to the thesis statement. Re-read the topic sentence for each body paragraph. Explain how the topic sentence for each body paragraph relates to the thesis statement.

10. Writing the conclusion

    Compare the thesis statement of the essay and the concluding paragraph. Check which of the following technique(s) the writer used to conclude the essay:
    - ☐ restate the thesis
    - ☐ summarize the main points
    - ☐ call for action on the part of the reader
    - ☐ make a prediction
    - ☐ pose a question

WRITING 2 ● **On Your Own**

Essay of Cause/Effect

Write Your Essay

Choose a topic from your field of study or from a subject you are interested in and which can be organized in a pattern of cause/effect. Examples of such topics are *the cause/effect of heart disease, the cause/effect of unemployment, the reason people volunteer, the benefit (effect) of being bilingual or bicultural, the effect on society of the cell phone/laptops/the Internet,* or *the advantage (effect) of recycling.* Follow the steps below to write an essay of cause/effect. You may choose to write about only the causes, only the effects, or both. Your audience is your instructor and classmates. The title should address the cause/effect aspect of your topic. After you finish writing your essay, read the sections on *Revising* and *Editing and Proofreading* below and complete the activities.

Steps:

1. Brainstorm the topic.

2. Narrow the topic.

3. Brainstorm and narrow the details.

4. Choose the text structure (cause/effect: explains the reason and/or result of some action, event, or situation).

5. Write the thesis statement.

6. Write the topic sentences for each body paragraph.

7. Organize the essay.

8. Write the introduction (a paragraph that includes a hook, general statements, and the thesis statement).

9. Write the body paragraphs (each paragraph includes a topic sentence and support).

10. Write the conclusion (a paragraph that restates the thesis, summarizes the main points, and/or offers final comments on the topic).

Revising

Follow the Steps

A. Use the checklist to revise the essay of cause/effect you wrote.

Revising Checklist

1. Assignment
   - ☐ follows the assignment to write an essay of cause/effect
   - ☐ addresses the instructor and classmates as the audience
   - ☐ follows the ten steps listed in the assignment

2. Introduction
   - ☐ contains a hook to capture the reader's attention
   - ☐ contains some general statements or background information about the topic
   - ☐ contains a thesis statement with the topic of the essay
   - ☐ Thesis statement includes a controlling idea.
   - ☐ Thesis statement gives a clue to the text structure.

3. Body
   - ☐ Each paragraph addresses the topic contained in the thesis statement.
   - ☐ Each paragraph focuses on one controlling idea in the thesis statement.
   - ☐ Each paragraph contains a topic sentence.
   - ☐ Each topic sentence is developed through general and specific support/details.
   - ☐ General and specific support/details are arranged in a logical order.
   - ☐ General and specific support/details follow the outline.
   - ☐ General and specific support/details are sufficient in number (not too many, not too few).

4. Conclusion
   - ☐ marks the end of the essay
   - ☐ offers the writer's final thoughts on the topic
   - ☐ restates the thesis or summarizes main points

B. Share your essay with a classmate. Ask your classmate to use the Revising Checklist to check your essay and give you some feedback. Make any changes to your essay that you feel are necessary. The changes you make should improve your essay.

ACTIVITY **31**

Editing and Proofreading

The Final Steps

A. Follow the steps below to edit and proofread the essay of cause/effect you wrote.

Editing and Proofreading Checklist

1. Grammar
   - ☐ Verb tenses are correct.
   - ☐ Each subject agrees with its verb (singular/plural).
   - ☐ Prepositions are correct.
   - ☐ Pronouns are correct.
   - ☐ No articles are missing (a, an, the).

2. Spelling
   - ☐ All the words are spelled correctly.
   - ☐ Abbreviations, if any, are used correctly.
   - ☐ First word of each sentence begins with a capital letter.
   - ☐ All proper nouns begin with a capital letter.

3. Punctuation
   - ☐ All sentences end with a punctuation mark.
   - ☐ Periods are after statements and question marks are after questions.
   - ☐ Commas are used correctly in sentences containing coordinating and subordinating conjunctions.

4. Sentences
   - ☐ All sentences are complete.
   - ☐ Each sentence has a subject and a verb.
   - ☐ There are no fragments.
   - ☐ Sentences contain balanced or parallel grammatical structures.

5. Format
   - ☐ Essay has a title.
   - ☐ All paragraphs are in essay format (first line is indented or there is one blank line between paragraphs).
   - ☐ All sentences are in paragraph format (not listed or numbered).
   - ☐ Writer's name is on the paper.
   - ☐ Paper is neat, clean, and legible (easily read).

B. Share your paragraph with a classmate. Ask your classmate to use the Editing and Proofreading Checklist to check your essay and mark any errors in grammar, spelling, punctuation, sentences, or format.

C. Fix any mistakes your essay contained. Proofread your essay one more time. Turn in your final draft to your instructor.

4 · From Language Arts: English Literature

Classes in English Literature expose students to a variety of works: fiction, poetry, and drama. Through novels and short stories, poems, and plays, students learn about the elements of literature including plot, setting, character, theme, and figures of speech. In addition, students write about what they have read, offering reactions, arguments, and critical analyses.

Using your general knowledge of literature, discuss the following questions with a partner or in a small group.

- What is your favorite type of literature? Why?
- Where do writers get their ideas?
- What, if any, are some universal symbols used in literature?

This chapter will help you understand some of the **key concepts** of English literature such as

- plot and theme
- point of view and tone
- similes and metaphors
- character and setting

Get Ready to Read

Agree or Disagree

Read the following statements and decide whether you agree or disagree. Circle your choice. Discuss your answers and your reasons for them with a partner.

1. Short stories are easy to read and understand because of their length.   AGREE   DISAGREE

2. The topics authors wrote about years ago are no longer popular.   AGREE   DISAGREE

3. Symbols used in literature mean the same thing to all readers.   AGREE   DISAGREE

4. All stories are told by a narrator.   AGREE   DISAGREE

5. Characters are presented through their actions and words.   AGREE   DISAGREE

Surveying and Predicting

Survey and Predict

A. Follow the steps below to survey Reading 1 below.

1. Read the title. Write it here. _____

2. Read the first line of the story.

3. From the title and first line, what do you think the story will focus on?
   _____

4. What is the value of an hour? Is it a lot of time or only a little time? _____
   _____

5. What are some things you can do in an hour? _____
   _____

6. This story was written in 1894. What do you think life was like then?
   _____

7. What kind of English do you think will be used in the story? Will it be different from the English we speak today? _____
   _____

8. What do you think the story will be about? _____
   _____

B. Share your survey answers with a partner and discuss what you think the reading will be about. Then circle the number of the statement below that matches your prediction.

1. The story will be about what happens during one hour of a person's life.

2. The story will be about all the things a person can do in one hour.

3. The story will be about a specific hour of the day.

C. Now read the story to see if your prediction is correct. Try to read as quickly as you can. Do not stop to look up words in your dictionary.

The Story of an Hour
by Kate Chopin (1894)

Knowing that Mrs. Mallard was afflicted with a heart trouble, great care was taken to break to her as gently as possible the news of her husband's death.

It was her sister Josephine who told her, in broken sentences; veiled hints that revealed in half concealing. Her husband's friend Richards was there, too, near her. It was he who had been in the newspaper office when intelligence of the railroad disaster was received, with Brently Mallard's name leading the list of "killed." He had only taken the time to assure himself of its truth by a second telegram, and had hastened to forestall any less careful, less tender friend in bearing the sad message.

She did not hear the story as many women have heard the same, with a paralyzed inability to accept its significance. She wept at once, with sudden, wild abandonment, in her sister's arms. When the storm of grief had spent itself, she went away to her room alone. She would have no one follow her.

There stood, facing the open window, a comfortable, roomy armchair. Into this she sank, pressed down by a physical exhaustion that haunted her body and seemed to reach into her soul.

She could see in the open square before her house the tops of trees that were all aquiver with the new spring life. The delicious breath of rain was in the air. In the street below, a peddler was crying his wares. The notes of a distant song which some one was singing reached her faintly, and countless sparrows were twittering in the eaves.

There were patches of blue sky showing here and there through the clouds that had met and piled one above the other in the west facing her window.

She sat with her head thrown back upon the cushion of the chair, quite motionless, except when a sob came up into her throat and shook her, as a child who has cried itself to sleep continues to sob in its dreams.

She was young, with a fair, calm face, whose lines bespoke repression and even a certain strength. But now there was a dull stare in her eyes, whose gaze was fixed away off yonder on one of those patches of blue sky. It was not a glance of reflection, but rather indicated a suspension of intelligent thought.

There was something coming to her and she was waiting for it, fearfully. What was it? She did not know; it was too subtle and elusive to name. But she felt it, creeping out of the sky, reaching toward her through the sounds, the scents, the color that filled the air.

Now her bosom rose and fell tumultuously. She was beginning to recognize this thing that was approaching to possess her, and she was striving to beat it back with her will—as powerless as her two white slender hands would have been.

When she abandoned herself a little whispered word escaped her slightly parted lips. She said it over and over under her breath: "Free, free, free!" The vacant stare and the look of terror that had followed it went from her eyes. They stayed keen and bright. Her pulses beat fast, and the coursing blood warmed and relaxed every inch of her body.

She did not stop to ask if it were not a monstrous joy that held her. A clear and exalted perception enabled her to dismiss the suggestion as trivial.

She knew that she would weep again when she saw the kind, tender hands folded in death; the face that had never looked save with love upon her, fixed and gray and dead. But she saw beyond that bitter moment a long procession of years to come that would belong to her absolutely. And she opened and spread her arms out to them in welcome.

There would be no one to live for during those coming years; she would live for herself. There would be no powerful will bending hers in that blind persistence with which men and women believe they have a right to impose a private will upon a fellow creature. A kind intention or a cruel intention made the act seem no less a crime as she looked upon it in that brief moment of illumination.

And yet she had loved him—sometimes. Often she had not. What did it matter! What could love, the unsolved mystery, count for in face of this possession of self-assertion which she suddenly recognized as the strongest impulse of her being.

"Free! Body and soul free!" she kept whispering.

Josephine was kneeling before the closed door with her lips to the keyhole, imploring for admission. "Louise, open the door! I beg; open the door—you will make yourself ill. What are you doing, Louise? For heaven's sake open the door."

"Go away. I am not making myself ill." No; she was drinking in a very elixir of life through that open window.

Her fancy was running riot along those days ahead of her. Spring days, and summer days, and all sorts of days that would be her own. She breathed a quick prayer that life might be long. It was only yesterday she had thought with a shudder that life might be long.

She arose at length and opened the door to her sister's importunities. There was a feverish triumph in her eyes, and she carried herself unwittingly like a goddess of Victory. She clasped her sister's waist, and together they descended the stairs. Richards stood waiting for them at the bottom.

Some one was opening the front door with a latchkey. It was Brently Mallard who entered, a little travel-stained, composedly carrying his grip-sack and umbrella. He had been far from the scene of the accident, and did not even know there had been one. He stood amazed at Josephine's piercing cry; at Richards' quick motion to screen him from the view of his wife.

But Richards was too late.

When the doctors came they said she had died of heart disease—of joy that kills.

Glossed Words

a face whose lines bespoke repression – (n.) lines in her face showed that she controlled her feelings

a very elixir of life – (n.) the answer/solution to everlasting life

aquiver – (adj.) shaking and moving

coursing blood – (n.) blood moving through her body

grip-sack – (n.) a small bag for holding clothes while traveling

Her fancy was running riot. – Her mind was going wild with ideas, visions of the future.

importunities – (n.) pleas, demands, requests

intelligence – (n.) news or information

joy – (n.) happiness, delight, pleasure

keen – (adj.) sharp

peddler crying his wares – (n.) street seller shouting out what he had for sale

screen – (v.) to hide

shudder – (v.) to shake

sob – (n.) a loud cry

veiled hints – (n.) thinly-covered hints/clues; information not stated directly

yonder – (adj.) in the distance, beyond

Summarizing

Share What You Read

Use two or three sentences to tell your partner what you thought the story was about. Then listen to your partner's sentences. Next, read the following statements and circle the number of the statement that best summarizes the story.

1. A woman learns her husband has died in a train accident, and she dies when she hears the news.

2. A woman learns her husband has died in a train accident, but she finds out it isn't true, and she dies because she is so happy to learn he is alive.

3. A woman learns her husband has died in a train accident, but she finds out it isn't true, and she dies because she is unhappy to learn he is alive.

ACTIVITY 4 **Check Your Comprehension**

Read the following statements. Circle the letter of the answer that best completes the statement.

1. Mrs. Mallard, Louise, was gently told of her husband's death because she
   a. was recently married to Brently Mallard.
   b. had a weak heart and couldn't take bad news.
   c. was paralyzed and unable to move.

2. When Mrs. Mallard first heard the news that her husband had been killed in a train disaster, she
   a. reacted the same way that many women would react.
   b. reacted as if nothing had happened.
   c. reacted differently from the way many women would react.

3. Alone in her room, Mrs. Mallard realizes that
   a. she had always loved her husband and that her life is now over, too.
   b. she lived for her husband and that she has no one to live for anymore.
   c. her husband's death means she is now free to live her own life.

4. Mrs. Mallard's sister, Josephine, asks her to open her bedroom door because she thinks
   a. Louise will cause herself to have a heart attack.
   b. Louise will jump out of the open window.
   c. Louise is sitting in her room, drinking.

5. When Mrs. Mallard goes downstairs, she thinks
   a. that her life is now over because she has lost her husband.
   b. that her whole life is ahead of her because she has lost her husband.
   c. that her sister will come to live with her now that she is alone.

6. Mrs. Mallard dies when she discovers her husband is alive because she
   a. realizes that she will not have the freedom she thought she would have.
   b. is overcome with joy when she sees him.
   c. realizes that she loves her husband more than she thought she did.

7. The doctors said that Mrs. Mallard died of a joy that kills because
   a. they didn't know that her heart was so weak.
   b. they knew how much she loved her husband.
   c. they didn't know how she really felt about her husband.

Academic Word List

 ACTIVITY 5 **Scan and Define**

A. Look at the ten words listed below. Scan the reading and underline the words from the list. Write the definitions for the words you know. Do not use a dictionary. The first one has been done for you.

1. abandonment _wildness, unrestraint, lack of control_

2. approach (v.) _____

3. assure _____

4. brief (adj.) _____

5. enable _____

6. impose _____

7. persistence _____

8. relax _____

9. reveal _____

10. suspension _____

B. Share your definitions with a partner and then with the rest of your classmates. As a group, try to complete the definitions for all ten words. Use a dictionary to check the definitions if you are unsure about them. Then complete the vocabulary activity.

 ACTIVITY 6

Vocabulary Challenge

A. Using your dictionary, work with a partner to find the missing word forms and complete the chart. If no form exists, draw a line in the space. The first one has been done for you.

Noun	Verb	Adjective	Adverb
1. abandonment	*abandon*	*abandoned*	---------
2.	approach		
3.	assure		
4.		brief	
5.	enable		
6.	impose		
7. persistence			
8.	relax		
9.	reveal		
10. suspension			

B. Read the definition of the words below. Then decide which meaning is the one used in the sentence. Put the definition number next to the sentence. The first one has been done for you.

1. **abandonment** *noun* **1.** the act of giving something up; **2.** the act of leaving someone or something; **3.** impulsiveness, uninhibitedness, freedom

    ____1____ a. The forced abandonment of her career after the accident led her into a deep depression.

    _____ b. The community was shocked by the perceived moral abandonment the town's young people displayed.

2. **approach** *verb* **1.** to move or come near or toward; **2.** to resemble or take after; **3.** to begin work on something

    _____ a. He approached the problem from a unique perspective and, amazingly, solved it!

_____ b. As the day of the wedding approached, both the bride and the groom began to have second thoughts about their decision.

3. **brief** _adjective_ **1.** short as in time or distance; **2.** concise and abrupt, succinct; **3.** very short (said of clothing)

_____ a. The telegram was brief, but the news had a tremendous impact on us nonetheless.

_____ b. As the summer drew to a close, so, too, did their brief romance.

4. **impose** _verb_ **1.** to interrupt, disturb, inconvenience; **2.** to require, force, or command; **3.** to take advantage of

_____ a. The state government has imposed yet another tax on gasoline.

_____ b. May I impose on you and ask for a small favor?

5. **relax** _verb_ **1.** to make or become less tight, to loosen; **2.** to make or become less strict, to soften; **3.** to rest from work; **4.** to become less tense

_____ a. The company relaxed its rules regarding the dress code for employees.

_____ b. I relax on weekends by spending time with my family and friends.

_____ c. Instead of feeling so upset, count to ten and relax when you find yourself losing patience.

_____ d. As they entered the playground area, the father relaxed his hold on his 3-year-old son.

6. **reveal** _verb_ **1.** to tell, announce, make known; **2.** to show, exhibit, or expose; **3.** to betray a confidence

_____ a. Removing layers of old varnish and paint from the table revealed the beautiful mahogany underneath.

_____ b. The name of the artist who was chosen to paint the mural was revealed in a ceremony at city hall today.

7. **suspension** _noun_ **1.** a temporary delay, a postponement; **2.** a system of support to absorb shocks in a vehicle; **3.** a stopping or end

_____ a. The suspension of the championship game was caused by severe lightning and heavy wind.

_____ b. Discovery of tainted dog and cat food resulted in the immediate suspension of all important animal products.

Making Inferences: Tone

Inference: drawing conclusions based on facts or information

Tone: the writer's attitude toward the subject

In Chapter 3, you learned that the main idea is not always stated directly in a passage, that it is sometimes implied. When the main idea is implied, it is up to you, the reader, to determine what the author wants you to know about the topic. You use the topic and the details the author provides to form a thesis statement or topic sentence in your own words.

The same skills you use to discover the implied main idea will help you identify or infer tone. Tone refers to the attitude the speaker or writer has about a subject. In conversation, tone is conveyed through the speaker's voice, through the intonation and emotion in the words and sentence structures the speaker uses. In conversation, tone is usually obvious and easy to infer.

In writing, tone is also conveyed through the specific words and sentence structures the writer uses, but it is sometimes difficult to infer the tone. Recognizing the writer's tone requires a careful study of the main idea and the details in addition to the words and sentence structures used in the reading. Adjectives and verbs offer clues to the tone writers convey in a passage. See the chart below for some examples.

Look at the two sample passages below.

1. Ann: *"I cannot believe how rude some salespeople are! They get annoyed if I interrupt their private telephone conversations to ask where an item in the store is located. They roll their eyes when I ask them to tell me a little bit about the product I am planning to purchase. They act as if they are doing <u>me</u> a favor by taking my money. From now on, I'm going to do all my shopping online!"*

   How does the speaker feel about salespeople? <u>angry</u>

   What words in the passage tell you that? <u>rude, private telephone conversations, roll their eyes, doing me a favor</u>

   What does the speaker believe or feel? <u>The speaker feels that salespeople don't want to give information or answer questions or take payment. The speaker has decided that shopping online is the solution because there won't be any rude salespeople to deal with.</u>

2. Introduction to a language book: *There are many ways to improve your speaking skills in a foreign language. First, practice imitating words and sounds you hear. This will help you learn the correct pronunciation and intonation of the language. Second, find someone who speaks that language as a first language. Spend time with that person so that you have an opportunity to use and acquire the language. Finally, take advantage of every opportunity that comes along to use the language. Read out loud, volunteer to answer in your language class, and practice, practice, practice!*

   How does the writer feel about learning a foreign language? <u>positive, optimistic</u>

   What words in the passage tell you that? <u>many ways to improve, will help you, an opportunity to use, take advantage</u>

   What does the writer believe or feel? <u>The writer is optimistic and believes that a person's speaking skills can be improved and offers some suggestions for doing that.</u>

Adjectives to Describe Tone			Verbs to Describe Tone	
amused	apologetic	helpless	beg	appreciate
angry	emotional	objective	demand	ask
apathetic	formal	patient	face	cry
certain	humorous	powerless	frown	disapprove
confident	informal	revengeful	insist	encourage
critical	ironic	sad	laugh	help
depressed	lonely	sarcastic	refuse	press
frightened	loving	serious	sigh	question
hopeful	negative	shocking	smile	sacrifice
neutral	polite	silly	sob	sink
optimistic	positive	sympathetic	weep	suggest
pessimistic	sick	understanding	whisper	surrender
respectful	surprising	upset	yell	try
rude	worried	weak		

Key Concepts 2: Reading and Writing Across the Disciplines

Infer the Tone

Read the passages from *The Story of an Hour* below and circle the letter of the group of adjectives that best describes the tone of the passage. Underline the words or phrases that help you infer the tone and explain the reasons for your choice.

1. There stood, facing the open window, a comfortable, roomy armchair. Into this she sank, pressed down by a physical exhaustion that haunted her body and seemed to reach into her soul. She sat with her head thrown back upon the cushion of the chair, quite motionless, except when a sob came up into her throat and shook her, as a child who has cried itself to sleep continues to sob in its dreams.

   a. upset, serious, sad   b. negative, shocking, pessimistic

2. There would be no one to live for during those coming years; she would live for herself. Spring days, and summer days, and all sorts of days that would be her own. She breathed a quick prayer that life might be long.

   a. hopeful, positive, optimistic   b. depressed, sad, lonely

3. Josephine was kneeling before the closed door with her lips to the keyhole, imploring for admission. "Louise, open the door! I beg; open the door—you will make yourself ill. What are you doing, Louise? For heaven's sake open the door."

   a. loving, sympathetic, understanding   b. worried, frightened, powerless

4. There was a feverish triumph in her eyes, and she carried herself unwittingly like a goddess of Victory. She clasped her sister's waist, and together they descended the stairs.

   a. confident, certain, positive   b. sick, weak, helpless

5. When the doctors came they said she had died of heart disease—of joy that kills.

   a. serious, emotional, upset   b. ironic, surprising, shocking

Making Inferences: Figurative Language

> **Figurative language:** a writing technique that conveys images through unusual or interesting comparisons

In addition to using specific words and sentence structures to convey their attitude or feeling about a topic, writers may also use figurative language. *Metaphors, similes,* and *symbols* are all examples of figurative language. Writers use them to explain or compare items that are dissimilar or, in the case of symbols, to represent something. Study the explanations and examples below.

Metaphor	Simile	Symbol
• comparing two dissimilar items without using *like* or *as* or *than*	• comparing two dissimilar items using *like* or *as*	• using an object to represent more than what it is
• Her family became her life.	• His smile was as bright as the sun.	• He gave her a red rose. (*rose* = flower; *rose* = love)

ACTIVITY 8

Metaphor, Simile, or Symbol

A. Read the lines below that are found in *The Story of an Hour*. Identify each underlined word or phrase as a metaphor or simile, and write the word *metaphor* or *simile* on the line. Explain the reason for your choice.

_____ 1. A sob came up into her throat and shook her, <u>as a child who has cried itself to sleep continues to sob in its dreams</u>

_____ 2. When the <u>storm of grief</u> had spent itself, she went away to her room alone.

_____ 3. She carried herself unwittingly <u>like a goddess of Victory.</u>

_____ 4. <u>The delicious breath of rain</u> was in the air.

_____ 5. And she was striving to beat it back with her will—<u>as powerless as her two white slender hands would have been.</u>

B. Read the following lines that are found in *The Story of an Hour.* Each underlined word or phrase is a symbol. Match the underlined word or phrase in Column A with what it symbolizes in Column B.

1. There were <u>patches of blue sky</u> showing here and there through <u>the clouds.</u>

2. She could see in the <u>open square before her house</u> the tops of trees that were all aquiver with <u>the new spring life.</u>

3. She was drinking in <u>a very elixir of life</u> through that open window.

Column A	Column B
_____ 1. patches of blue sky	a. a new beginning
_____ 2. the clouds	b. her future
_____ 3. open square before her house	c. the darkness of her past life
_____ 4. the new spring life	d. the hope of a bright future
_____ 5. a very elixir of life	e. a cure for her unhappy life

Identifying Text Structure—*Literature*

Literature takes many forms. Poetry, prose, and drama are all classified as literature, and yet they differ in numerous ways. Poetry is written in verse form, prose in paragraph form, and drama as dialogue, for example. The readings in this chapter offer three forms: a short story (fictional prose), a poem (poetry), and a newspaper article (nonfictional prose). Literature may use a variety of text structures, but narration and description are two common patterns. Study the examples, taken from different forms of literature, below.

<u>Short Story</u>

A Great Day

Jan woke up that morning knowing that something great was going to happen to her that day. She felt it as soon as she had opened her eyes. She felt it again as she got out of bed and headed for the shower. The feeling came to her once more as she headed out the door to work. As she stepped off the bus in front of the office building where she worked, she looked up at the blue sky and smiled, failing to notice the gaping hole in the street where someone had removed the grate. It was, indeed, a "grate" day for Jan.

<u>Poetry</u>

The Lama (1931)

The one-l lama   And I will bet
He's a priest.   A silk pajama
The two-l llama,   There isn't any
He's a beast.   Three-l llama.

Ogden Nash (1902–1971)

Poet Ogden Nash

Rev. John Cross, Jr.

1925–2007

Dug through rubble after 1963 church bombing

Associated Press

ATLANTA – The Rev. John Cross Jr., who dug through the rubble of his Alabama church looking for survivors of a bombing, then presided over a funeral for some of the youngest victims of civil rights era violence, has died. He was 82.

Key Words—*Literature*

Elements: parts or aspects of a story, poem, or other work of literature

Although it is important to recognize the form or text structure of literature, it is the elements of literature that help the reader interpret and understand the writer's purpose. The tables below list some major elements for each of the three forms of literature in this chapter. Think of these elements as some of the *key words* of literature.

Fictional Prose

characters—people in the story (protagonist is main character; antagonist is force acting against the main character)

imagery—descriptions in the story (metaphors, similes)

plot—the series of events that occur and that include conflict in the story; includes foreshadowing (clues to what will happen in the story)

point of view—who is telling the story; the narrator

setting—when and where the story takes place

symbols—objects that represent more than the literal objects themselves

theme—idea(s) important to the story

tone—feelings resulting from the story (irony, joy, sadness)

In *The Story of an Hour,* Louise Mallard is the protagonist, the main **character**. Through **imagery** in the story, we learn that, at first, she is saddened by the news of her husband's death ("storm of grief"*)* but later is excited about the new life she is beginning ("the new spring life"*)*. The story's **plot** begins with the news that Louise's husband has been killed in a train accident. Louise, alone in her room, realizes that her husband's death means she can begin a new life. As she comes downstairs, her husband walks in the door. The story ends with the death of Mrs. Mallard. The writer uses a third-person **narrator** to tell the story, someone who is not a character. The **setting** of the story is in the Mallard's house; the exact time is unknown, but based on when the story was written, we assume it took place in the late 1800s. **Symbols** in the story include the clouds and the blue sky Louise sees from her window. One of the

themes of the story is identity; now that Louise is no longer Brently Mallard's wife, she can live for herself and make her own decisions. The **tone** of the story is ironic; instead of dying because of the death of her husband, Louise died after discovering he was still alive.

Poetry

figures of speech—expressions to communicate feelings and associations; includes similes and metaphors

form—the structure of the individual lines; grouped in a verse or stanza, sonnet or haiku, for example

imagery—words that describe or appeal to the reader's senses

sound—the words that are chosen and which create a rhythm

symbols—objects that represent more than the literal objects themselves

theme—the main idea of the poem

tone—the speaker's attitude about the topic, ideas, or events (irony, joy, sadness)

voice—the speaker, who is describing the topic or ideas or events

word order—placing a word in a specific order to emphasize its meaning or effect

---

Poetry shares many of the same key words associated with fictional prose: **figures of speech, imagery, symbols, theme, tone,** and **voice**. In addition, poems have specific **forms**; a poem of fourteen lines with a specific rhyme scheme (pattern) is called a *sonnet;* a poem without a regular line length or pattern of rhyme is referred to as *free verse.* The **sound** of a poem creates a rhythm: repeating consonant or vowels sounds (She sells seashells/It's a sweet treat to eat) are examples of ways this is done. **Word order** may differ from the usual format to provide emphasis: *All alone I came* vs. *I came all alone.*

Nonfictional Prose

language—vocabulary and sentence structure used

structure—how the work is divided into sections or parts: paragraphs, chapters, volumes, etc.

style—formal or informal

theme—main idea or thesis of the work

tone—the writer's attitude about the topic: critical, humorous, serious, factual, emotional, etc.

voice—the writer, who is telling the story or events

Nonfictional prose has fewer key words and shares them with both fictional prose and poetry. Nonfictional prose, for example, has **theme, tone,** and **voice.** The **structure** of nonfictional prose is similar to **form** in poetry: it refers to how the work is divided. News articles are divided into paragraphs; books are divided into chapters. The **language** and **style** of nonfictional prose refer to the vocabulary used and the formal or informal aspect of the writing. A scientific journal article is written in a formal style; a human-interest story in a newspaper is written in an informal style.

ACTIVITY 9

Recognize Key Words

Read the following literature excerpts and circle the letter of the key word that best represents the information given. More than one answer may be possible for some of the excerpts. Discuss the reason for your choice with a partner.

1. "There stood, facing the open window, a comfortable, roomy armchair."
   a. character   b. plot   c. setting

2. "Oh, my love is like a red, red rose."
   a. figure of speech   b. tone   c. word order

3. "The Lakewood High School choir is holding its spring concert at 8:00 pm in the auditorium tonight."
   a. voice   b. language   c. theme

4. "The new U.S. President will be sworn into office next January."
   a. style   b. tone   c. theme

5. "I have seen roses damasked red and white, / But no such roses see I in her cheeks."
   a. sound   b. word order   c. figure of speech

6. "She was young, with a fair, calm face, whose lines bespoke repression and even a certain strength."
   a. imagery   b. character   c. plot

7. "Someone was opening the front door with a latchkey."
   a. character   b. symbolism   c. plot

8. "Is life so dear, or peace so sweet, as to be purchased at the price of chains and slavery? . . . I know not what course others may take; but as for me, give me liberty or give me death!"
   a. style   b. structure   c. tone

ACTIVITY 10

Use Key Words

For each of the readings listed below, select the key word that identifies the information given. Then use both the key word and the information in a sentence. The first one has been done for you.

A Great Day

1. Jan _character; Jan is the main character in the short story "A Great Day."_

2. gets up, goes to work, falls in a hole _____

   _____

3. home, bus, street _____

   _____

"The Lama"

4. funny, humorous _____

   _____

5. priest and beast; pajama and llama _____

   _____

6. eight lines _____

_____

"Rev. John Cross, Jr.—Dug Through Rubble"

7. paragraph _____

_____

8. formal _____

_____

9. serious, factual _____

_____

READING 2 ● On Your Own

In the first section of this chapter, you learned about making inferences and the elements of literature. You practiced the skills and strategies of surveying, predicting, and summarizing with Reading 1. In this section you will practice these same skills with two new readings. You will also practice using context to guess the meaning of unfamiliar words.

Get Ready to Read

Agree or Disagree

Read the following statements and decide whether you agree or disagree. Discuss your answers and your reasons for them with a partner.

1. Poetry is difficult to understand.   AGREE   DISAGREE

2. Poetry is not usually about political or social issues.   AGREE   DISAGREE

3. Newspaper articles contain only facts, not opinions.   AGREE   DISAGREE

4. Newspaper articles are written in a specific style.   AGREE   DISAGREE

5. Poetry can be influenced by news articles.   AGREE   DISAGREE

Survey and Predict

A. Using the following steps, survey Reading 2a and predict what the reading will be about.

    1. Read the title and related information (poet, date).

    2. Read the first four lines (first stanza).

B. Write your prediction here. _____

_____

C. Now read the poem to see if your prediction is correct. Try to read as quickly as you can. Do not stop to look up words in your dictionary.

Ballad of Birmingham (1969)
by Dudley Randall (1914–2000)

(On the bombing of a church in
Birmingham, Alabama, 1963)

"Mother dear, may I go downtown
Instead of out to play,
And march the streets of Birmingham
In a Freedom march today?"

"No, baby, no, you may not go,
For the dogs are fierce and wild,
And clubs and hoses, guns and jails
Aren't good for a little child."

"But, mother, I won't be alone.
Other children will go with me,
And march the streets of Birmingham
To make our country free."

"No, baby, no, you may not go,
For I fear those guns will fire.
But you may go to church instead
And sing in the children's choir."

She has combed and brushed her night-dark hair,
And bathed rose petal sweet,
And drawn white gloves on her small brown hands,
And white shoes on her feet.

The mother smiled to know her child
Was in the sacred place,
But that smile was the last smile
To come upon her face.

For when she heard the explosion,
Her eyes grew wet and wild.
She raced through the streets of Birmingham
Calling for her child.

She clawed through bits of glass and brick,
Then lifted out a shoe.
"O, here's the shoe my baby wore,
But, baby, where are you?"

Glossed Words

clawed – (v.) dug or tore at or through
drawn – (v.) put on (put gloves on her hands)
fierce – (adj.) dangerous, vicious, violent
raced – (v.) ran, hurried
sacred – (adj.) holy, saintly

ACTIVITY **13**

Summarizing

Share What You Read

Use two or three sentences to tell your partner what you thought the poem was about. Then listen to your partner's sentences. If you disagree, go back and find support for your summary. Write your summary statement below.

Summary: _____

_____

Check Your Comprehension

Read the statements and then circle the correct answer or answers. Sometimes more than one answer is possible.

1. The two speakers in the poem are
   a. a mother and her child.
   b. a mother and her son.
   c. a mother and her daughter.

2. Why does the child want to go downtown?
   a. to march for freedom
   b. to see the dogs
   c. to go to church

3. Why does the mother send her child to the church?
   a. So she can sing in the children's church choir.
   b. It's safer than marching in the streets.
   c. She has to go to work.

4. What happens to the child?
   a. The mother finds her alive and well.
   b. The mother finds her child's shoe.
   c. The child dies in the church bombing.

5. What is the tone of the ballad?
   a. critical
   b. respectful
   c. ironic

Survey and Predict

A. Using the following steps, survey Reading 2b and predict what the reading will be about.

1. Read the title and related information (publication, date).

2. Read the first paragraph and identify the main idea.

3. Read the headings

4. Look for any graphic or visual aids in the reading.

5. Look for key terms in bold.

6. Read the last paragraph.

B. Write your prediction here. _____

_____

C. Now read the news article to see if your prediction is correct. Try to read as quickly as you can. Do not stop to look up words in your dictionary.

Vocabulary Note: The modern Civil Rights movement in the U.S. began in the mid-1950s. This newspaper article, written in 1963, uses the word "Negro" in its report of the bombing. It was later, during the 1960s, that the terms "Black" and "Afro-American" replaced the term "Negro." Today, the terms "African-American" and "Black" are both widely used.

Six Dead After Church Bombing

Blast Kills Four Children; Riots Follow Two Youths Slain; State Reinforces Birmingham Police

United Press International
September 16, 1963.

Birmingham, Sept. 15 – A bomb hurled from a passing car blasted a crowded Negro church today, killing four girls in their Sunday school classes and triggering outbreaks of violence that left two more persons dead in the streets.

Two Negro youths were killed in outbreaks of shooting seven hours after the 16th Street Baptist Church was bombed, and a third was wounded.

Five Fires Reported

Police reported at least five fires in Negro business establishments tonight. An official said some are being set, including one at a mop factory touched off by gasoline thrown on the building. The fires were brought under control and there were no injuries.

Meanwhile, NAACP Executive Secretary Roy Wilkins wired President Kennedy that unless the Federal Government offers more than "picayune and piecemeal aid against this type of bestiality" Negroes will "employ such methods as our desperation may dictate in defense of the lives of our people." Reinforced police units patrolled the city and 500 battle-dressed National Guardsmen stood by at an armory.

City police shot a 16-year-old Negro to death when he refused to heed their commands to halt after they caught him stoning cars. A 13-year-old Negro boy was shot and killed as he rode his bicycle in a suburban area north of the city.

Police Battle Crowd

Downtown streets were deserted after dark and police urged white and Negro parents to keep their children off the streets.

Thousands of hysterical Negroes poured into the area around the church this morning and police fought for two hours, firing rifles into the air to control them. When the crowd broke up, scattered shootings and stonings erupted through the city during the afternoon and tonight.

The Negro youth killed by police was Johnny Robinson, 16. They said he fled down an alley when they caught him stoning cars. They shot him when he refused to halt. The 13-year-old boy killed outside the city was Virgil Ware. He was shot at about the same time as Robinson.

Shortly after the bombing police broke up a rally of white students protesting the desegregation of three Birmingham schools last week. A motorcade of militant adult segregationists apparently en route to the student rally was disbanded.

Police patrols, augmented by 300 State troopers sent into the city by Gov. George C. Wallace, quickly broke up all gatherings of white and Negroes. Wallace sent the troopers and ordered 500 National Guardsmen to stand by at Birmingham armories.

A few hours later, police picked up two white men, questioned them about the bombing and released them.

Reverend Martin Luther King, Jr. Pleads to Negroes

The Rev. Martin Luther King, Jr. wired President Kennedy from Atlanta that he was going to Birmingham to plead with Negroes to "remain non-violent." But he said that unless "immediate Federal steps are taken" there will be "in Birmingham and Alabama the worst racial holocaust this Nation has ever seen."

Dozens of survivors, their faces dripping blood from the glass that flew out of the church's stained glass windows, staggered around the building in a cloud of white dust raised by the explosion. The blast crushed two nearby cars like toys and blew out windows blocks away.

Negroes stoned cars in other sections of Birmingham and police exchanged shots with a Negro firing wild shotgun blasts two blocks from the church.

It took officers two hours to disperse the screaming, surging crowd of 2,000 Negroes who ran to the church at the sound of the blast.

At least 20 persons were hurt badly enough by the blast to be treated at hospitals. Many more, cut and bruised by flying debris, were treated privately.

Mayor Boutwell Reacts

Mayor Albert Boutwell, tears streaming down his cheeks, announced the city had asked for help. "It is a tragic event," Boutwell said. "It is just sickening that a few individuals could commit such a horrible atrocity. The occurrence of such a thing has so gravely concerned the public . . . " His voice broke and he could not go on. "While the situation appears to be well under control of federal law enforcement officers at this time, the possibility of further trouble exists," Boutwell and Moore said in their telegram.

President Kennedy, yachting off Newport, R.I., was notified by radio-telephone and Attorney General Robert F. Kennedy ordered his chief civil rights troubleshooter, Burke Marshall, to Birmingham. At least 25 FBI agents, including bomb experts from Washington, were being rushed in.

Witnesses to Bombing

City Police Inspector W.J. Haley said as many as 15 sticks of dynamite must have been used. "We have talked to witnesses who say they saw a car drive by and then speed away just before the bomb hit," he said.

In Montgomery, Wallace said he had a similar report and said the descriptions of the car's occupants did not make clear their race. But he served notice "on those responsible that every law enforcement agency of this State will be used to apprehend them."

As police struggled to hold back the crowd, the blasted church's pastor, the Rev. John H. Cross, grabbed a megaphone and walked back and forth, telling the crowd: "The police are doing everything they can. Please go home." "The Lord is our shepherd," he sobbed. "We shall not want."

The only stained glass window in the church that remained in its frame showed Christ leading a group of little children. The face of Christ was blown out.

After the police dispersed the hysterical crowds, workmen with pickaxes went into the wrecked basement of the church. Parts of brightly painted children's furniture were strewn about in one Sunday School room, and blood stained the floors. Chunks of concrete the size of footballs littered the basement.

The bomb apparently went off in an unoccupied basement room and blew down the wall, sending stone and debris flying like shrapnel into a room where children were assembling for closing prayers following Sunday School. Bibles and song books lay shredded and scattered through the church.

The coroner's office identified the dead as Denise McNair, 11; Carol Robertson, 14; Cynthia Wesley, 14, and Addie Mae Collins, 10.

As the crowd came outside and watched the victims being carried out, one youth broke away and tried to touch one of the blanket-covered forms. "This is my sister," he cried. "My God, she's dead." Police took the hysterical boy away.

Mamie Grier, superintendent of the Sunday School, said when the bomb went off "people began screaming, almost stampeding" to get outside. The wounded walked around in a daze, she said.

Fourth in Four Weeks

It was the fourth bombing in four weeks in Birmingham, and the third since the current school desegregation crisis came to a boil Sept. 4.

Desegregation of schools in Birmingham, Mobile, and Tuskegee was finally brought about last Wednesday when President Kennedy federalized the National Guard. Some of the Guardsmen in Birmingham are still under Federal orders. Wallace said the ones he alerted today were units of the Guard "not now federalized."

The City of Birmingham has offered a $52,000 reward for the arrest of the bombers, and Wallace today offered another $5,000.

Dr. King Berates Wallace

But Dr. King wired Wallace that "the blood of four little children . . . is on your hands. Your irresponsible and misguided actions have created in Birmingham and Alabama the atmosphere that has induced continued violence and now murder."

Glossed Words

augmented – (v.) supplemented, increased, added to

battle-dressed – (adj.) wearing clothing for fighting in a war

bestiality – (n.) brutality

bomb – (n.) an explosive device

debris – (n.) trash, ruins from a destructive force

deserted – (adj.) empty, desolate

disperse – (v.) to break up and send away (said of a crowd of people)

heed – (v.) to obey

hurled – (v.) thrown with force

militant adult segregationists – (n. ph.) aggressive group of people who believe in keeping people of different races separate

mop – (n.) an instrument or piece of equipment used to clean/wash the floor

outbreak – (n.) sudden eruption or explosion

picayune and piecemeal – (adj.) small, unimportant and piece by piece (a little at a time)

staggered – (v.) walked with unsteady or unsure movement

stained glass window – (n. ph.) a window of colored glass with an etched design; church windows often depict religious scenes or saintly figures

stoning – (v.) throwing stones and rocks

touched off – (v.) started, set off

troubleshooter – (n.) one who investigates and offers a solution

wired – (v.) sent a telegram

wounded – (n.) injured and hurt people

Summarizing

Share What You Read

Use two or three sentences to tell your partner what you thought the newspaper article was about. Then listen to your partner's sentences. If you disagree, go back and find support for your summary. Write your summary statement below.

Summary: _____

_____

Check Your Comprehension

Read the statements and then circle the correct answer or answers. Sometimes more than one answer is possible.

1. The *Washington Post* news article states that
   a. four children were killed in a church bombing.
   b. two teenagers were shot after the bombing.
   c. some people were burned in a factory fire.

2. After the bombing, Alabama State troopers and National Guardsmen were sent to the city by
   a. Rev. Martin Luther King, Jr.
   b. President John F. Kennedy.
   c. Governor George C. Wallace.

3. The Rev. Martin Luther King, Jr. went to Birmingham to
   a. plead for non-violence from the African-American community.
   b. protest the church bombing and the murder of the children.
   c. help clear the debris from the bombing.

4. The bombing that occurred on September 15, 1963,
   a. was the first in a series of bombings.
   b. was the fourth in four weeks in Birmingham.
   c. was the third since September 4th of that year.

5. The reason for the bombing was attributed to
   a. the murder of two young African-American teenagers.
   b. the desegregation of schools in Birmingham, Mobile, and Tuskegee.
   c. the federalization of the National Guard by President Kennedy.

6. The connection between the poem and the news article is that
   a. they are both about the same event.
   b. they are about two similar events.
   c. they are about two unrelated events.

Academic Word List

Scan and Define

A. Look at the ten words listed below. Scan Reading 2b and underline the words from the list. Write the definitions for the words you know. Do not use a dictionary. The first one has been done for you.

1. apparently <u>in all likelihood, most probably</u>

2. civil _____

3. federal _____

4. finally _____

5. induce _____

6. injuries _____

7. occurrence _____

8. release (v.) _____

9. survivors _____

10. trigger (v.) _____

B. Share your definitions with a partner and then with the rest of your classmates. As a group, try to complete the definitions for all ten words. Use a dictionary to check the definitions if you are unsure about them. Then complete the vocabulary activity.

Vocabulary Challenge

A. Word analogies are pairs of words that share a relationship or have something in common. Look at the first pair of words and determine the relationship between them. Then supply a word from the Academic Word List above to complete the second pair that shows the same relationship. You may have to change the form of the word. Note: The parts of an analogy are separated by colons; analogies are read as follows: *Dead **is to** fatalities **as** alive **is to** survivors.*

Key Concepts 2: Reading and Writing Across the Disciplines

1. dead : fatalities:: alive : <u>survivors</u>

2. beginning : initially :: end : _____

3. city : municipal :: national : _____

4. armed forces : military :: citizens : _____

5. stopping : ending :: starting : _____

6. confirmed : definitely :: unconfirmed : _____

7. cars : damage :: people : _____

8. hold : let go :: detain : _____

B. Replace the underlined word in the sentences below with one from the Academic Word List above. The first one has been done for you.

Corrupt Official Arrested

federal

Crime City – Judge John M. Swindler, a (1) ~~national~~ judge, was arrested at his home last night by local authorities and charged with accepting bribes. (2) <u>Evidently</u>, authorities received a tip from an anonymous caller. The call (3) <u>started</u> an investigation into Swindler's finances. Because the charges filed against the judge are criminal, it is also possible that he will be the subject of (4) <u>non-criminal</u> action as well.

    The charges stem from accepting cash and luxury items in return for favorable judgments in his court. One case in particular involves awarding a large settlement to the plaintiff in a wrongful death suit. (5) <u>People injured but who did not die as a result</u> of the accident were awarded hundreds of thousands of dollars for (6) <u>physical harm</u> they sustained in the accident in addition to an award for "pain and suffering."

    Asked to comment, the district attorney said, "After an eight-month investigation into Swindler's activities, we were (7) <u>at last</u> able to charge him. The investigation suggests that there were multiple (8) <u>occasions</u> of the judge's accepting bribes."

    After entering a plea of "not guilty" and posting bail in the amount of $200,000, Judge Swindler was (9) <u>let out</u> late last night. Calls to his home and office were not returned. No court date has yet been set.

Using Context to Guess Meaning—*Inference*

While reading, you will sometimes come across an unfamiliar word for which there is no obvious context clue. In that case, you may be able to use your background knowledge and personal experiences to guess the meaning. You will, in a sense, have to "read between the lines" to get the meaning of a word. Study the examples below.

1. *It was he who had been in the newspaper office when **intelligence** of the railroad disaster was received, with Brently Mallard's name leading the list of "killed."*

You are probably familiar with the word *intelligence,* but the meaning you understand (smartness) doesn't fit the context of this sentence. However, your personal experience includes having heard of disasters such as earthquakes, hurricanes, plane crashes, etc. You know that when a disaster happens, the news of it is always reported to the media: television, radio, newspapers. Thus, you can infer that the meaning of *intelligence* in this sentence is *news.*

2. *City police shot a 16-year-old Negro to death when he refused to **heed** their commands to **halt** after they caught him stoning cars.*

Your background knowledge about police more than likely includes knowing that when the police tell you to do something, you need to obey them. In this sentence, *heed their commands* means just that—obey their command, do what they say. What do you think the police told the young man to do? Consider his choice: run or stop. Would the police tell him to run? Again, your background knowledge tells you that the police would probably not tell the teenager to run. Thus, you infer the word *halt* means "to stop." In addition, the structure *to* + word indicates that the word *halt* is a verb.

Guess Meaning From Context

Read the sentences below. Use the information in each sentence and your background knowledge and life experiences to determine the meaning of the word in bold. Share your definitions with a partner and explain how you inferred the meanings.

1. "No, baby, no, you may not go, / For the dogs are fierce and wild, / And **clubs** and hoses, guns and jails / Aren't good for a little child."

   clubs = _____

2. She **clawed** through bits of glass and brick, / Then lifted out a shoe. / "O, here's the shoe my baby wore, / But, baby, where are you?"

   clawed = _____

3. Downtown streets were **deserted** after dark and police **urged** white and Negro parents to keep their children off the streets.

   deserted = _____

   urged = _____

4. The City of Birmingham has offered a $52,000 **reward** for the arrest of the bombers, and Wallace today offered another $5,000.

   reward = _____

5. She could see in the open square before her house the tops of trees that were all **aquiver** with the new spring life.

   aquiver = _____

6. Her pulses beat fast, and the **coursing** blood warmed and relaxed every inch of her body.

    coursing = _____

7. It was Brently Mallard who entered, a little travel-stained, composedly carrying his **grip-sack** and umbrella.

    grip-sack = _____

8. Shortly after the bombing police broke up a **rally** of white students protesting the desegregation of three Birmingham schools last week.

    rally = _____

9. President Kennedy, **yachting** off Newport, Rhode Island, was notified by radio-telephone, and Attorney General Robert F. Kennedy ordered his chief civil rights **troubleshooter**, Burke Marshall, to Birmingham.

    yachting = _____

    troubleshooter = _____

10. The Rev. Martin Luther King, Jr. **wired** President Kennedy from Atlanta that he was going to Birmingham to plead with Negroes to "remain non-violent." But he said that unless "immediate Federal steps are taken" there will be "in Birmingham and Alabama the worst racial **holocaust** this Nation has everseen."

    wired = _____

    holocaust = _____

WRITING 1A • ## Skills and Strategies

In this section, you will learn some skills and strategies associated with the writing process. It includes the grammar of participial adjectives, which is one of the grammatical structures used in the readings. In this section, you will practice the different steps in the writing process and will write a reaction essay.

The Grammar of Participial Adjectives

Participles can function both as verbs and adjectives. Participial adjectives describe both people and things. The present (-*ing*) form is used to refer to the person/thing that causes the emotion. It has an active sense. The past (usually -*ed*) form is used to refer to the person that feels the emotion or the thing that is affected. It has a passive sense. Study the participial adjectives in the chart below.

Verb	Present Participial Adjective (cause of the feeling)	Past Participial Adjective (receiver of the feeling)
bore	The movie was extremely **boring.** The **boring** movie lasted two hours	We were **bored** by the movie. The **bored** audience got up and left.
interest	The short story was very **interesting**. We read the **interesting** short story in class.	The entire class was **interested** in the story. The **interested** students listened
confuse	Participial adjectives are **confusing.** I don't understand these **confusing** structures.	The class was **confused** by the lesson. The **confused** students asked lots of questions.
crowd	The **crowding** vegetation kept the roses from growing.	Public transportation eased traffic on the **crowded** streets.
pass	The **passing** years strengthened their love.	The **passed** legislation included a Patient's Bill of Rights.
break	The **breaking** news interrupted the TV movie.	Their **broken** promises were too many to count.

ACTIVITY 21

Recognize Participial Adjectives

Read the sentences and underline the participial adjectives. Identify them as present or past participles.

1. Reinforced police units patrolled the city and 500 battle-dressed National Guardsmen stood by at an armory.

2. When the crowd broke up, scattered shootings and stonings erupted through the city during the afternoon and night.

3. She was watching the approaching storm, which was visible through the open window in her bedroom.

4. The restrained look on her face made her seem much stronger than she was; her family was amazed by her strength after she had heard such overwhelming news about her husband.

5. The twittering sparrows gave her a feeling of hope, as did the trees that were aquiver with new spring life.

 ACTIVITY 22

Use Participial Adjectives

A. Read the sentences and choose the correct form of the participial adjective in parentheses.

1. It was her sister Josephine who told her, in *breaking / broken* sentences, that her husband had died.

2. When she abandoned herself, a little *whispering / whispered* word escaped her slightly (*parting / parted*) lips.

3. He stood amazed at Josephine's *piercing / pierced* cry; at Richard's quick motion to screen him from the view of his wife.

4. A bomb hurled from a *passing / passed* car blasted a *crowding / crowded* church, killing four girls.

5. Downtown streets were *deserting / deserted* after dark and police urged parents to keep their children off the streets.

6. It took officers two hours to disperse the *screaming / screamed, surging / surged* crowd who ran to the church.

B. Write sentences of your own using the following participial adjectives.

1. amazing _____

_____

2. closed _____

_____

3. misguided _____

_____

4. continuing _____

_____

Sentence Essentials

Sentence Errors

Writers, to add variety to their writing, use a combination of sentence types: simple, compound, complex, and compound-complex. (See Sentence Essentials in Chapters 1 and 2 to review sentence types.) Sometimes, however, in their quest for variety, writers introduce errors into their writing. This section highlights some of the most common sentence errors and shows how to correct them.

Fragments

Fragment: incomplete sentence

A sentence fragment is an incomplete sentence. It often lacks a subject or a verb. Sentence fragments often begin with a subordinating conjunction, but they are not connected to an independent clause. To correct a sentence fragment, add a subject or a verb, or connect the fragment to an independent clause. Look at the examples below.

Fragment	Reason	Correction
Living for herself would find joy.	missing a subject	Living for herself, **she** would find joy.
Ideas of all kinds rushing through her head.	missing an auxiliary verb	Ideas of all kinds **were** rushing through her head.
Although sometimes she had loved him.	dependent clause	Although sometimes she had loved him, **often she had not.**

Correct Fragments

Correct each fragment by adding a subject or verb, or connecting it to an independent clause.

1. While she knew she would cry when she saw him. _____
   _____

2. The streets of Birmingham crowded after the blast. _____
   _____

3. Running for safety after the bomb destroyed the church basement. _____
   _____

Run-on Sentences

Run-on: two sentences combined with no punctuation

Combining two independent clauses without using any connectors or punctuation will result in a run-on sentence. One way to correct a run-on sentence is to make two separate sentences: insert a period (and add a capital letter) between the two clauses. Another way to correct a run-on is to insert a semicolon between the two clauses. A third possible correction is to add a conjunction and appropriate punctuation. Look at the examples below.

Run-on Sentence	Correction
Someone was opening the front door with a latchkey it was Brently Mallard who entered.	Someone was opening the front door with a latchkey. **It** was Brently Mallard who entered.
She went away to her room alone she would have no one follow her.	She went away to her room alone**;** she would have no one follow her.
There was a feverish triumph in her eyes she carried herself unwittingly like a goddess of Victory.	There was a feverish triumph in her eyes**,** **and** she carried herself unwittingly like a goddess of Victory.

Correct Run-on Sentences

Correct the run-on sentences by separating them or by connecting them with a semicolon or conjunction.

1. The stained glass window that was still intact showed Christ leading a group of little children the face of Christ was blown out.

2. There was something coming to her she did not know what it was it was too subtle to name.

3. She opened the door she clasped her sister's waist together they descended the stairs.

Comma Splices

> **Comma splice:** two sentences combined with a comma

Combining two independent clauses using only a comma to connect them results in a comma splice. Comma splices are corrected exactly the same way that run-on sentences are corrected: inserting a period, inserting a semicolon, or adding a conjunction and appropriate punctuation. Look at the examples below.

Comma Splice	Correction
The delicious breath of rain was in the air, in the street below, a peddler was crying his wares	The delicious breath of rain was in the air. **In** the street below, a peddler was crying his wares.
Her husband's friend Richards was there, it was he who had been in the office when the news came.	Her husband's friend Richards was there**;** it was he who had been in the office when the news came.
The notes of a distant song reached her, countless sparrows were twittering in the eaves.	The notes of a distant song reached her**, and** countless sparrows were twittering in the eaves.

Correct Comma Splices

Correct the comma splices by inserting the correct punctuation or appropriate conjunction.

1. She went away to her room, she would have no one follow her.

2. Her eyes grew wet and wild, she raced through the streets of Birmingham calling for her child.

3. The city of Birmingham has offered a $52,000 reward for the arrest of them bomber, Governor Wallace offered another $5,000.

Identify and Correct Sentence Errors

Read the sentences below. Put a *C* in the blank if the sentence is correct. If the sentence is incorrect, put an *F* in the blank if the error is a fragment, *RO* if it is a run-on sentence, or *CS* if it is a comma splice. On a separate sheet of paper, correct all sentences that contain errors. The first one has been done for you.

___F___ 1. And sing in the children's choir. <u>You may sing in the children's choir.</u>

_____ 2. I won't be alone other children will go with me.

_____ 3. May I go downtown instead of out to play?

_____ 4. The fires were brought under control there were no injuries.

_____ 5. City police shot a 16-year-old youth to death, a 13-year-old boy was shot and killed, too.

_____ 6. Hurt badly enough by the blast to be treated at hospitals.

_____ 7. Many more, cut and bruised by flying debris, were treated privately.

_____ 8. Attorney General Robert F. Kennedy ordered Burke Marshall to Birmingham.

_____ 9. At least 25 FBI agents, including bomb experts from Washington.

_____ 10. After the police dispersed the hysterical crowds.

Combining and Separating Sentences

For some writers, it is not always clear when two sentences should be combined or when long sentences should be separated into two or more shorter ones. This uncertainty often leads to sentence errors of the types presented above.

Generally, we combine two sentences when they contain related ideas. If the ideas are of equal importance, combine them in a compound sentence; if the ideas are not of equal importance, create a complex sentence. In a complex sentence, be sure to state the main or most important idea in the independent clause, and place the minor or less important idea in the dependent clause. (See Sentence Essentials in Chapter 3.)

Using too many simple sentences in your writing makes it uninteresting to read. On the other hand, connecting multiple compound sentences or stringing together sentences with multiple subordinate clauses results in writing that is difficult to read and understand. Your writing needs to contain a balance of sentence types.

Combine or Separate Sentences

Correct the sentence errors by either combining or separating the sentences below. You will need to add, delete, or change the sentences in order to correct them. There is more than one way to correct an error. Share your answers with a partner.

1. The crowd came outside. The crowd watched the victims being carried out. One young boy broke away from the crowd. He tried to touch one of the blanket-covered forms. It was his sister. _____
_____
_____

2. The bomb apparently went off in an unoccupied basement room, and it blew down the wall, and it sent stone and debris flying like shrapnel into a room where children were assembling for closing prayers after Sunday School, and bibles and song books lay shredded and scattered through the church. _____

_____

_____

_____

3. President Kennedy was yachting off Newport, Rhode Island, but he was notified by radio-telephone, and Attorney General Robert F. Kennedy ordered his chief civil rights troubleshooter, Burke Marshall, to go to Birmingham, and at least 25 FBI agents, including bomb experts from Washington, were being rushed in as well.

_____

_____

_____

4. City police shot a 16-year-old Negro to death. He refused to obey their command to stop. They caught him stoning cars. _____

_____

5. Shortly after the bombing, the police broke up a rally. At the rally, a group of white students protested. They protested the desegregation of three Birmingham schools. The schools were desegregated last week. _____

_____

_____

6. Police reported at least five fires in Negro business establishments tonight, and an official said that some fires are being set, including one fire at a mop factory, which was started by gasoline thrown on the building, but the fires were brought under control, and there were no injuries. _____

_____

_____

Other Types of Sentence Errors

In addition to the types of sentence errors above, there are "in-sentence" errors you need to watch for. Some of the most common errors are listed below.

Subject-Verb Agreement

Subjects and verbs must agree in number. Look at the examples below.

Sentence	Explanation
Someone was opening the door.	singular (indefinite) pronoun
A vacant **stare and** a **look** of terror **were** in her eyes.	compound subject
There **were birds** outside her window.	subject is *birds* (follows *there*)
A long **procession** of years **was** ahead of her.	subject is *procession*; *years* is object of preposition *of*
Love for her husband **was** no longer in her heart.	noncount noun

Word Placement

Words must be placed near the words or phrases they modify. Look at the examples below.

Examples	Explanation
She was young, with a **fair, calm face.**	adjective + noun
Her pulses **beat fast.**	verb + adverb
It was **only yesterday** she had thought life would be long.	limiting modifier + word modified
Kneeling before the closed door, **Josephine** pleaded with Louise.	modifier of unstated subject (unstated subject = stated subject)
She saw the **trees that were all aquiver with new spring life.**	noun + adjective clause
Exhaustion seemed **to reach** into her soul.	to + verb

Punctuation

Periods, commas, semicolons, and colons have different uses. Some of the most common uses are listed below.

Periods

- end sentences

  Great care was taken to break the news to her as gently as possible.

- come after abbreviations, titles

  Mr. Brently Mallard walked in the front door.

Commas

- separate a series of three or more

  She saw the rain, the birds, and the trees through her window.

- used with a conjunction, join two independent clauses

  She went away to her room alone, and she would have no one follow her.

- come after introductory phrases or clauses

  After a moment, she rose and unlocked the door.

- set off nonrestrictive adjective clauses

  Brently Mallard, who had not been killed, opened the front door and entered.

- come after transitional words or connectors

  Josephine thought Louise would make herself ill; however, Louise felt joy and happiness.

- introduce a quote or direct speech

  Her sister cried, "Louise, open the door!"

Semicolons
- connect two independent clauses

  She went away to her room alone; she would have no one follow her.
- come before transitional words or connectors

  Josephine thought Louise would make herself ill; however, Louise felt joy and happiness.
- separate a series of items that contains commas

  She knew she would weep when she saw the kind, tender hands folded in death; the face that had never looked save with love upon her.

Colons
- come between independent clauses if the second clause explains or summarizes the first clause

  She suddenly realized what she was feeling: It was the feeling of freedom.
- introduce a list

  Her fancy was running riot along those days ahead of her: spring days, summer days, and all sorts of days that would be her own.
- introduce a quote or direct speech

  She said it over and over under her breath: "Free, free, free!"

ACTIVITY 28

Correct the Error

Read the sentences and rewrite them, correcting the error in each. The type of error is identified with *SV* (subject-verb agreement), *W* (word placement), or *P* (punctuation).

1. Mrs. Mallard was a woman not very healthy. (W) _____

   _____

2. When Mrs. Mallard heard the news about her husband; she wept and ran to her room. (P) _____

   _____

3. Alone in her room, Mrs. Mallard realizes that her husband's death mean she is now free. (SV) _____

   _____

4. When Mrs. Mallard goes downstairs, she think that her whole life is ahead of her. (SV) _____

   _____

5. Mrs. Mallard dies when she discovers her husband is alive, because she realizes that she is no longer free. (P) _____

   _____

6. Because they didn't know how she really felt the doctors said that Mrs. Mallard died of a joy that kills. (P) _____

   _____

7. Always Mrs. Mallard had loved her husband. (W) _____

   _____

8. She clasped her sister's waist and together they descended the stairs. (P) _____
_____
_____

9. Feeling better, the door opened and Louise faced her sister Josephine. (W) _____
_____
_____

10. There were patches of sky blue showing here and there through the clouds. (W)
_____
_____

 ACTIVITY 29

Spot the Error

Read the sentences. Identify and correct the error in each sentence. Types of errors include subject-verb agreement, word placement, and punctuation.

1. There would be no one to live for during those coming years, she would live for herself.

2. Louise realizes that her life in the years to come are going to be filled with joy.

3. She breathed a prayer quick that her life might be long.

4. Josephine begs her sister Louise to not keep the door locked because Josephine is worried about her.

5. She did not know what she was feeling; because it was too subtle and elusive to name.

6. The doctors who come to the house says Louise has died from joy, but it's untrue.

7. Only she had loved him sometimes.

8. Brently Mallard stood amazed at Josephine's cry piercing.

9. Josephine fears that her sister will die who has a weak heart.

10. Louise knew there was a bitter moment ahead, however, she would still have years that would belong to her alone.

Making the Connection

The body of a passage offers the reader support for the thesis statement. It contains the details about the topic that the author believes are important. It is the writer's job to present as much support as is needed to fully develop the thesis and to present the support in a clear and logical order. For the reader, focusing on the controlling idea of the thesis statement is key to evaluating the support the passage might be expected to contain. For the writer, focusing on the controlling idea is key to developing sufficient and effective support for the thesis statement. The details of a passage can include examples, facts, statistics, descriptions, and personal experiences.

Get Ready to Write

Body and Support Sentences

Once you have formulated your thesis statement, your focus turns to developing the body of your essay. The body of your essay is where you present the major points in support of your thesis statement. Typically, the body of your essay will have as many paragraphs as there are major points or controlling ideas in your thesis statement. For example, to support the thesis statement *After reading "The Story of an Hour," I felt shock and sadness,* the writer would need a minimum of two body paragraphs: one to explain the feeling of shock and one to explain the feeling of sadness.

 ACTIVITY 30

Determine the Number and Topic of Body Paragraphs

Read the following thesis statements and list the number of body paragraphs and the topic of each that you would expect to find in the body of the essay.

1. There are three types of figurative language writers use: metaphors, similes, and symbols.

    Number of paragraphs: _____

    Topics: _____

2. Poetry, prose, and drama are all classified as forms of literature.

    Number of paragraphs: _____

    Topics: _____

3. Character, setting, plot, and theme are all elements of fictional prose.

    Number of paragraphs: _____

    Topics: _____

4. The main character in the story was kind, generous, and optimistic about the future.

    Number of paragraphs: _____

    Topics: _____

5. The newspaper article about the demonstration reported both views on the issue.

    Number of paragraphs: _____

    Topics: _____

Topic Sentences for Body Paragraphs

Each paragraph in the body of the essay develops one major point or controlling idea in your thesis statement. Beginning the paragraph with a clear topic sentence helps the reader anticipate the information the paragraph will present. Study the examples below.

Thesis statement: *There are three types of figurative language writers use: metaphors, similes, and symbols.*

Topic sentence for body paragraph 1: *A metaphor is a comparison of two dissimilar items without using the words **like, as,** or **than.***

Topic sentence for body paragraph 2: *A simile is a comparison of two dissimilar items using the words **like** or **as.***

Topic sentence for body paragraph 3: *A symbol is an object that represents more than what it is.*

In these examples, each topic sentence introduces one of the controlling ideas from the thesis statement. The topic sentences in the examples are in the form of definitions. The remainder of each paragraph will present support for its topic sentence by providing details and examples.

Write Topic Sentences

Write a topic sentence for each of the main points or controlling ideas in the thesis statements below.

1. Poetry, prose, and drama are all classified as forms of literature.
   a. _____
   b. _____
   c. _____

2. The main character in the story was kind, generous, and optimistic about the future.
   a. _____
   b. _____
   c. _____

3. The newspaper article about the demonstration reported both views of the issue: schools should be integrated and schools should be segregated.
   a. _____
   b. _____

4. After reading the news article on the church bombing, I found it to contain misinformation and bias.
   a. _____
   b. _____

General Support for the Topic Sentence

Once you have chosen your topic sentences for the body paragraphs of your essay, you will need to support them. Your support will usually consist of general statements followed by specific details or examples. The ideas for your general and specific support can come from brainstorming and/or research.

Examples of general support for the topic sentence, *An analogy is a comparison of an unknown item to one that is known,* are listed below.

Topic sentence: *An analogy is a comparison of an unknown item to one that is known.*

General support: *An analogy is often used when trying to explain a complex subject or a concept that is abstract.* (explains when analogies are used)

   An analogy is usually a long, point-by-point comparison. It is longer than a metaphor or a simile. (adds to the definition given in the topic sentence)

   Analogies add interest to writing by giving the reader new meaning to an everyday object or concept. (explains the purpose and/or effect of using analogies)

ACTIVITY 32

Choose General Support

Read each topic sentence and the statements that follow. Put an X in front of each statement that is an example of general support.

1. A metaphor is a comparison of two dissimilar items using the words *is* or *are.*
    _____ a. Metaphors can be used to express emotions and feelings.
    _____ b. Metaphors can make ordinary writing more interesting.
    _____ c. *My life is a nightmare* is an example of a metaphor.

2. A simile is a comparison of two dissimilar items using the words *like* or *as.*
    _____ a. Similes can be used to make a point through exaggeration.
    _____ b. *The fish I caught was as big as a whale* is a simile.
    _____ c. Using similes is one way to make simple descriptions come alive.

3. A symbol is an object that represents more than what it is.
    _____ a. The overuse of symbols in a story can turn it into a cliché.
    _____ b. An open window can be a symbol of freedom
    _____ c. Symbols take the reader beyond the character or setting of a story.

Specific Support for the Topic Sentence

While general support for your topic sentence is needed, it is often not enough. General support can be strengthened by the addition of specific details. Specific details often include facts, statistics, examples, and even experiences.

Examples of specific support for analogies are listed below.

General support: *An analogy is often used when trying to explain a complex subject or a concept that is abstract.*
Specific support: *For example, analogies are helpful when trying to explain the meanings of freedom, truth, or love.*

General support: *An analogy is usually a long, point-by-point comparison. It is longer than a metaphor or a simile.*
Specific support: *To illustrate, imagine a writer wants to explain how to write an essay. The writer might compare writing an essay to building a house. The foundation of the house would represent the thesis statement, for example.*

General support: *Analogies add interest to writing by giving the reader new meaning to an everyday object or concept.*
Specific support: *For example, after reading an analogy of how writing an essay is like building a house, the reader may understand the process more clearly.*

 ACTIVITY 33

Choose Specific Support

Read each topic sentence and the statements that follow. Put an X in front of each statement that is an example of specific support.

1. A metaphor is a comparison of two dissimilar items using the words *is* or *are.*
    _____ a. For example, the author wrote that "The fire that was love had gone out of their marriage years ago."
    _____ b. Metaphors can make ordinary writing more interesting.
    _____ c. *My life is a nightmare* is an example of a metaphor.

2. A simile is a comparison of two dissimilar items using the words *like* or *as*.
   _____ a. Similes can be used to make a point through exaggeration.
   _____ b. *The fish I caught was as big as a whale* is a simile.
   _____ c. A simile such as "she wore her love like a jewel" can make a simple description come alive.

3. A symbol is an object that represents more than what it is.
   _____ a. The overuse of symbols in a story can turn it into a cliché.
   _____ b. Walking through the woods could symbolize a character's life journey.
   _____ c. The use of green in a story may range in meaning from jealousy to riches to nature.

Quotations as Support

Depending on the type of essay you are writing and the points you want to support, your essay may include quotations from outside sources. You might quote an expert on a particular subject or quote facts and statistics about the subject. If your assignment is to read an article or literary selection, however, you will quote the article or selection itself as support for your thesis statement.

Outside Sources

Writer Kate Chopin

Including quotations in your essay from experts, people knowledgeable about a particular subject, is a good way to support your thesis statement. When you include a direct quote from an expert, you must identify the expert and enclose that person's exact words in quotation marks. See the basic rules for quotations below.

1. *Dr. Leonard Reed, Professor of Literature at Prose University, said, "Kate Chopin wrote about subjects that are still relevant today—perhaps even more relevant to women today than they were 100 years ago."*

The quotation identifies the expert, Dr. Leonard Reed, and includes the exact words he said. Only the exact words he said are enclosed in quotation marks. The quotation is introduced with a reporting verb, *said*, followed by a comma and the beginning quotation mark. The end punctuation, a period, is inside the quotation mark at the end of the sentence.

2. *"Kate Chopin wrote about subjects that are still relevant today—perhaps even more relevant to women today than they were 100 years ago," said Dr. Leonard Reed, Professor of Literature at Prose University.*

For quotations ending with the reporting verb and the name of the speaker, the quotation is followed by a comma, which is inside the quotation marks. A period ends the entire sentence.

3. *"Kate Chopin wrote about subjects that are still relevant today," said Dr. Leonard Reed, Professor of Literature at Prose University, "perhaps even more relevant to women today than they were 100 years ago."*

For quotations that are split, the first half of the quotation is followed by a comma and quotations marks; following this is the reporting verb, the name of the speaker, and another comma. The second half of the quote begins with quotation marks, followed by the remainder of the quote. Do not begin the second half of the quote with a capital letter. The end punctuation, a period, goes inside the quotation marks.

4. *"Is Kate Chopin's writing still relevant today?" the reporter asked Dr. Leonard Reed, Professor of Literature at Prose University. He replied, "Absolutely!"*

Did Dr. Reed say, "Kate Chopin's writing is still relevant today"?

Punctuation marks that are part of the quote go inside the quotation marks. If they apply to the entire sentence, place them outside the quotation marks.

Verbs commonly used to introduce quotations include *announce, ask, agree, claim, explain, note, remark, report, say, show, state, tell, think, warn,* and *write.*

Quote Outside Sources

Read the statements below. Rewrite them as direct quotes, using the name of the expert provided in parentheses. Choose a reporting verb for your quote.

1. The difficulty of literature is not to write, but to write what you mean. (Robert Louis Stevenson, Scottish author) _____
   _____

2. Men seldom make passes at girls who wear glasses. (Dorothy Parker, U.S. author, poet, and humorist) _____
   _____

3. If you don't have the time to read, you don't have the time or the tools to write. (Stephen King, U.S. novelist) _____
   _____

4. Feet, why do I need them if I have wings to fly? (Frida Khalo, Mexican artist) _____
   _____

5. Will you succeed? Yes, you will indeed! (Dr. Seuss, U.S. author of children's books) _____
   _____

Selection Itself

Sometimes you will need to reference words, phrases, or sentences from the selection you are writing about. Enclose the exact quotation in quotation marks. See the examples below.

Chopin's descriptions of Louise's having "a feverish triumph in her eyes" as she "carried herself unwittingly like a goddess of Victory" downstairs made me realize that Louise was strong enough to take care of herself and that her life without Brently would be a happy one for her.

It was exciting to see the change in Louise, especially after she realized that Brently's death meant she was "'Free! Body and soul free!'"

In the first example, quotation marks set off specific phrases from the story. In the second example, the quotation is from one of the characters in a story. The double quotation marks indicate that the quotation is from the story; the single quotation marks indicate that the character spoke those exact words.

Note: You will practice using quotes (direct and indirect) again in Chapter 7.

Citations

If you quote outside sources in your essay, you will need to cite your sources in your essay. There are two types of citations: in-text and references. The APA (American Psychological Association) style is used for social sciences. The MLA (Modern

Language Association) style is used for humanities courses. Your instructor will indicate which style to use for a particular course. (See Appendix 7 on page 293 for basic guidelines for using the APA style.)

In-text

The purpose of in-text citations is to state the source of the information or ideas the writer has just used. It provides enough information for the reader to find the complete source in the reference section at the end of the paper. In-text citations are used whether you paraphrase or quote the source. MLA style for in-text citations includes the name of the author and the page number. See the examples below.

Kate Chopin's short stories routinely shocked her audience, and she is often considered to be among the first feminist writers of the twentieth century (Smith, 28).

According to Dr. Dale Smith, Kate Chopin's short stories routinely shocked her audience, and she is often considered to be among the first feminist writers of the twentieth century (28).

Rewrite Citations

Read the statements and insert the source information given in parentheses.

1. Understanding the elements of literature is key to interpreting and understanding the writer's purpose. (Ramon Leyendo / 35 – insert within statement)

2. Literature uses a variety of text structures, but narration and description are two common patterns. (Anne Taylor / 199 – insert at end of statement)

3. "There would be no one to live for during those coming years; she would live for herself." (Kate Chopin / 2 – insert at end of statement)

4. "It is only through suffering and sorrow that one can appreciate the true feelings of happiness and joy." (Emily Wise / 12 – insert within statement)

5. Academic reading and writing are skills that can be improved only through practice, and because they require time and attention to detail, many students give up and never learn to master either skill. (W. B. Cheater / 19–20 – insert at end of statement)

References

Each source that you cited in your essay or paper must be listed at the end of your document. The purpose of the Works Cited page in MLA or References page in APA style is to provide the reader with the exact source and location of your information. There are numerous guidebooks and online sites that outline the different formats for citing references in the MLA and/or APA styles. Below are some general guidelines for MLA style formats.

Books

a. Book – Author

Last name, First name. Title. Location: Publisher, Year of Publication.

Andrea, Alfred H., and James H. Overfield. The Human Record: Sources of Global History. Boston: Houghton Mifflin, 2005.

b. Edited book – no author

Last name, First name, ed. Title. Location: Publisher, Year of Publication.

Lauter, Paul, ed. The Heath Anthology of American Literature: Concise Edition. Boston: Houghton Mifflin, 2004.

c. Edited book – with author

Last name, First name. Title. Ed. First name Last name. Location: Publisher, Year of Publication.

Shakespeare, William. The Complete Works of Shakespeare. Ed. David Bevington; New York: Longman, 2006.

Articles

a. Last name, First name. "Title of article." Title of Journal volume number.issue number (Year of publication): page numbers.

Dell, Frank. "Literature of Today." Journal of Literary Issues 6.4 (2003): 66–73.

b. Newspaper

Last name, First name. "Title of article." Title of newspaper Date: Section and page numbers.

Wales, Lester. "Academic Skills at Work." Our Country News 23 May 2007: A3.

Electronic Sources

a. Web site

Author. "Title of Web Page." Title of the Site. Editor. Date and/or Version Number. Name of Sponsoring Institution. Date of Access <http://Web address>.

Lorentz, M. "Life of the Buddha." Emuseum @ Minnesota State University, Mankato. 2007. Minnesota State University, Mankato. 1 Sept. 2008 <http://www.mnsu.edu/emuseum/cultural/religion/Buddhism/history.html>.

b. Online Periodical

Last name, First name. "Title of article." Title of online journal volume and issue number (Date of online publication). Date of access <http://Web address>

Ellis, Barry, and Harold Green. "Cite that Quote!" Online Sources 15 (2002). 18 October 2005 http://www.onlinesources.edu.

 Write References

Use the information in the chart to write MLA references on a separate sheet of paper.

Source	Publisher	Year	Title	Author	Location	Other
Web site	—	1/8/05 and 3/4/06	Writing in Five Easy Steps	Dave Bishop	http://www.davebishopwriting.com	
Book	Longtime Books, Inc.	4/03	Building Academic Skills	Melanie Hodges	St. Louis, MO	
Article	Journal of Reading	9/07	Barriers to Academic Reading	Ben Brown	London	Volume 6, Issue 4
Online periodical	Online and Inline	3/15/07 and 12/28/07	Finding Reliable Sources Online	Johann Stein	http://www.writingforwriters.edu	Volume 12
Newspaper	The Center City News	5/10/08	New School Curriculum	Edna Bucher	Center City, ID	Section 6A

Synthesizing

In Chapter 2, you read about and practiced synthesizing information from two sources about extended families. In this chapter you will practice synthesizing information from two sources about the bombing of the Sixteenth Street Baptist Church in Birmingham, Alabama. Before you begin the activity, review the steps in the process below.

1. Read the original source documents.

2. Choose the information that you want to include. Note the source.

3. Put information with similar ideas together.

4. Paraphrase, summarize, or quote the information.

5. Organize the information in a logical order.

6. Rewrite the information as a paragraph, combining it with your own ideas.

7. Add transitions and make other changes as necessary.

Practice Synthesizing

Follow the steps listed above to synthesize the information in the two paragraphs below. Each paragraph is a news article about the church bombing in Birmingham, Alabama, on September 15, 1963.

1. Read the original source documents.

Paragraph 1—*Today's News*

Six people are dead after a church bombing in Birmingham, AL, on September 15, 1963. Four of the dead were girls attending church; two were boys who died after the bombing. The four dead girls were Denise McNair, Carol Robertson, Cynthia Wesley, and Addie Mae Collins. The two boys shot and killed by the police were Johnny Robinson and Virgil Ware. After the bombing, survivors staggered around the church, and cars in other parts of the city were stoned. Near the church, thousands of people poured into the area, and police fought the crowds for two hours. They also broke up a rally of white students protesting desegregation and disbanded a motorcade of militant adult segregationists. Witnesses to the bombing said they saw a car drive by and speed away before the blast, but the race of the occupants was unclear. Workmen with pickaxes entered the building after the blast, which was caused by a bomb exploding in a basement room. This was the fourth bombing in Birmingham in four weeks. Desegregation was brought about last week, with National Guard sent in by the President. A reward for the arrest of the bombers has been established.

Paragraph 2—*The Daily News*

After the church bombing in Birmingham, AL, in which four young girls lost their lives, the FBI was in charge of solving the murders and bringing the criminals to justice. However, after five years, no one had been charged with the crime and the case remained unsolved. Alabama prosecutors reopened the case after discovering that evidence had been blocked by FBI Director Herbert Hoover. Finally, in 1977, a member of the Ku Klux Klan, Robert Chambliss, who had been identified by a witness as the person who placed the dynamite under the church steps, was charged with murder and found guilty. He was sentenced to life in prison and died there in 1985. In 2000, the

FBI announced that three other members of the KKK were also involved in the church bombing. They identified the men as Herman Cash, Bobby Frank Cherry, and Thomas Blanton. Herman Cash died in 1994 without having been charged with the crime. The two remaining men, Cherry and Blanton, were charged with murder in 2000. Blanton was convicted of four counts of murder in 2001 and sentenced to life in prison. Cherry was found guilty of four counts of murder in 2002 and sentenced to life imprisonment; he died in 2004. The tragedy of the church bombing, which shocked the nation, brought to light the civil rights struggles in the 1960s and brought international attention to the struggle and to the town of Birmingham, AL, as well.

2. Choose the information that you want to include. Note the source.

3. Put information with similar ideas together.

4. Paraphrase or summarize the information.

5. Organize the information in a logical order.

6. Rewrite the information as a paragraph, combining it with your own ideas.

7. Add transitions and make other changes as necessary.

How Did They Do That?

This section of the chapter focuses on essays of reaction/response. It begins with the characteristics of a reaction/response essay, describes its structure, and offers questions for brainstorming. In this section, you will read one writer's reaction to the short story, "Runaway," by Alice Munro. Finally, you will follow the steps in the writing process to identify the key elements in the writer's essay.

Essays of Reaction/Response
Essays of reaction/response

- are your personal reaction to something: a piece of literature or art or music, a movie or play, a television or news program, a seminar or course taken, or even a common everyday object
- are not simply a summary or a description of the work/item; do not just retell what happens in the movie; do not just physically describe a piece of art
- include your personal feelings, opinions, and/or thoughts about the work/item
- can relate the work/item to your own life or personal experience
- typically contain quotes or paraphrases from the work (poem, short story, news article) as support for the thesis statement
- can be a response to a character, symbol, theme, imagery or description, or even to the language used in the work
- may be subjective and informal
- may be analytical and present an argument
- use present tense to describe and discuss the work
- are written in first person because they are personal

Parts of a Reaction/Response Essay
The structure or format of a reaction/response essay is similar to other types of essays insofar as it has an introduction, body, and conclusion. The content and focus, however, are quite different.

The introduction

- identifies the prompt: the title, the author or artist, the year of publication
- briefly summarizes or describes the work (refer to summary writing in Chapter 2 for help)
- includes the thesis statement

The body

- discusses your reaction/response
- supports your reaction with material or examples from the work
- discusses one topic per paragraph
- begins with a topic sentence

The conclusion

- offers your final thoughts
- may state whether you liked or disliked it
- may state whether or not you recommend it to others

Brainstorming for an Essay of Reaction/Response

Following are some questions to ask yourself while brainstorming for your essay of reaction/response.

Literature/Film

- How do you feel about the work?
- Do you like it? Why or why not?
- What significance does the work have for you?
- Can you identify with the situation and/or the character(s)?
- How do you feel about the characters?
- Does one of the characters remind you of someone you know or of yourself?
- What is your evaluation of the work?
- How does the story relate to your life?
- How does the work relate to real life or to real events in life that you have observed?
- How is it similar to an experience you have had?
- What theme does the work discuss?
- What, if any, symbolism is used in the work?
- Is there irony in the work? How is it used?

Art/Music

- How do you feel about the work?
- Do you like it? Why or why not?
- Does the work trigger an emotional response in you?
- What significance does the work have for you?
- Can you identify with the work?
- What idea is the artist/composer trying to communicate?
- Does the artist/composer succeed?
- Does the work remind you of someone or something?

Seminar/Course/Workshop

- What did you know about the topic before you attended?
- What new facts have you learned from the course?
- Does your experience add to the information you learned?
- What is your reaction to the topic?
- What is your reaction to the speaker?
- Did the course meet your expectations?
- How will you use what you have learned?
- Do you recommend the course to others? Why or why not?

News Program/News Article

- Was the topic relevant to you as a viewer/reader? Why or why not?
- How were the facts presented?
- Were the facts presented clearly?
- Was there bias? If so, what was the bias?
- Was the speaker/reporter accurate and knowledgeable?
- Do you agree with the content? Why or why not?
- Did the program/article confirm or change your beliefs about the issue?
- What was the purpose of the program/article? Did it achieve its goal?
- Was the language used formal or informal?
- What did you learn from the program/article?

Common Everyday Objects

- What is the importance or relevance of this object to you?
- Has this object changed your life in some way? How?
- Does the object remind you of a person or time that was important to you? What is it?
- How do you feel about this object? Is it useful, frivolous, necessary?
- Does the object evoke any feelings or emotions in you? If so, what are they?

 ACTIVITY **38**

Follow the Writer's Steps

Review Activity 28, Follow the Writer's Steps, in Chapter 3, which outlines the steps the writer took to develop an essay. Then read the following essay of reaction/response and complete the activity.

"Runaway" Mirrors Real Life Runaway

The short story "Runaway" was written by Canadian author Alice Munro and was published in a book of short stories by the same name in 2004. "Runaway" is a story about a woman named Clara, who feels trapped in her marriage to her husband Clark, a controlling and often unfriendly man. The setting of the story is in Canada, where Clark and Clara run a trail-riding business and board horses. Business is not going well, and neither is Clark and Carla's marriage. With the help of her neighbor Sylvia, Clara leaves Clark. She takes a bus to Toronto but after only two stops on the route, changes her mind about leaving. She calls Clark, who picks her up and takes her back home. Clark is angry at Sylvia and tells her not to interfere in his life with

Carla. Soon after Clark's visit, Sylvia sells her home and moves into town. As the story ends, Carla continues to stay with her husband. Reading this story made me realize that people may run away for different reasons, but the one thing they have in common is the belief that running away is the answer to their problems.

As the story begins, Sylvia is returning from Greece, where she has gone after the death of her husband. She tells Clara, "And then I figured out what there was to do, and there were just these few simple things but they could fill the day." Without her husband, her life was empty; Greece was a place for her to run away to in order not to feel the emptiness and loneliness of her life without her husband. However, going to Greece does not solve her problems, and she returns home. I have seen this same reaction in people who have suffered a loss in their life: they cannot face the change this loss brings, and so they run away to a new place, thinking that their lives will suddenly become "whole" again. They find, however, that the loss continues to exist.

The character Clark seems to have been running away from problems his entire life, moving from one place to another and moving from one job to another. For example, "He had altogether lost touch with his family. He had been an attendant in a mental hospital, a disc jockey on a radio station, a member of a road crew on the highway, an apprentice barber, and a salesman in an Army Surplus store." His personality causes him to have problems with customers and clerks; he often has Clara talk to the customers or deal with business owners after his temper causes fights with them. In real life, too, there are many "Clarks." These are people who cannot get along with others. They fight with their families and stop all communication with them. They have conflicts on the job, and disagreements with their bosses or with customers cost them their job. Instead of changing their own behavior, they believe the answer is to move to a new place or a new job.

Clara, the main character in the story, first runs away from her problems when she leaves home to marry Clark. She wants a different life from the one her parents live, and she knows they do not approve of her relationship with him. "So, naturally, Carla had to run away with Clark. The way her parents behaved, they were practically guaranteeing it." Many young people who fight with their parents believe that running away is the solution. They find out, however, that their problems do not end. For Carla, her problem is now her unhappy marriage to Clark. Once again she tries to solve her problem by running away. Her return to an unhappy and unhealthy situation is common among women who are abused by their husbands. They try to run away, only to return because they believe there is no place else to go or because they fear being alone.

In real life, as in "Runaway," people try to escape the loss or emptiness in their life, flee conflict with family and employers, or evade an unhappy life by running away. They do not want to face the truth and struggle to find a solution, and yet that is the only way to solve problems—by staying and facing them. None of the characters in this story is able to do this, just as happens in real life. Despite the sadness I felt for the characters because of their inability to face their problems, I enjoyed reading "Runaway" and was able to relate it to people I know in real life.

1. Circle the topic the writer brainstormed and used in the essay.

2. Underline the narrowed topic in the essay.

3. List some of the key words that identify the text structure. _____

_____

4. Write the thesis statement here. _____

   _____

5. Draw two lines under the topic discussed in each body paragraph.

6. Put parentheses around examples the writer used for support in each body paragraph.

7. Identify the technique the writer used to conclude the essay. _____

   _____

● **On Your Own**

Essay of Reaction/Response

Write Your Essay

Respond to either Reading 1, *The Story of an Hour,* or to Reading 2, "Ballad of Birmingham" or "Six Dead After Church Bombing." Your audience is your instructor and classmates. Your title will refer to the story, poem, or news article to which you are reacting/responding. After you finish writing your essay, read the sections on *Revising* and *Editing and Proofreading* below and complete the activities.

Refer to *Writing 2: On Your Own* in Chapter 3 for the steps to follow in writing your essay. In step 4, choose the text structure for reaction/response, which describes or explains your personal reaction to the reading. In step 8, writing the introduction, identify the prompt/stimulus, include a brief summary or description of the reading, and write the thesis statement.

Revising

Follow the Steps

A. Use the checklist to revise the essay of reaction/response you wrote.

Revising Checklist

1. Assignment
   - ☐ follows the assignment to write an essay of reaction/response
   - ☐ addresses the instructor and classmates as the audience
   - ☐ follows the ten steps listed in the assignment

2. Introduction
   - ☐ identifies what the writer is responding to
   - ☐ contains a brief summary or description of the work
   - ☐ contains a thesis statement with the topic of the essay
   - ☐ Thesis statement includes a controlling idea.
   - ☐ Thesis statement gives a clue to the text structure.

3. Body
   - ☐ Each paragraph addresses the topic contained in the thesis statement.
   - ☐ Each paragraph focuses on one controlling idea in the thesis statement.
   - ☐ Each paragraph contains a topic sentence.
   - ☐ Each topic sentence is developed through general and specific support/details.
   - ☐ General and specific support/details are arranged in a logical order.
   - ☐ General and specific support/details follow the outline.
   - ☐ General and specific support/details are sufficient in number (not too many, not too few).

4. Conclusion
   - ☐ marks the end of the essay
   - ☐ offers the writer's final thoughts on the topic
   - ☐ restates the thesis, summarizes main points, calls for action, makes a prediction, or poses a question

---

B. Share your essay with a classmate. Ask your classmate to use the Revising Checklist to check your essay and give you some feedback. Make any changes to your essay that you feel are necessary. The changes you make should improve your essay.

Editing and Proofreading

ACTIVITY 41

The Final Steps

A. Follow the steps below to edit and proofread the essay of reaction/response you wrote.

Editing and Proofreading Checklist

1. Grammar

   ☐ Verb tenses are correct.

   ☐ Each subject agrees with its verb (singular/plural).

   ☐ Prepositions are correct.

   ☐ Pronouns are correct.

   ☐ No articles are missing (*a, an, the*).

2. Spelling

   ☐ All the words are spelled correctly.

   ☐ Abbreviations, if any, are used correctly.

   ☐ First word of each sentence begins with a capital letter.

   ☐ All proper nouns begin with a capital letter.

3. Punctuation

   ☐ All sentences end with a punctuation mark.

   ☐ Periods are after statements and question marks are after questions.

   ☐ Commas are used correctly in sentences containing coordinating and subordinating conjunctions.

   ☐ Material used from the source is correctly quoted.

4. Sentences

   ☐ All sentences are complete.

   ☐ Each sentence has a subject and a verb.

   ☐ There are no fragments, run-on sentences, or comma splices.

   ☐ Sentences contain balanced or parallel grammatical structures.

5. Format

   ☐ Essay has a title.

   ☐ All paragraphs are in essay format (first line is indented or there is one blank line between paragraphs).

   ☐ All sentences are in paragraph format (not listed or numbered).

   ☐ Writer's name is on the paper.

   ☐ Paper is neat, clean, and legible (easily read).

B. Share your paragraph with a classmate. Ask your classmate to use the Editing and Proofreading Checklist to check your essay and mark any errors in grammar, spelling, punctuation, sentences, or format.

C. Fix any mistakes your essay contained. Proofread your essay one more time. Turn in your final draft to your instructor.

5 | From Mathematics: Applied Mathematics

Applied mathematics means using mathematical techniques to solve problems encountered in everyday situations. Applied math is used to solve real-world problems in science, business, technology, and even medicine. Creating systems of identification by assigning social security numbers or drivers' license numbers, for instance, is just one example of how government uses applied mathematics.

Using your general knowledge, discuss with a partner or in a small group the role math plays in the following topics:

- voting systems and elections
- polls and surveys
- population growth
- simple and compound interest

This chapter will help you understand some of the **key concepts** of applied mathematics such as

- weighted systems
- quotas
- probabilities
- outcomes

Skills and Strategies

Get Ready to Read

ACTIVITY **1**

True or False

Read the following statements and decide if they are true or false. Share your answers with a classmate.

1. Voting methods and votes cast are equally important in an election.   TRUE   FALSE

2. It is possible to be elected President in the United States with less than 50 percent of the popular vote.   TRUE   FALSE

3. Stockholders have as many votes as they have shares of stock.   TRUE   FALSE

4. The *plurality method* means the candidate receiving the most votes is selected.   TRUE   FALSE

5. Weighted voting is less fair than simple majority voting.   TRUE   FALSE

Surveying and Predicting

ACTIVITY **2**

Survey and Predict

A. Follow the steps below to survey Reading 1 below.

1. Read the title. Write it here. _____

2. Read the first paragraph. Write one or two words which tell the topic or what the paragraph is about. _____

3. Write the main idea here. _____
   _____

4. Read the headings, the titles of the sections in the reading.

5. Look for any graphic or visual aids in the reading. Graphic aids are charts, graphs, pictures, maps, diagrams, etc.

6. Look for key (important) terms related to the topic. They are usually in bold.

B. Share your survey answers with a partner and discuss what you think the reading will be about. Then circle the number of the statement below that matches your prediction.

1. The passage will summarize how the President is elected in the United States.

2. The passage will describe the best voting systems currently in use.

3. The passage will use examples to explain weighted voting systems.

C. Now read the passage to see if your prediction is correct. Try to read as quickly as you can. Do not stop to look up words in your dictionary.

Reading 1

Weighted Voting Systems

The United States is a constitutional democracy. As citizens of a constitutional democracy, we consider our right to vote to be sacred. We want a voice in the decisions that affect us, but we seldom realize that the outcome of a vote depends as much on the voting methods as on the actual votes cast. In some voting systems, each voter has an equal voice in determining the outcome of an election, since each voter has a single vote. However, in many voting systems this is not the case. In a weighted voting system, any particular voter might have more than one vote.

Business Decisions by Vote

For example, in the business world, major decisions may be made by a vote of the stockholders, where each stockholder has a number of votes equal to the number of shares of stock held. The Council of the European Union, which is the principal law-making body of the 25-member European Union (EU-25)*, uses a voting system in which each member state of the EU-25 is assigned a number of votes roughly proportional to its population.

Elections by Electoral College

In our own national politics, the election of the President is not by a direct vote of the people, but by the electoral college. Under this unique system, each state has a number of votes equal to the number of its U.S. senators plus the number of its U.S. representatives, with a minimum of three votes. The District of Columbia also has three votes in the electoral college. Currently, 538 electoral votes are possible and 270 votes are needed to win the presidential election.

Generally, all the electoral college votes of a particular state go to the same presidential candidate, the candidate who received the greatest number of

*as of 2006

votes by that state's voters. Usually, no single state has had a sufficient number of electoral votes to change the outcome of the presidential election. However, in the 2000 presidential election, 25 of the states that cast electoral votes for George W. Bush had enough votes that had any one of them gone for Al Gore instead of George Bush, Al Gore would have won the election.

Of the 30 states casting electoral votes for Bush, 25 had four or more votes. In four of these 25 states, the margin of victory for Bush was 3 percent or less. If a **plurality** of voters in any one of these states had voted for Gore rather than Bush, the state's electoral voters would have gone to Gore rather than to Bush, and Bush would have lost the election. In the 2000 presidential race, New Hampshire (where Bush won 4 electoral votes by a margin of only 1 percent) had as much power as Texas (where Bush won 32 electoral votes by a margin of 21 percent).

In an election it is possible to determine a **quantitative** measure of the power of voters in a system in which voters cast votes with different weights, as the states do in the electoral college.

Weighted Votes

Because it can be confusing to talk about voters having more than one vote, we speak instead about the **weight** assigned to each voter. For example, in the electoral college system, a state's weight is its number of electoral votes (the number of senators plus the number of representatives). In an election held by company stockholders, the voter's weight is the number of shares of stock owned by that voter. The voters and their respective weights can be listed in a table as shown here:

Voter	Weight
Angie	9
Roberta	12
Carlos	8
Darrell	11

Use of Notations

For mathematical purposes, the voters' names are unimportant; all we really need to know are the number of voters and their weights. That minimal information is usually recorded as a sequence of numbers in **square brackets** with the weights listed in decreasing order of size. The crucial mathematical information from the table above is captured in the following notation: [12, 11, 9, 8].

To denote the voters and their weights, we generally use **subscripts**. The voter with weight 12 is simply called the "first voter" and is given the name P_1. The weight of this first voter is represented by $W_1 = 12$. The voter with weight 11 is called the "second voter," is denoted as P_2, and has weight $W_2 = 11$. The remaining voters and their weights are represented in a similar manner.

Simple Majority

In a vote, simple yes/no questions are commonly called motions. Assume that a final decision of "no" defeats the motion and leaves the status quo (the current situation) unchanged, while a decision of "yes" passes the motion and changes the status quo. Generally speaking, for a motion to pass, voters whose weights total *more* than half the total weight must vote "yes" on that motion. In presidential elections, for example, the winning candidate must receive at least 270 electoral votes, which is one more than half the total 538 electoral votes. The requirement that a candidate must receive one more than half of the votes is called a **simple majority.**

Supermajority

Sometimes, however, the threshold for changing the status quo may be set even higher than one more than half the total weight. This requirement is called a **supermajority**. For example, it is common for legislative bodies to require a two-thirds vote to pass constitutional amendments. In fact, a two-thirds vote is necessary in both the House and Senate chambers to override a presidential veto.

The weight required to pass a motion and effect a change is called the **quota**. For instance, the weighted voting system represented by the sequence of weights [12, 11, 9, 8] has a total weight of $12 + 11 + 9 + 8 = 40$. Half the total weight is $40/2 = 20$. Requiring a weight of more than half the total weight means setting a quota greater than 20. Because the weights we are using are whole numbers, the natural choice for a simple majority is a quota of 21.

The quota for a particular system is usually added to the **notation** listing the weights. In this way, all the mathematically important information about the weighted voting system can be compactly expressed. A weighted voting system with a quota of 21 and weights [12, 11, 9, 8] will be represented by [21: 12, 11, 9, 8] where a colon or vertical bar is used to separate the quota from the weights.

Key Concept Words

notation – (n.) a set of numbers that describes mathematical information

plurality – (n.) in an election with three or more candidates, the number of votes received by the winner when the winner receives fewer than half of the total votes

quantitative – (adj.) able to be measured

quota – (n.) a required amount

simple majority – (n.) one more than half of the votes

square brackets – (n.) symbols used to denote mathematical notations: [ ]

subscript – (n.) a character or symbol written below and next to a number: S_1

supermajority – (n.) requirement for more than a simple majority (one more than half the votes)

weight – (n.) an assigned value

Glossed Words

cast – (v.) to vote; **electoral college** – (n.) a group of electors who are chosen by their respective states to elect the President and Vice President of the United States; **override** – (v.) to overrule or take precedence over; to declare null and void; **roughly** – (adv.) not exactly; approximately; **sacred** – (adj.) highly respected and valued; **status quo** – (n.) the current situation; **stockholders** – (n.) those who own stocks or shares in a company/corporation; **threshold** – (n.) the place or point that must be passed or met

Summarizing

Share What You Read

Use two or three sentences to tell your partner what you thought the reading was about. Then listen to your partner's sentences. Next, read the following statements and circle the number of the statement that best summarizes the reading.

1. Weighted voting systems, used in business and politics, use different methods to determine the winner.

2. Weighted voting systems, used in business and politics, may or may not be fair.

3. Weighted voting systems, used in business and politics, can lead to surprising results.

Check Your Comprehension

Read the following statements. Circle the word(s) that best complete(s) the statement.

1. In a weighted voting system, any particular voter might have *one / more than one* vote.

2. In the United States, the President is not elected by *a direct vote / the electoral college*.

3. A *supermajority / simple majority* is the requirement that a candidate must receive one more than half of the votes.

4. The weight required to pass a motion and effect a change is called a quota. Requiring a weight of more than half the total weight means that if a sequence of weights totals 40, the quota must be at least *20 / 21* for a simple majority.

5. Mathematical information from a table of voters and their weighted votes is correctly depicted in the following notation: *[14, 9, 8, 6] / [6, 8, 9, 14]*.

6. In a vote, simple yes/no questions are commonly called *status quo / motions*.

7. Legislative bodies may require a two-thirds vote to pass a constitutional amendment or to override a presidential veto. This requirement is called a *supermajority / simple majority.*

8. In an election, it is possible to determine the *qualitative / quantitative* measure of the power of voters in a system in which voters cast votes with different weights, such as in the electoral college.

Academic Word List

ACTIVITY 5

Scan and Define

A. Look at the ten words listed below. Scan the reading and underline the words from the list. Write the definitions for the words you know. Do not use a dictionary. The first one has been done for you.

1. affect _to influence or change; to move (emotionally)_____

2. amendments _____

3. assume _____

4. denote _____

5. major (adj.) _____

6. margin _____

7. outcome _____

8. plus (conj.) _____

9. principal (adj.)_____

10. sufficient_____

B. Share your definitions with a partner and then with the rest of your classmates. As a group, try to complete the definitions for all ten words. Use a dictionary to check the definitions if you are unsure about them. Then complete the vocabulary activity.

ACTIVITY 6

Vocabulary Challenge

A. Read the definition of the words below. Then decide which meaning is the one used in the sentence. Put the definition number next to the sentence. The first one has been done for you.

1. **affect** *verb* **1.** to influence or cause a change in; **2.** to pretend or feign (as in an accent); **3.** to touch or move someone emotionally
   ___1___ a. Decisions that affect our lives should never be made lightly.
   _____ b. His volunteer work affected him deeply, and he gave up his banking career to spend more time helping the poor.

2. **assume** *verb* **1.** to take for granted or presume; **2.** to believe something is true; **3.** to pretend (as in an identity); **4.** to take on responsibility
   _____ a. Ms. Nichols recently assumed the duties of managing editor for *Math Magazine.*
   _____ b. Despite her broken heart, Ella assumed an air of indifference about her breakup with Ron.
   _____ c. I didn't call them because I assumed they would remember to come.

3. **margin** *noun* **1.** the border or edge of a page; **2.** the amount of profit a company makes; **3.** the amount in excess of what is needed
   _____ a. The vote was close; the motion passed by only a small margin.
   _____ b. I spent this afternoon reviewing the notes I made in the margin of my history text.

4. **major** *adjective* **1.** greater in size, amount, or number; **2.** more important or significant, principal; **3.** very serious or of great concern

_____ a. Major decisions in companies are commonly made by a vote of the stockholders.

_____ b. He was diagnosed with a major illness last fall but has recovered fully.

_____ c. A major portion of the contributions will be sent to charitable organizations in the South.

B. Read the statements and then circle the correct answer or answers. Sometimes more than one answer is possible. The first one has been done for you.

1. In the United States, legislative bodies require a two-thirds vote to pass a constitutional <u>amendment</u>. In this sentence, *amendment* means
   a. a law in the constitution
   b. a change in the constitution
   c. a new constitution

2. The word *mother* <u>denotes</u> *female parent*, but it connotes *love* and *nurturing*. In this sentence, the word *denote* is used to explain
   a. the meaning of a word
   b. the feeling associated by a word
   c. the history of a word

3. In an election, an <u>outcome</u> in which a candidate must receive one (vote) more than half of the votes is called a *simple majority*. In this sentence, *outcome* has the same meaning as
   a. an announcement
   b. a result
   c. a vote

4. The Council of the European Union is the <u>principal</u> law-making body of the European Union. In this sentence, *principal* means
   a. chief
   b. important
   c. secondary

5. In the electoral college, each state has a number of votes equal to the number of its U.S. senators <u>plus</u> the number of its U.S. representatives, with a minimum of three votes. In this sentence, *plus* means
   a. increased by
   b. along with
   c. added to

6. Usually, no single state has had a <u>sufficient</u> number of electoral votes to change the outcome of the presidential election. The meaning of *sufficient* in this sentence is
   a. satisfactory
   b. adequate
   c. enough

Reading Details: Tables, Charts, and Graphs

In previous chapters, you learned that the main idea of a reading can be stated or implied and that it is often found in the introductory paragraph. Each paragraph in the reading includes a topic sentence that contains the main idea for that particular paragraph. The remainder of the paragraph contains the *details*, the information the writer provides to support the main idea of the paragraph and that contributes to the overall main idea of the reading.

The details of a reading are usually presented as written text. However, sometimes details are expressed visually—that is, they are presented in tables, charts, or graphs. Such visuals present a lot of information in a concise way. It is much easier to read numbers, for example, when they are presented in a visual format than when they are written in the text. As a reader, you can use visuals or graphic aids to get an overview of the content of a chapter or reading passage before you begin to read.

Putting Visuals into Words

To ensure you fully understand the information presented in a table, chart, or graph, try to describe or explain it. Include the title of the visual and the data it describes before summarizing the actual data presented. The following activity shows examples of commonly used tables, charts, and graphs and the kinds of information they present. Accompanying the graphics are activities to help you practice summarizing the information they contain.

 ACTIVITY 7

Understanding Visuals

A. Describe or explain Figure 1 in your own words. Share your description with a partner. The first one has been done for you.

Table—presents data or information in rows and columns

Name	Reading Grade Level	Math Grade Level	English Grade Level
Alex	10.6	12.0	11.8
Brian	11.2	12.0	10.9
Claire	10.7	11.9	12.0

Figure 1. Student Grade Levels

1. Description/Explanation: Figure 1 is titled Student Grade Levels. The table shows the student grade levels in reading, math, and English for three students: Alex, Brian, and Claire. Alex's scores are 10.6 in reading, 12.0 in math, and 11.8 in English. Brian's scores are 11.2 in reading, 12.0 in math, and 10.9 in English. Claire has a 10.7 reading level, 11.9 math level, and 12.0 English level. Alex scored the lowest in reading, and Brian scored the highest. Claire scored the highest in English.

B. Describe or explain Figure 2 and either Figure 3 or 4 in your own words. Share your description with a partner.

Chart—presents data in order to see or compare relationships or to see steps in a process

Reading Test Content

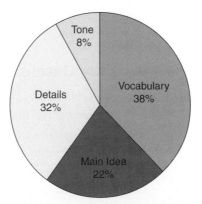

Figure 2. Reading Test Content

Pie Chart

1. Description/Explanation: _____

_____

_____

Key Concepts 2: Reading and Writing Across the Disciplines

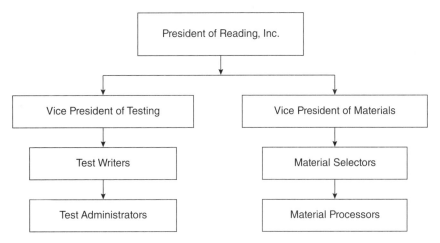

Figure 3. Organizational Chart for Reading, Inc.

Flow Chart

2. Description/Explanation: _____

_____

_____

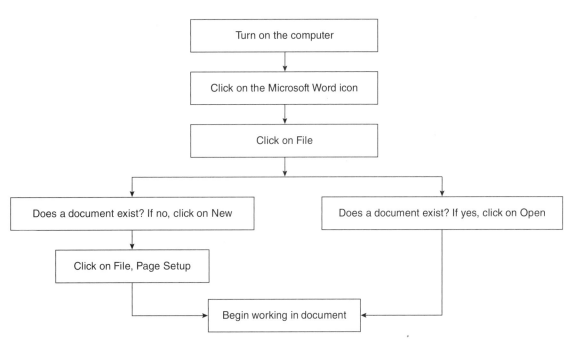

Figure 4. Opening a Microsoft™ Word Document

Flow Chart

3. Description/Explanation: _____

_____

_____

C. Look at the information presented in Figure 5. Then read the statements below. If the statement is true, put a *T* in the blank; if the statement is false, put an *F* in the blank. Change the false statements to make them true.

Graph—presents data in order to see or compare changes or relationships

Bar Graph

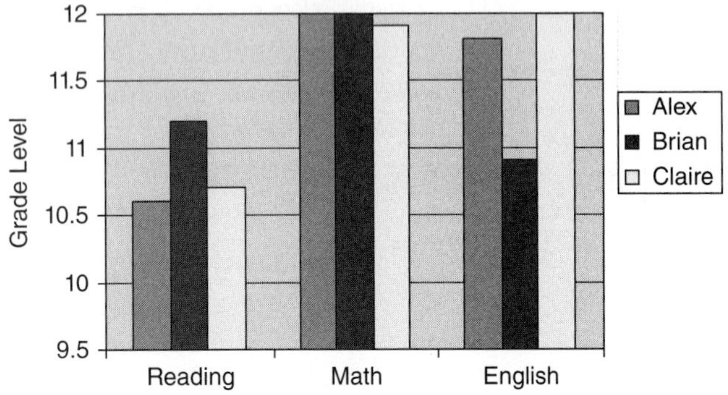

_____ 1. Figure 5 represents the grade levels for three students in reading, math, and English.

_____ 2. Brian has the highest score in all three subjects.

_____ 3. All three students scored above 10.5 in all three subjects.

_____ 4. Alex has the highest reading score of the three students.

_____ 5. None of the students scored above 12.0 in any subject.

_____ 6. Claire scored lower in math than in English.

_____ 7. None of the three students scored below 11.0 in English.

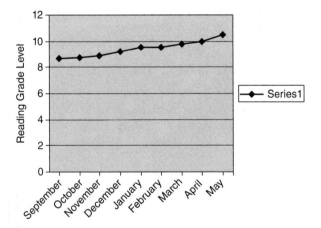

Figure 5. Student Grade Levels

D. Look at the information presented in Figure 6. Write three true statements and two false statements about the line graph. Ask a classmate to determine which of the statements are true and which are false.

Figure 6. Reading Grade Level Averages for School Year 2005

Line Graph

1. _____

2. _____

3. _____

4. _____

5. _____

Choose a Visual

Read the statements below and decide what kind of visual would best represent the information or data: a table, a pie chart, a flow chart, a bar graph, or a line graph. On a separate sheet of paper, make a sketch of the visual and label the principal parts.

1. Out of every dollar you earn, 30 cents goes toward housing costs, 15 cents goes toward food, 10 cents goes toward utilities and other housing-related costs, 20 cents goes toward taxes, 15 cents goes toward savings, 5 cents goes toward entertainment, and 5 cents goes for all other expenses.

2. Of the three people running for elective office, Mr. Anderson received 26% of the vote in Texas, 18% of the vote in Oklahoma, and 44% of the vote in Nebraska. Mr. Bowers, on the other hand, received just 17% of the vote in Texas, 43% in Oklahoma, and 22% in Nebraska. Ms. Collins received 57% of the vote in Texas, 39% in Oklahoma, and 34% in Nebraska.

3. In order to be accepted into a university, a student must first submit an application. Accompanying the application are transcripts from high school and/or other colleges attended; standardized test scores as required; and an application fee of $30. After the application has been reviewed, the student must wait to find out whether or not he or she has been accepted. If the student is accepted, the next step in the process is to speak with an advisor to choose classes. If the student is not accepted, the student may reapply the next semester, write a letter of appeal, or apply to a new college.

Identifying Text Structure—*Exemplification*

> **Exemplification:** using examples to explain terms or concepts

In order to explain difficult topics or concepts, writers often turn to examples. Examples are easy for readers to understand, and they add interest to the reading as well. In Reading 1, the writer's goal is to explain the role of mathematics in selection processes. In order to explain the mathematical concept of weighted systems, the writer uses the examples of decision-making in business and presidential elections in the United States. Because these are examples most readers know something about, the writer's message is clear to the reader. This format follows the text structure of *exemplification.* This type of text structure can also be used for personal topics; in this case, examples may contribute more to the interest of the reading than to an explanation of a concept or process.

As a reader, recognizing the text structure of exemplification will help you follow the writer's explanation and improve your understanding of a difficult concept. Sometimes an example will reinforce what you already know about a topic, while at other times it may introduce new information.

Key Words—*Exemplification*

Good readers recognize the key words that are used with different text structures. Recognizing key words speeds up your reading and improves your comprehension of the material. Some commonly used key words associated with the pattern of exemplification are listed in the table below.

as an example	for example	specifically
as an illustration	for instance	such as
consider (the situation)	imagine that	to demonstrate
e.g. (for example)	in the case of	to illustrate

Recognize Key Words

Read the following sentences. Match the sentence in Column A with its example in Column B. Circle the key word(s) used in the example.

Column A	Column B
_____ 1. This requirement is called a *supermajority*.	a. To illustrate, a weighted voting system with a quota of 21 and weights [12,11,9,8] will be represented by [21: 12,11,9,8].
_____ 2. The quota for a particular system is usually added to the notation listing the weights.	b. In U.S. presidential elections specifically, the winning candidate must receive at least 270 electoral votes, which is one more than half the total 538 electoral votes.
_____ 3. In a weighted voting system, any particular voter might have more than one vote.	c. In the case of the 2000 pr esidential race, New Hampshire (where Bush won 4 electoral votes by a margin of 1 percent) had as much power as Texas (where Bush won 32 electoral votes by a margin of 21 percent).
_____ 4. Generally, all the electoral college votes of a particular state go to the same presidential candidate, the candidate who received the greatest number of votes by that state's voters.	d. For example, it is common for legislative bodies to require a two-thirds vote to pass constitutional amendments.
_____ 5. The requirement that a candidate must receive one more than half of the votes is called a *simple majority*.	e. Consider the business world, where major decisions may be made by a vote of the stockholders, each stockholder having a number of votes equal to the number of share of stock held.

ACTIVITY 10

Use Key Words

Read the sentences and fill in the blanks with one of the key words from the box on page 175. There may be more than one answer possible.

1. To denote the voters and their weights, we generally use subscripts. _____, a voter with weight 12 is simply called the "first voter" and is given the name P_1. The weight of this first voter is represented by $W_1 = 12$.

2. We seldom realize that the outcome of a vote depends as much on the voting methods as on the actual votes cast. In some voting systems, _____, each voter has a single vote. However, in many voting systems this is not the case.

3. When voting in an election, the voters' names are important. This is not the case in mathematics, however. _____ mathematics, all we really need to know are the number of voters and their weights.

4. There are many popular voting systems. The plurality method and the Borda count method, _____, are two.

5. Different voting methods have been tried, some with more success than others. Take France _____. In an election between Chirac and LePen in 2002, the winning candidate did not have majority support. In addition to calls for reform, it also led to the idea of letting voters rank their preferences for president rather than simply voting for one candidate.

In the first section of this chapter, you were introduced to reading tables, charts, and graphs. You practiced the skills and strategies of surveying, predicting, and summarizing with Reading 1. In this section you will practice these same skills with a new reading. You will also practice using context to guess the meaning of unfamiliar words.

Get Ready to Read

Believe It or Not

Read the following statements and put an X in front of the ones that you believe. Discuss your answers with a partner.

_____ 1. The probability of winning the lottery is very small.

_____ 2. Mathematical formulas can be used to determine the probability of an event.

_____ 3. People who win the jackpots in casinos have a "system" for winning.

_____ 4. An event with 90 percent probability is more likely to occur than one with 10 percent.

_____ 5. Probability can be used to get a high score on a test.

Survey and Predict

A. Using the following steps, survey Reading 2 and predict what the reading will be about.

1. Read the title.

2. Read the first paragraph and identify the main idea.

3. Read the headings.

4. Look for any graphic or visual aids in the reading.

5. Look for key terms in bold.

6. Read the last paragraph.

B. Write your prediction here: _____

_____

C. Now read the passage to see if your prediction is correct. Try to read as quickly as you can. Do not stop to look up words in your dictionary.

Computing Probabilities in Simple Experiments

Probability is the mathematics of chance, and the terminology used in probability theory is often heard in daily life. For example, you may hear on the radio, "The probability of precipitation today is 80 percent." This statement should be interpreted as meaning that on 80 percent of past days that had atmospheric conditions like those of today, it rained at some time. The intuitive interpretation might be "carry an umbrella."

Sample Spaces and Events

To study probability in a mathematically precise way, we need special terminology and notation. Making an observation or taking a measurement of some act, such as flipping a coin, is called an **experiment**. An **outcome** is one of the possible results of an experiment, such as getting a head when flipping a coin. The set of all possible outcomes is called the **sample space**. Finally, an **event** is any collection of the possible outcomes—that is, an event is a subset of the sample space.

Examples of *experiments* include rolling a die and recording the number of dots showing on the top face, tossing a coin three times and recording the results in order, or spinning a spinner twice and recording the colors of the regions where it comes to rest in order.

Examples of an *outcome*, one of the possible results, for each of the above experiments could include {3} as the number of dots on the die, {HTT} as the results of flipping a coin three times where *H* means *heads* and *T* means *tails*, or {RY} as the results of spinning a spinner twice where *R* means *red* and *Y* means *yellow*.

The *sample space*—all possible outcomes—for the die experiment includes six possible outcomes: {1, 2, 3, 4, 5, 6}, where numerals represent the number of dots showing on the top of the die. There are eight possible outcomes in the *sample space* for the coin-

toss experiment: {HHH, HHT, HTH, THH, TTH, THT, HTT, TTT}. If the spinner comprised four colors—blue, red, green, and yellow—the *sample space* for the third experiment would include: {RR, RY, RG, RB, YR, YY, YG, YB, GR, GY, GG, GB, BR, BY, BG, BB}.

Finally, an example of an *event*, or any collection of the possible outcomes, for the die experiment is {2, 4, 6}. For the coin toss, an *event* might be {HTH, HTT, TTH, TTT}, the event of getting a tail on the second coin. An example of an *event* for the spinner experiment is {RR, YY, GG, BB}.

Experimental Probability

One way to find the probability of an event is to conduct a series of experiments. For example, if we wanted to know the probability of "heads" landing face up when a coin is tossed, we could toss a coin repeatedly. To find the probability of heads landing face up in this experiment, we would record the number of times heads appears face up when the coin is tossed and divide that number by the total number of times the coin is tossed. This leads to the definition of **experimental probability**, which is the relative frequency with which an event occurs in a particular sequence of trials.

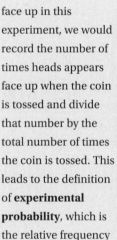

Experiments have shown that a coin tossed hundreds of times will land "heads up" approximately 50 percent of the times it is tossed. Based on such experiments, we say that the probability of a coin landing "heads up" is ½ (or 0.5 or 50%). Note that experimental probabilities may differ from one set of observations to another. One person tossing a coin 1,000 times could get heads 507 times while another person performing the same experiment 1,000 times might get heads only 480 times.

The probability of an event can be reported as a fraction, a decimal, or a percentage, as illustrated above. This number must be between zero and one, inclusive, if expressed as a fraction or a decimal; it must be between 0 percent and 100 percent, inclusive, if expressed as a percentage. The greater the probability, the more likely the event is to occur. An event with a probability of 0 is expected never to occur. An event with probability 1 is a "sure thing" and is expected to happen every time the experiment is repeated.

Imagine an experiment which consists of tossing two coins 500 times and recording the results. The table below gives the observed results and the experimental probability of each outcome. Let E be the event of getting a head on the first coin. Our task is to find the experimental probability of E is {HH, HT}.

Outcome	Frequency	Experimental Probability
HH	137	137/500
HT	115	115/500
TH	108	108/500
TT	140	140/500
	Total: 500	*Total:* 500/500 = 1.00

From the table, we see that a head showed on the first coin $137 + 115 = 252$ times. Thus, the experimental probability of E is $137 + 115/500 = 252/500 = 0.504$.

Theoretical Probability

The advantage of finding a probability experimentally is that it can be done by simply performing experiments. The disadvantage is that the experimental probability will depend on the particular set of repetitions of the experiment and hence may need to be recomputed when more experiments are performed. Rare outcomes may not appear at all in the list of actual observations. Furthermore, repeating the experiment many times may be time-consuming or tedious.

In many cases we can determine what fraction of the time an event is likely to occur without actually performing experiments. For example, you already knew that a coin is going to land heads up about ½ of the time and that a die is going to land showing three dots 1/6 of the time. The probability of event E, if all the outcomes in the sample space S are equally likely to occur, is $P(E)$ = number of outcomes in E / number of outcomes in S.

We cannot be sure that a real-world coin or die is perfectly balanced, so we cannot be sure that the outcomes in the sample space are equally likely. Thus, when we apply the above definition, we are computing **theoretical probabilities**. When we deal with theoretical probabilities of an ideal coin or ideal die, we refer to them as a **fair coin** or a **fair die**.

Key Concept Words

event – (n.) a collection of the possible outcomes

experiment – (n.) making an observation or taking a measurement of an act

experimental probability – (n.) the relative frequency with which an event occurs in a particular sequence of trials

fair coin – (n.) an ideal coin, one that is perfectly balanced

fair die – (n.) an ideal six-sided cube, one that is perfectly balanced

outcome – (n.) – one of the possible results

sample space – (n.) the set of all possible outcomes

theoretical probability – (n.) determining what fraction of the time an event is likely to occur without actually performing the experiments

Glossed Words

dot – (n.) a small, dark circle or round mark; **flipping a coin** – (v.) throwing a coin into the air; **heads / tails** – (n.) the two sides of a coin; **inclusive** – (adj.) including the first and last items; from beginning to end; **intuitive** – (adj.) instinctive, not learned; **rare** – (adj.) uncommon, unusual, infrequent; **tedious** – (adj.) boring or dull, unexciting; **toss** – (v.) to flip a coin; to throw

Summarizing

Share What You Read

Use two or three sentences to tell your partner what you thought the reading was about. Then listen to your partner's sentences. If you disagree, go back and find support for your summary. Write your summary statement below.

Summary: _____

_____

Check Your Comprehension

Match the words in Column A with the definitions in Column B.

_____ 1. experiment   a. all possible outcomes

_____ 2. outcome   b. the chance that a specific outcome will occur

_____ 3. sample space   c. the side of a coin opposite the head

_____ 4. die   d. a perfectly balanced six-sided cube

_____ 5. probability   e. an observation or measurement of some action

_____ 6. fair die   f. a six-sided cube with a range of 1–6 dots on a side

_____ 7. tails   g. one of the possible results of an experiment

Academic Word List

Scan and Define

A. Look at the ten words listed below. Scan the reading and underline the words from the list. Write the definitions for the words you know. Do not use a dictionary. The first one has been done for you.

1. approximately _nearly, almost, roughly_____

2. compute _____

3. conduct (v.) _____

4. furthermore _____

5. hence _____

6. interpret _____

7. precise _____

8. region _____

9. sequence (n.) _____

10. series _____

B. Share your definitions with a partner and then with the rest of your classmates. As a group, try to complete the definitions for all ten words. Use a dictionary to check the definitions if you are unsure about them. Then complete the vocabulary activity.

ACTIVITY 16 **Vocabulary Challenge**

A. Using your dictionary, work with a partner to find the missing word forms and complete the chart. If no form exists, draw a line in the space. The first one has been done for you.

Noun	Verb	Adjective	Adverb
1. *approximation*	*approximate*	*approximate*	approximately
2.	compute		
3.	conduct		
4.			furthermore
5.			hence
6.	interpret		
7.		precise	
8. region			
9. sequence			
10. series			

B. Circle the word that best completes the sentence.

1. If you toss a coin hundreds of times, it will land "heads up" *precisely / approximately* 50 percent of the times it is tossed.

2. *Conducting / Interpreting* observations and recording the outcomes precisely is called an experiment.

3. A person's chances of being struck by lightning are approximately 1 in 700,000. Ray Cleveland, a forest ranger from Virginia, was struck by lightning seven times between 1942 and 1983. *Furthermore, / Hence,* he could be called a "human lightning conductor."

4. If a weather forecaster predicts a 80 percent chance of rain, the forecast can be *interpreted / computed* as meaning that, in the past, on 80 percent of the days with similar atmospheric conditions, it rained at some time.

5. One way to find the probability of an event is to conduct a *series / sequence* of experiments.

6. Dr. David Blackwell has made important contributions to probability, statistics, game theory, and set theory. *Furthermore, / Hence,* he was a dedicated teacher.

7. An example of an experiment is spinning a spinner twice and recording, in order, the colors of the *regions / sequence* where it comes to rest.

8. Experimental probability is the relative frequency with which an event occurs in a particular *computing / sequence* of trials.

Using Context to Guess Meaning—*Examples*

When writers introduce new ideas or terms in their writing, they often provide examples. While examples may serve as support for main ideas and topics in a passage, they also clarify concepts and provide explanation. As the reader, you can use these examples to define unfamiliar terms or concepts.

Examples are often introduced with the phrases *for example, for instance, to illustrate,* or *such as.* Read the following sentences to see how an example is used to explain the word in bold.

*In a **weighted** voting system, any particular voter might have more than one vote. For example, in the business world, major decisions may be made by a vote of the stockholders, where each stockholder has a number of votes equal to the number of shares of stock held.*

From the example, the reader is able to understand that the term *weighted* means that something—in this case, the number of votes each person has—has been adjusted to reflect a specific value. In business, the vote of a person who holds 100 shares of stock has 10 times as much weight as the vote of a person who holds 10 shares of stock.

Guess Meaning from Context

Use the examples below to define the terms and/or concepts in bold. Underline the key words and then write the definition of the terms in your own words.

1. **Probability** is the mathematics of chance, and the terminology used in probability theory is often heard in daily life. For example, you may hear on the radio, "The probability of precipitation today is 80 percent." How likely it is that this event (rain) will occur? The statement should be interpreted as meaning that on 80 percent of past days that had atmospheric conditions like those of today, it rained at some time.

   probability = _____

2. Experiments can be used to compute probabilities. An experiment can be simple, such as tossing a coin three times and recording the results in order. An **outcome** for the experiment could include {HTT}, where *H* means *heads* and *T* means *tails*. The **sample space** for the experiment includes {HHH, HHT, HTH, THH, TTH, THT, HTT, TTT}.

   outcome = _____

   sample space = _____

3. Some elections call for a **simple majority**. For instance, in the U.S. presidential election, the winning candidate must receive at least 270 electoral votes, which is one more than half the total 538 electoral votes.

   simple majority = _____

4. For other elections, a **supermajority** is required. A legislative body may have a requirement such as a two-thirds vote to pass constitutional amendments, for instance. In this case, the requirement is higher than one more than half the total weight.

   supermajority = _____

5. A group of stockholders wants to pass a motion to fire one of the board members. In order to pass the motion, there needs to be a **quota**. To illustrate how the quota is determined, imagine that there are four voters with respective weights of 12, 11, 9, and 8. The total weight is 40; half the total weight is 20. Requiring a weight of more than half the total weight (40) means setting a quota greater than 20. Thus, for a simple majority, the quota is 21.

   quota = _____

Key Concepts 2: Reading and Writing Across the Disciplines

In this section, you will learn some skills and strategies associated with the writing process. It includes the grammar of adjective clauses, which is one of the grammatical structures used in the readings. In this section, you will practice the different steps in the writing process and will write an essay of exemplification.

The Grammar of Adjective Clauses

Like adjectives, adjective clauses modify a noun in a sentence. Adjective clauses are dependent clauses and are connected to independent clauses by relative pronouns or relative adverbs. Study the relative pronouns and relative adverbs and their use in adjective clauses in the chart below. The nouns modified by the adjective clauses are in bold.

Relative Pronoun	Use	Adjective Clause
who / that	subject (people)	In business, **people** *who vote on major decisions* are called stockholders. People choose the **candidate** *that best represents their beliefs and values.*
which	subject (things) object (things)	The electoral **votes**, *which equal the number of senators and U.S. representatives*, decide the winner. Winning the presidential election requires a minimum of 270 electoral **votes**, *which the electoral college awards the month after the election.*
whom that	object (people) object (things)	The **candidate** *to whom the most votes go* is declared the winner. The **states** *that candidates visit the most often* are those with the most electoral votes.
whose	subject/object (possessive)	The **candidate** *whose platform is the most popular* will win the people's votes. The **candidate** *whose platform the people find problematic* will lose the election.

Relative Adverb	Use	Adjective Clause
when	object (time)	I need to know the **time** *when the polls open* so I can get there early.
where	object (place)	They decided to hold the board meeting in the **city** *where most of the stockholders lived* in order to increase attendance.

ACTIVITY 18

Recognize Adjective Clauses

Underline the adjective clauses in the sentences below and on the following page. Circle the noun that each adjective clause modifies. There may be more than one in a sentence.

1. In the 2000 presidential race, New Hampshire, where Bush won four electoral votes by a margin of only 1 percent, had as much power as Texas, where Bush won 32 electoral votes by a margin of 21 percent.

2. Generally speaking, for a motion to pass, voters whose weights total *more* than half the total weight must vote "yes" on that motion.

3. A forecast that says there is an 80 percent chance of rain today really means "take your umbrella today."

4. An event, which is any collection of possible outcomes in an experiment, is a subset of all of the possible outcomes.

5. This leads to the definition of *experimental probability*, which is the relative frequency with which an event occurs in a particular sequence of trials.

Use Adjective Clauses

A. Read the sentences and circle the relative pronoun or adverb that best completes the sentence.

1. I wonder whether mathematicians *who / whose* study probability ever buy lottery tickets.

2. An event *which / where* has a probability of 0 is expected never to occur, and one *which / who* has a probability of 1 is a "sure thing" and is expected to happen every time the experiment is repeated.

3. When we deal with theoretical probabilities, we compute probabilities based on an ideal coin, *when / which* we refer to as a fair coin.

4. The Council of the European Union, *which / where* is the principal law-making body of the European Union, uses a voting system in which each member state is assigned a number of votes proportional to its population.

5. In a weighted voting system, for example, a stockholder *which / that* owns 1,000 shares of stocks has the equivalent number of votes, 1,000.

B. Fill in the blank with the correct relative pronoun or adverb. The first one has been done for you. Sometimes more than one answer is possible.

1. The United States is a country ____*whose*____ citizens consider their right to vote to be sacred.

2. U.S. citizens want a voice in the decisions _____ affect them.

3. The election of the President of the United States is not determined by a direct vote of the people _____ vote for their favorite candidate on the first Tuesday in November.

4. The President is chosen by the electoral college, _____ is composed of people _____ represent their respective states.

5. The last election _____ I voted in was not much of a contest between the candidates.

6. After the election, the electors meet in their respective state capitals _____ they cast their electoral votes.

7. In an election it is possible to determine a quantitative measure of the power of voters in a system in _____ voters cast votes with different weights.

Sentence Essentials

Dependent Clauses: Adjective Clauses

A dependent clause, when connected to an independent clause, forms a complex sentence. As mentioned in previous Sentence Essentials sections, there are three types of dependent clauses: adjective, adverb, and noun clauses. This section will focus on writing sentences that contain adjective clauses.

Adjective clauses

- function as adjectives by modifying nouns or pronouns
- begin with a relative pronoun or relative adverb (*who, which, that, whose, when, where*)
- are placed after the noun in the sentence they modify
- can be restrictive: contain information essential to the meaning of the sentence
- can be nonrestrictive: add information that is not essential to the meaning of the sentence

Adjective clauses give additional information—a description or explanation or definition—about a noun in the independent clause. Sentences containing adjective clauses add variety and coherence to your writing.

Independent clause:	In business, people are called stockholders.
Additional information:	People vote on major decisions.
Sentence with adjective clause:	In business, people [**who** *vote on major decisions*] are called stockholders.

How to Form Adjective Clauses

First, determine which noun in the sentence the adjective clause will modify. Then choose the correct relative pronoun or adverb—see The Grammar of Adjective Clauses in the previous section for help choosing the correct pronoun/adverb. Insert the relative pronoun/adverb (along with the remaining part of the clause) after the noun in the sentence. See the example below.

Clauses to be connected: We want a voice in the decisions. The decisions affect us.

1. Determine the noun the adjective clause will modify: *decisions* (in the first sentence).

2. Choose relative pronoun: *which* (*decisions* is a thing; it is used as a subject in the adjective clause). Replace *the decisions* (in the second sentence) with the pronoun *which*.

3. Insert the pronoun after the noun: We want a voice in the *decisions which*.

4. Insert the remaining part of the clause: We want a voice in the decisions which *affect us*.

Connect Clauses

Connect the two clauses with the relative pronoun or adverb in parentheses. Do not repeat the underlined word or phrase you replace with the relative pronoun or adverb. The first one has been done for you.

1. The United States is a country. <u>Its</u> citizens consider their right to vote to be sacred. (whose) <u>The United States is a country whose citizens consider their right to vote to be sacred.</u>

2. The United States is a country. <u>In the United States,</u> presidential elections are held every four years. (where) _____

3. Generally, all the electoral votes go to the candidate. The candidate receives the greatest number of votes by that state's voters. (who) _____

4. In an election, it is possible to measure the quantitative power of voters in a system. Voters cast votes with different weights in the system. (in which) _____

5. People probably don't play the lottery. People truly understand the concept of probability. (who) _____

6. Imagine an experiment. The experiment consists of tossing two coins 500 times and recording the results. (which) _____

7. Game theory is studied by scientists. It provides scientists opportunities to study social interaction among people. (for whom) _____

8. Mathematicians and economists are just two groups of researchers. Researchers have used game theory to study the behavior of politicians, voters, consumers, and even terrorists. (who) _____

Two Types of Adjective Clauses: Restrictive and Nonrestrictive

There are two types of adjective clauses: restrictive and nonrestrictive. In a sentence with a restrictive adjective clause, the information that describes, explains, or defines the noun is needed to understand the meaning of the sentence. In contrast, in a sentence with a nonrestrictive adjective clause, the information that describes, explains, or defines the noun is not needed to understand the meaning of the sentence. It simply provides extra information.

In the sentence, *Weather forecasters who work at the National Hurricane Center in Miami issue tropical storm warnings and watches,* the underlined adjective clause restricts the group of weather forecasters that is being defined. That is, only specific weather forecasters issue tropical storm warnings and watches. Who are they? They are the forecasters who work at the National Hurricane Center in Miami. Other forecasters do not issue tropical storm warnings and watches.

In the sentence, *Weather forecasters, who make predictions based on weather patterns, use sophisticated equipment to gather information,* the underlined clause provides additional information about weather forecasters. We know that weather forecasters predict the weather. Thus, the adjective clause is about forecasters in general, not about a specific group of forecasters. The important idea in the sentence is that weather forecasters use sophisticated equipment to gather weather information.

Note: The relative pronoun *that* is not used in nonrestrictive adjective clauses; use *which* for things and *who* for people.

Identify Restrictive and Nonrestrictive Clauses

Read the sentences and underline the adjective clauses. If they are restrictive, put *R* in the blank; if they are non-restrictive, put *NR* in the blank.

_____ 1. Mathematicians, who study numbers, have many career options.

_____ 2. One of the possible results of an experiment that mathematicians perform is called an outcome.

_____ 3. Probability theory, which can be experimental or theoretical, deals with the occurrence of random events.

_____ 4. Imagine an experiment which consists of tossing two coins 500 times and recording the results.

_____ 5. A fair coin is a coin which is perfectly balanced.

Punctuation of Restrictive and Nonrestrictive Adjective Clauses

When the information in the adjective clause is required to identify the specific noun in the sentence, no special punctuation is required. However, when the information in the adjective clause is not essential to understand the meaning of the sentence, the adjective clause is set off by commas.

Restrictive

The four candidates campaigned in several Midwest states over the last two weeks. One candidate spent time in Minnesota, one in Iowa, one in Wisconsin, and one in Michigan. The candidate **who campaigned in Michigan last week** was the winner.

Nonrestrictive

The candidate campaigned in the Midwest over the last two weeks. The candidate spent time in Minnesota, Iowa, Wisconsin, and Michigan. The candidate, **who campaigned in Michigan last week**, was the winner.

The restrictive adjective clause describes which of the four candidates won the election. The nonrestrictive adjective clause does not need to describe which candidate won because there is only one candidate mentioned. The additional information, the fact that the candidate was in Michigan last week, is not needed to identify the candidate.

Explain the Difference

Read the sentences and answer the questions that follow. The first one has been done for you.

1. A. The voters' names, which are unimportant for mathematical purposes, are listed in a table.
   B. The voters' names which are unimportant for mathematical purposes are listed in a table.

   Which sentence states that all of the names are listed in the table? _Sentence A_ _means that all of the names are listed in the table._

   Which sentence states that only some of the names are listed in the table? _Sentence B states only the unimportant names are in the table; the names which_ _are important are not listed._

2. A. The city, where the ballots were cast, had eight people running for mayor.
   B. The city where the ballots were cast had eight people running for mayor.

   Which sentence is part of a conversation about many cities? _____

   _____

   Which sentence is part of a conversation about one city? _____

   _____

3. A. The members of the Senate committee, who sponsored the legislation, needed a two-thirds majority vote to pass the constitutional amendment.
   B. The members of the Senate committee who sponsored the legislation needed a two-thirds majority vote to pass the constitutional amendment.

   Which sentence states that some of the committee members sponsored the legislation? _____

   _____

   Which sentence states that all of the committee members sponsored the legislation? _____

   _____

4. A. People, who win the jackpots in casinos, have a "system" for winning.
   B. People who win the jackpots in casinos have a "system" for winning.

   Which sentence is about a specific group of people? _____

   _____

5. Ray Cleveland, who is a forest ranger from Virginia, was struck by lightning seven times between 1942 and 1983.

   Why is the adjective clause in this sentence nonrestrictive? _____

   _____

 ACTIVITY 23

Punctuate Complex Sentences Containing Adjective Clauses

Read the sentences and underline the adjective clauses. If a clause is nonrestrictive, insert commas to set off the information that is not essential to the meaning of the sentence.

1. In the 2000 presidential race, New Hampshire where Bush won four electoral votes by a margin of only 1 percent had as much power as Texas.

2. In order to study probability in a mathematically precise way, we need special terminology and notation that can describe it.

3. People that like math are often viewed as nerds or geeks.

4. John who was a gambler studied mathematical probability in hopes of beating the Las Vegas casinos.

5. An event with a probability of 0 is one which is expected never to occur.

6. This leads to the definition of experimental probability which is the relative frequency with which an event occurs in a particular sequence of trials.

7. Students who are looking for careers in mathematics should consider becoming teachers, statisticians, or computer scientists.

Write Sentences Containing Adjective Clauses

Write sentences which contain adjective clauses. The sentences can be about any topic.

1. _____
2. _____
3. _____
4. _____

Spot the Error

Each sentence contains an error common to adjective clauses: incorrect pronoun or incorrect punctuation. Find the error and correct it.

1. Blaise Pascal who was a French mathematician had an interest in probability.

2. People which study mathematics might want to consider a career in finance.

3. The President of the United States who is elected by the electoral college needs 270 votes to win.

4. After an election, electors meet in their respective state capitals which they cast their electoral votes.

5. The requirement, that he explained, is called a simple majority.

6. The Council of the European Union, that is the principal law-making body of the European Union, uses a weighted voting system.

7. Voters, who go to the polls, are exercising their right as citizens of this country.

Blaise Pascal, mathematician

Adjective Clauses vs. Adverb Clauses and Noun Clauses

The three clauses have some words in common: adjective and noun clauses can both use *who, which,* and *that,* for example. Adjective and adverb clauses can both use *when*. It is not the relative pronoun or relative adverb that identifies the type of clause it is; it is the function of the clause that identifies its type. Adjective clauses modify the noun or pronoun in the main clause; adverb clauses function as adverbs and may tell time, place, manner, reason, or result, for example; noun clauses function as nouns and can be subjects or objects. Look at the examples below; the first clause in each example is the adjective clause.

Adjective Clause vs. Adverb Clause

On the day **when** people voted for George Bush or Al Gore, U.S. major networks had a difficult time projecting a winner. (modifies noun *day*)

Thus, **when** we apply the above definition, we are computing theoretical probabilities. (tells at whatever time)

Adjective Clause vs. Noun Clause

We want a voice in the decisions **that** affect us. (modifies noun *decisions*)

You already know **that** a coin is going to land heads up about one half of the time. (object of verb *know*)

Making the Connection

Good readers evaluate the details of a passage while they are reading. They consider the type of details offered and the source of the details. They look for sufficient examples and consider the validity of opinions that are offered on the subject. Writers must keep this in mind as they build support for their main idea. Offering facts that can be verified, statistics that give weight to your argument, examples that are relevant to the topic, and citations from credible sources are all ways to effectively support your ideas.

WRITING 1B • The Process

Get Ready to Write

Body and Support Sentences

The previous chapter introduced the use of quotations as a way to support the thesis statement of an essay. Citing the opinion of an expert or quoting something from the article you are writing about adds to the overall strength of your essay. While citing the opinion of an expert serves as factual support for your thesis statement, stating your own opinion does not.

Facts and Opinions

Facts are statements that are accepted as true and that can be verified or proven. *The President of the United States is chosen by the electoral college* is an example of a fact. Opinions, on the other hand, are statements that reflect someone's personal belief or feeling about a subject. *The President of the United States is the best president this country has ever had* is an opinion. Any personal opinion expressed in an essay must be supported with facts.

Fact or Opinion

Read the following statements. If the statement is a fact, put *F* on the line; if it is an opinion, put *O* on the line. For each opinion, suggest what kind of facts could serve to support it.

_____ 1. A two-thirds vote in both houses of Congress is necessary to override a presidential veto.

_____ 2. The President was right to veto the bill sent to him by Congress.

_____ 3. The lottery is a great way to win money.

_____ 4. The weather forecaster stated that the chance of rain today was 80 percent.

_____ 5. The Senate vote to override the President's veto of the bill was 62 to 38.

_____ 6. If the law bans cell phone use in downtown areas, there will be fewer accidents.

_____ 7. I have a 50–50 chance of getting this question, no. 7, correct.

Statistics

Citing statistics is another way to provide strong support for an essay. Statistics, which are numerical facts, may be written or may be presented visually in an essay. A visual presentation includes tables, charts, or graphs and has the advantage of presenting a lot of information in a concise way. When citing statistics in your writing, be sure to include the source of your information.

Using Details from Graphics

The information contained in graphics—tables, charts, and graphs—can be used as general or specific support for the thesis statement or topic sentence in an essay. General support includes the overall idea(s) represented by the graphic; specific support includes numbers and percents. Look at the example below.

State	Population	Electoral Votes
California	36,500,000	55
Georgia	9,400,000	15
Hawaii	1,300,000	4
Illinois	12,800,000	21
New York	19,300,000	31

Figure 7. U.S. Population and Electoral Votes (U.S. Census Bureau, 2006)

Table Information:

The table in Figure 7 shows the figures for the U.S. population and corresponding electoral votes for five states: California, Georgia, Hawaii, Illinois, and New York.

General Support:

a. Of the five states included in the chart, California has the largest population and the largest number of electoral votes.

b. California has almost twice the population of New York.

c. The population of Illinois is larger than that of Georgia and Hawaii combined.

d. New York has more than twice as many electoral votes as Georgia has.

Specific Support:

a. According to the chart, California, with a population of 36,500,000, has 55 electoral votes. Hawaii, with a population of 1,300,000, has only four electoral votes.

b. California's population of 36,500,000 is almost twice as large as New York's, which is 19,300,000.

c. Illinois has a population of 12,800,000, Georgia's is 9,400,000, and Hawaii's is 1,300,000.

d. New York has 31 electoral votes, while Georgia has 15.

Write General and Specific Details

Look at the charts below. For each chart, describe the overall information presented. Then write general and specific details.

1.

Percent of Math Majors	Occupation	Starting Salary
27%	Teacher	$35,000
18%	Statisticians	$49,000
16%	Research Analysts	$50,000
39%	Other	$42,000

Figure 8. Sample Occupations and Starting Salaries for Math Majors

Table Information: _____

_____

General Support:

   a. _____

   b. _____

   c. _____

Specific Support:

   a. _____

   b. _____

   c. _____

2.

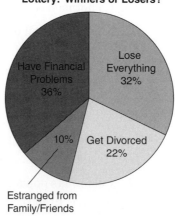

Figure 9. What Happens to Lottery Winners

Chart Information: _____

_____

General Support:

   a. _____

   b. _____

   c. _____

Specific Support:

a. _____

b. _____

c. _____

Synthesizing

In previous chapters, you practiced synthesizing information from two written sources. Synthesizing information can also include combining facts and statistics from charts and graphs with information from other sources. Place the information, either general or specific, after the sentence it supports.

Read the paragraph below and study the chart; then see how information from both was incorporated into one paragraph. Information based on or taken from the table is in bold.

Paragraph:

People dream of winning the lottery. They believe that once they have money, their lives will change for the better. They are correct on one point: their lives will change. Unfortunately, for many lottery winners, their lives become filled with unhappiness as an indirect result of winning the lottery. Having millions of dollars does not guarantee happiness. Indeed, winning the lottery can have negative effects on personal relationships. Winners must deal with family and friends who feel entitled to some of the winnings based on their relationship with the winners. In addition, winning an enormous amount of money does not always improve a person's financial situation. People who buy lottery tickets with the hope of winning should have in place a plan to deal with the resultant change in their lives in case they do win.

Table:

The Downside of Winning the Lottery	
Have financial problems	36%
Lose everything	32%
Get divorced	22%
Estranged from family and friends	10%

Figure 10. Type and percent of problems lottery winners experience (D. Force Institute)

Synthesized paragraph:

People dream of winning the lottery. They believe that once they have money, their lives will change for the better. They are correct on one point: their lives will change. Unfortunately, for many lottery winners, their lives become filled with unhappiness as an indirect result of winning the lottery. Having millions of dollars does not guarantee happiness. Indeed, winning the lottery can have negative effects on personal relationships. **People who are married sometimes end up getting divorced. According to D. Force Institute, for example, 22 percent of people who win the lottery end up getting divorced**. Even if a couple remains married after winning the lottery, winners must deal with family and friends who feel entitled to some of the winnings based on their relationship with the winners.

In fact, 10 percent of lottery winners end up being estranged from their family and friends. In addition, winning an enormous amount of money does not always improve a person's financial situation, **and, in some cases, worsens it. Statistics from the Institute show that 36 percent of those winning the lottery suffer some kind of financial problem after winning. Even more surprising is the fact that almost one-third, 32 percent of winners end up losing everything.** People who buy lottery tickets with the hope of winning should have in place a plan to deal with the resultant change in their lives in case they win.

Synthesize Information from Graphics

Read the paragraph below and study the chart. On a separate sheet of paper, write a paragraph which synthesizes information from the paragraph and the chart.

Paragraph:

People tend to complain about the government and its elected officials on a regular basis. Some might complain because they are looking for someone to blame for the high taxes they pay and the low standard of living they have. Others might complain because their political views are opposite those of the elected officials, and they disagree with current political policies. No matter the reason, there is one thing people can do to express their pleasure or displeasure with their elected representatives at the federal, state, and local levels: vote. Everyone who is a citizen of this country has the right to vote but must first register to vote in the community in which he or she lives. Voting is not only one of the rights of the citizens of a country but also one of the responsibilities. Although many people threaten to vote elected officials out of office, when it comes time to go to the polls, the number of voters who go is surprisingly lower than might be expected. However, the numbers tend to be higher in presidential election years, which are every four years.

Presidential Election Year	Total U.S. Population (18 years and older)	Citizen Population	Citizens Registered		Citizens Voted	
			Number	Percent	Number	Percent
2004	215,694	197,005	142,070	72.1	125,736	63.8
2000	202,609	186,366	129,549	69.5	110,826	59.5
1996	193,651	179,935	127,661	70.9	105,017	58.4

Figure 11. Reported Rates of Voting and Registration: 1996 to 2004 (numbers in thousands) (U.S. Census Bureau, Current Population Survey, November 1996, 2000, and 2004)

How Did They Do That?

This section of the chapter focuses on exemplification essays. It begins with the characteristics of an exemplification essay and describes its structure. In this section you will follow the steps in the writing process to identify the key elements in Reading 1, "Weighted Voting Systems," to see how the writer used exemplification to develop the essay.

Essays of Exemplification/Illustration

Essays of exemplification/illustration

- are often used to explain abstract terms or concepts
- are also used to explain terms or ideas that may be unfamiliar to the reader
- can be used to persuade/convince or entertain/amuse the reader
- can consist of one extended example or multiple short examples
- often relate examples through anecdotes or short narratives
- use key words such as *for example, for instance, to illustrate*
- often use facts, statistics, and quotes
- may pose a question in the conclusion

Parts of an Exemplification/Illustration Essay

The introduction and conclusion of an exemplification/illustration essay are similar in format to other types of essays. The structure of the body of the essay, however, is different.

The introduction

- begins with a hook to attract the reader's attention
- provides general information related to the topic
- ends with a thesis statement

The body

- discusses one aspect of an example per paragraph if the essay is one extended example
- discusses one example per paragraph if the essay uses multiple examples

The conclusion

- signals the end of the essay
- includes a restatement of the thesis, summary of the main points, or poses a question
- offers a final comment about the topic

Examples Used for the Essay

- must be relevant to the topic
- need to support the thesis statement and topic sentences
- must be specific and well developed
- are very detailed or specific if the essay uses only one example
- are less detailed if the essay uses multiple examples
- may be presented in order from least → most important or least → most familiar

ACTIVITY 29

Follow the Writer's Steps

Review Activity 28, *Follow the Writer's Steps,* in Chapter 3, which outlines the steps the writer took to develop an essay. Then refer to Reading 1, "Weighted Voting Systems," in this chapter to complete the activity.

1. Circle the topic the writer brainstormed and used in the essay.

2. Underline the narrowed topic in the essay.

3. List some of the key words that identify the text structure. _____
   _____

4. Write the thesis statement here. _____
   _____

5. Identify the writer's use of examples as either one extended example or multiple examples. Write the example(s) here. _____
   _____

6. Draw two lines under the topic discussed in each body paragraph.

7. Put parentheses around four facts, statistics, or quotes the writer used to support the example(s) used in the essay

8. Identify the order the example(s) are presented (least → most important, most → least important, least → most familiar, or most → least familiar). _____
   _____

9. Identify the technique the writer used to conclude the essay. _____
   _____

WRITING 2 ● **On Your Own**

Essay of Exemplification/Illustration

ACTIVITY 30

Write Your Essay

Choose a topic from your field of study or from a subject you are interested in and which can be explained using examples/illustrations. Examples of such topics are *ethical advertising in business, problems which arise from differing cultural values, adolescence as a difficult stage in life, someone who represents a model entrepreneur/ activist/environmentalist, gender stereotypes, someone you know who is superstitious, why humor is hard to understand in a second language,* or a common expression or saying such as *What goes around, comes around* or *All good things come in threes.*

Follow the steps below to write an essay of exemplification/illustration. You may choose to use one extended example or multiple short examples. Your audience is your instructor and classmates. Your title will refer to the concept or term you are explaining. After you finish writing your essay, read the sections on *Revising* and *Editing and Proofreading* and complete the activities.

Refer to *Writing 2: On Your Own* in Chapter 3 for the steps to follow in writing your essay. In step 4, choose the text structure for exemplification, which explains a term or concept through an example. In step 9, writing the body paragraphs, each paragraph may be a separate example or a part of one extended example.

Key Concepts 2: Reading and Writing Across the Disciplines

Revising

Follow the Steps

A. Use the checklist to revise the essay of exemplification/illustration you wrote.

Revising Checklist

1. Assignment
   - ☐ follows the assignment to write an essay of exemplification/illustration
   - ☐ addresses the instructor and classmates as the audience
   - ☐ follows the ten steps listed in the assignment

2. Introduction
   - ☐ contains a hook to capture the reader's attention
   - ☐ contains some general statements or background information about the topic
   - ☐ contains a thesis statement with the topic of the essay
   - ☐ Thesis statement includes a controlling idea.
   - ☐ Thesis statement gives a clue to the text structure.

3. Body
   - ☐ Each paragraph discusses one aspect of the example if essay is an extended example. OR
   - ☐ Each paragraph discusses one example if essay uses multiple examples.
   - ☐ Each paragraph contains a topic sentence.
   - ☐ Each topic sentence is developed through general and specific support/details.
   - ☐ General and specific support/details are arranged in a logical order.
   - ☐ General and specific support/details follow the outline.
   - ☐ General and specific support/details are sufficient in number (not too many, not too few).

4. Conclusion
   - ☐ marks the end of the essay
   - ☐ offers the writer's final thoughts on the topic
   - ☐ restates the thesis, summarizes main points, or poses a question

---

B. Share your essay with a classmate. Ask your classmate to use the Revising Checklist to check your essay and give you some feedback. Make any changes to your essay that you feel are necessary. The changes you make should improve your essay.

ACTIVITY 32

Editing and Proofreading

The Final Steps

A. Follow the steps below to edit and proofread the essay of exemplification/ illustration you wrote.

> **Editing and Proofreading Checklist**
>
> 1. Grammar
>   - ☐ Verb tenses are correct.
>   - ☐ Each subject agrees with its verb (singular/plural).
>   - ☐ Prepositions are correct.
>   - ☐ Pronouns are correct.
>   - ☐ No articles are missing (*a, an, the*).
> 2. Spelling
>   - ☐ All the words are spelled correctly.
>   - ☐ Abbreviations, if any, are used correctly.
>   - ☐ First word of each sentence begins with a capital letter.
>   - ☐ All proper nouns begin with a capital letter.
> 3. Punctuation
>   - ☐ All sentences end with a punctuation mark.
>   - ☐ Periods are after statements and question marks are after questions.
>   - ☐ Commas are used correctly in sentences containing coordinating and subordinating conjunctions.
> 4. Sentences
>   - ☐ All sentences are complete.
>   - ☐ Each sentence has a subject and a verb.
>   - ☐ There are no fragments, run-on sentences, or comma splices.
>   - ☐ Sentences contain balanced or parallel grammatical structures.
> 5. Format
>   - ☐ Essay has a title.
>   - ☐ All paragraphs are in essay format (first line is indented or there is one blank line between paragraphs).
>   - ☐ All sentences are in paragraph format (not listed or numbered).
>   - ☐ Writer's name is on the paper.
>   - ☐ Paper is neat, clean, and legible (easily read).

B. Share your paragraph with a classmate. Ask your classmate to use the Editing and Proofreading Checklist to check your essay and mark any errors in grammar, spelling, punctuation, sentences, or format.

C. Fix any mistakes your essay contained. Proofread your essay one more time. Turn in your final draft to your instructor.

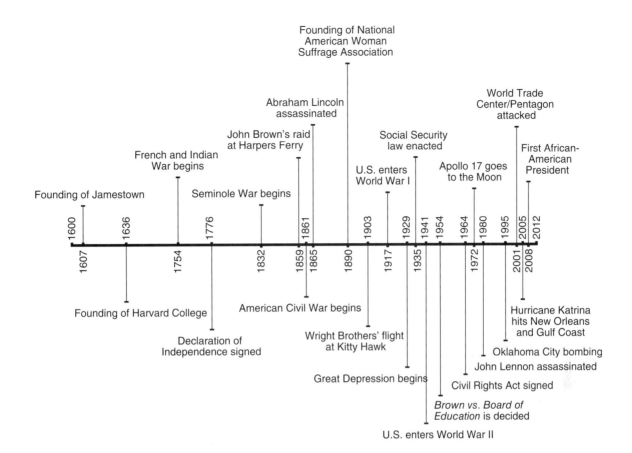

Founding of National
American Woman
Suffrage Association

Abraham Lincoln
assassinated

World Trade
Center/Pentagon
attacked

John Brown's raid
at Harpers Ferry

Social Security
law enacted

First African-
American
President

French and Indian
War begins

U.S. enters
World War I

Apollo 17 goes
to the Moon

Founding of Jamestown

Seminole War begins

1600 1636 1776 1861 1903 1929 1941 1954 1964 1980 1995 2005 2012

1607 1754 1832 1859 1865 1890 1917 1935 1972 2001 2008

Founding of Harvard College

American Civil War begins

Hurricane Katrina
hits New Orleans
and Gulf Coast

Declaration of
Independence signed

Wright Brothers' flight
at Kitty Hawk

Oklahoma City bombing
John Lennon assassinated

Great Depression begins

Civil Rights Act signed

*Brown vs. Board of
Education* is decided

U.S. enters World War II

6 · From History: American History

American history began long before the founding of Jamestown in 1607;
it began with the Native Americans who lived here thousands of years
earlier. Students who enroll in American history courses will learn about the
discoveries and wars and challenges and changes the country experienced as
it made its way through time.

Using your knowledge about the United States, discuss the following
questions with a partner or in a small group.

- Which historical events helped shape the United States as a country?

- What are some of the wars in which the United States has fought?

- What are some important cultural and political changes the United
States has experienced?

This chapter will help you understand some of the **key concepts** of
American history during the 1960s such as

- the counterculture

- political activism

- consumer capitalism

- the women's liberation movement

Get Ready to Read

Familiar or Unfamiliar

Read the following facts about American history in the 1960s and put a check next to those you are familiar with. Share your answers with a classmate.

_____ 1. John F. Kennedy became the youngest man and first Catholic to be elected President in 1960.

_____ 2. There were large-scale antiwar and civil rights protests during the 1960s.

_____ 3. In 1965, César Chávez organized a national boycott of grapes, which resulted in better working conditions for farm workers.

_____ 4. Women began organizing in order to fight sexual discrimination, demanding social equality with men.

_____ 5. The counterculture of the hippies attracted many young people who challenged the mainstream culture and values of their parents and the "establishment."

Surveying and Predicting

Survey and Predict

A. Follow the steps below to survey Reading 1 below.

1. Read the title. Write it here. _____

2. Read the first paragraph. Write one or two words that tell the topic or what the paragraph is about. _____

3. Write the main idea here. _____

_____

4. Read the headings, the titles of the sections in the reading.

5. Look for any graphic or visual aids in the reading. Graphic aids are charts, graphs, pictures, maps, diagrams, etc.

6. Look for key (important) terms related to the topic. They are usually in bold.

7. Read the last paragraph. It is a summary of the entire reading.

B. Share your survey answers with a partner and discuss what you think the reading will be about. Then circle the number of the statement below that matches your prediction.

1. The passage will compare the counterculture and mainstream culture of the 1960s.

2. The passage will outline the history of the hippie counterculture.

3. The passage will explain the counterculture of the hippie.

C. Now read the passage to see if your prediction is correct. Try to read as quickly as you can. Do not stop to look up words in your dictionary.

Guy Strait, "What Is a Hippie?"

While some young people gravitated to the political movements of the sixties, others were attracted to the **counterculture**. Like their predecessors the **Beats**, the "hippies" or "flower children" challenged traditional views of sexuality and capitalism. Seeking self-realization through the abandonment of inhibitions and the pursuit of pleasure, **hippies** were heterosexually adventurous. Hoping to broaden their perspectives, they smoked marijuana and took hallucinogens like LSD. Adopting a "live free" philosophy, they wore clothing from thrift stores, avoided conventional jobs, and, in some cases, moved to rural communes. Their public use of obscene language flouted decorum.

Music

Rock music was an integral element of the counterculture. Some artists, like Bob Dylan and Phil Ochs, used music as a tool of social protest. Others, like The Beatles, The Doors, and The Grateful Dead, celebrated sensuality and **mysticism**. In August 1969, almost 400,000 people attended Woodstock, a music festival in upstate New York. The peaceful crowd spent three days frolicking in the rain, having sex, and taking drugs. Since most of the attendees were not true hippies, Woodstock demonstrated how deeply the counterculture had pervaded **mainstream culture**. By 1969, many young Americans had adopted long hair, flamboyant fashions, and freer attitudes toward sex and drugs.

View of Counterculture

Many Americans loathed the counterculture and viewed the hippies as parasitic and immoral. Indeed, there were negative elements of the lifestyle. Some hippies abused the welfare system or resorted to theft. Reports of venereal disease and rape complicated

notions of "free love." Jimi Hendrix, Janis Joplin, Jim Morrison, and hundreds of others died of drug overdoses. The Altamont music festival, held on December 6, 1969, in Livermore, California, was as violent as Woodstock had been peaceful. Hired as security guards, Hell's Angels motorcycle gang members fought with concertgoers and killed a man as the Rolling Stones sang, "Sympathy for the Devil" onstage. By the time the concert ended, four people were dead. Depending on one's perspective, either Woodstock or Altamont exemplified the counterculture.

In this 1967 essay, Guy Strait, a San Francisco–based journalist, explains the counterculture.

What is a Hippie?

It is strange and disturbing to watch the straight (i.e., mainstream) community's angry, sometimes violent reaction to the hippies. There are many reasons for this. The principal one is appearance. The hippies dress strangely. They dress this way because they have thrown a lot of middle-class notions out the window and with them the most sensitive **middle-class dogma**: the neutral appearance.

The straight world is a jungle of taboos, fears, and personality games. People in that jungle prey on each other mercilessly. Therefore, to survive in any jungle requires good protective coloring: the camouflage of respectable appearance. The anonymity of middle-class dress is like a flag of **truce**. It means (whether true or not): "I'm not one of the predators." It is in the nature of an assurance of harmlessness. Unusual or bright-colored clothing then becomes an alarm, a danger signal to the fearful and their armed truce with the rest of mankind. They see it as a challenge. They are fearful, unsure of themselves, and fear sours into anger. It is but a step to thinking that the anger is "good." The oldest fallacy in the world is that anything that makes you angry must be bad.

The sin of the hippies is that they will not play the straight game of **camouflage**. Their non-participation, in effect, exposes them as another **tribe**, whose disregard of straight taboos of dress makes them seem to be capable of anything, and therefore a danger. That danger moreover is felt clear up to city hall, that **shrine of Squaredom**. Why else, I submit, does the Health Department of this city have such a tender solicitude about the living conditions of human beings at the Haight when they have ignored the conditions at Hunter's Point, the Mission and the Fillmore?

Many people cannot understand the hippies' rejection of everything that is commonly expected of the individual in regard to employment and life goals: steady lucrative employment, and the accumulation through the years of possessions and money, building (always building) security for the future. It is precisely this **security hypochondria**, *this checking of bank book rather than pulses,* this worrying over budgets instead of medicine cabinets, that drives the youth of today away. It is this frantic concern with money that also drives the young into the Haight-Ashbury. They have seen their parents slave for years, wasting away a lifetime to make sure that the house was paid off, that the kids got through school in order to get "good" jobs so that they could join the frantic scramble, later on. The parents' reward for this struggle is that they wind up old and tired, alienated from their children, and just as often each parent from the other.

It has been demonstrated over and over again throughout history by the best possible people that very little is required for happiness. It is the fight for money and possessions and the prestige they bring that sets people at odds, and that is what makes the world hard. We are the richest nation in the world, with the highest living standard. By our own fond illusions about prosperity we should also be the happiest. Are we? Suicides, racial violence, and the exodus of the young from comfortable homes suggest otherwise. The terrible truth is that our prosperity is the bringer of misery. We have been brainwashed by the advertising industry into being the most dissatisfied people in the world. We are told we must all be handsome or beautiful, sexually devastating, and owners of a staggering amount of recreational gadgetry or doomed to frustration. The result is that most of us are frustrated. It is exactly this that the hippie avoids like poison. He wants no part of self-defeating goals.

Future Outlook

It is very likely that the hippie will go hungry and suffer exposure, and perhaps freak out. But he considers these far less dangerous than the kind of **dehumanization** society tried to wreak on him before his rebellion. He has escaped from a culture where the machine is god, and men judge each other by mechanical standards of efficiency and usefulness. He sees a madness in the constant fight to sell more washing machines, cars, toilet paper, girdles, and gadgets than the other fellow. He is equally horrified at the grim ruthlessness of the men who participate in that fight.

Key Concept Words

Beats – (n.) shortened form of "beatniks," the people of the 1950s who rebelled against the existing, traditional culture

camouflage – (n.) a disguise or change in appearance to conceal oneself from others, usually one's enemies

counterculture – (n.) culture (especially in the 1960s and '70s) that opposed the values of the existing, traditional culture

dehumanization – (n.) loss of human qualities

hippie – (n.) person who abandons traditional culture and conventional society

mainstream culture – (n.) culture that most people follow, one of traditional values

middle-class dogma – (n.) the set of beliefs of society's middle class

mysticism – (n.) belief that one can learn "spiritual truth" or communicate with God through meditation

security hypochondria – (n.) unfounded or abnormal fears and anxiety about having enough for the future

shrine of Squaredom – (n.) a slang expression used to refer to a place considered sacred and, in this case, for people who are "square"—old-fashioned or conservative

tribe – (n.) a group of people living together as a community, often having common ancestors

truce – (n.) an agreement to temporarily stop fighting

Glossed Words

a tender solicitude – (n.) a sensitive concern or caring for others; **alienated** – (v.) withdrawn from, apart from; **frolicking** – (v.) playing happily; **gadgets** – (n.) small objects or tools; **loathed** – (v.) hated, detested; **lucrative** – (adj.) profitable; well-paying or money-making; **pervaded** – (v.) spread to or became a part of; **predator** – (n.) one who exploits others; **prestige** – (n.) the power to influence or impress people due to one's reputation or power; **rape** – (n.) the crime of forcing someone to have sex without his or her consent; **resort** – (v.) to turn to or use; **venereal disease** – (n.) a contagious sexual disease or infection

Summarizing

Share What You Read

Use two or three sentences to tell your partner what you thought the reading was about. Then listen to your partner's sentences. Next, read the following statements and circle the number of the statement that best summarizes the reading.

1. The counterculture of the hippie began in the early 1960s when young people started taking drugs and "lived free."

2. The counterculture of the hippie challenged the traditional views of mainstream culture in an effort to find peace and happiness.

3. Members of the mainstream culture often reacted angrily and violently toward the hippies and their counterculture.

Check Your Comprehension

Read each statement and circle whether it is *True (T)* or *False (F)*. Change a false statement to make it true.

T / F   1. Many people react to the hippies' unusual or bright-colored clothing with feelings of alarm.

T / F   2. Hippies believe that fighting for money and material possessions sets people against each other.

T / F   3. The same young people who became political activists were also attracted to the counterculture.

T / F   4. The music festival Woodstock was attended by 400,000 hippies.

T / F   5. Members of the middle class believed that a person's appearance should be neutral and, thus, not offensive to anyone.

T / F   6. The United States has the highest living standard and, based on our ideas of prosperity, we are the happiest nation in the world.

T / F   7. Hippies believe that the advertising industry is responsible for making people miserable.

T / F   8. Hippies would prefer to experience the physical problems of hunger and exposure than to live in a world where they are judged by what material possessions they have.

T / F   9. The San Francisco Health Department is equally concerned about living conditions in the Haight district and the Hunter's Point district.

T / F   10. Hippies see that their parents are happy after years of working to pay for their home and their children's education.

Academic Word List

Scan and Define

A. Look at the ten words listed below. Scan the reading and underline the words from the list. Write the definitions for the words you know. Do not use a dictionary. The first one has been done for you.

1. constant (adj.) _staying the same, not changing_ _____

2. element _____

3. expose _____

4. ignore _____

5. inhibitions _____

6. integral _____

7. neutral _____

8. notions _____

9. reaction _____

10. seek _____

B. Share your definitions with a partner and then with the rest of your classmates. As a group, try to complete the definitions for all ten words. Use a dictionary to check the definitions if you are unsure about them. Then complete the vocabulary activity.

Vocabulary Challenge

A. Read the sentences and the words that follow them. Circle the letter of the word that most closely matches the meaning of the underlined word. The first one has been done for you.

1. The hippies' non-participation <u>exposes</u> them as another tribe, whose disregard of straight taboos of dress makes them seem to be capable of anything, and therefore a danger.
   a. shows   b. endangers   c. reveals

2. Rock music was an <u>integral</u> element of the counterculture.
   a. essential   b. complete   c. aggregate

3. The hippies dress this way (strangely) because they have thrown a lot of middle-class notions out the window and with them the most sensitive middle-class dogma: the <u>neutral</u> appearance.
   a. dull   b. disinterested   c. impartial

4. The hippie sees a madness in the <u>constant</u> fight to sell more washing machines, cars, toilet paper, girdles, and gadgets than the other fellow.
   a. continual   b. uniform   c. faithful

5. <u>Seeking</u> self-realization through the abandonment of inhibitions and the pursuit of pleasure, the hippies were heterosexually adventurous.
   a. Hunting   b. Requesting   c. Pursuing

6. Many Americans loathed the counterculture and viewed the hippies as parasitic and immoral. Indeed, there were negative <u>elements</u> of the lifestyle.
   a. details   b. aspects   c. chemicals

B. Circle the word that best completes the sentence.

1. The hippies of the 1960s, in an effort to avoid becoming their parents, *ignored / sought* a lifestyle that included a "live free" philosophy.

2. The music festival Woodstock provided hippies and non-hippies alike with an opportunity to experiment with drugs and sex as they sought to abandon *inhibitions / reactions* instilled in them by mainstream culture.

3. Members of the mainstream culture had different *elements / notions* of the meaning behind the hippies' pursuit of pleasure and "free love."

4. Members of the middle class were often confused by the appearance and behavior of the hippies, and the hippies were as equally confused by the strong, negative *reaction / notion* they experienced from the mainstream community.

5. During the 1960s, both young people and their parents *sought / ignored* what they felt was lacking in their lives, whether it was self-realization or security for the future.

Drawing Conclusions

Fallacies: errors in reasoning

Reading is an interactive process. As you read, you try to predict what the writer is going to say, and you evaluate the writer's support for the main idea presented in the reading. You make inferences and draw conclusions based on the details or evidence the writer supplies.

Sometimes the evidence (support for the main idea) that the writer provides is strong, and it leads you to accept the writer's conclusion. Other times, the evidence may not support the writer's conclusion. The evidence may be weak or may even contain an error in reasoning or logic. As the reader, it is your job to evaluate the writer's support and to recognize weak or faulty logic.

Some common errors in reasoning, often called *logical fallacies,* include

- hasty generalization—drawing conclusions based on little evidence

    People who were lazy and into drugs moved to San Francisco to become hippies in the '60s.

- false cause—saying that because one event followed another, the first event caused the second

    The Beatles came to the United States with their new music and long hair. Not too long after that, the hippie movement started. Thus, The Beatles were responsible for the hippie movement.

- weak analogy—comparing two things that aren't really alike and drawing a conclusion

    Listening to rock music is like taking drugs. Both are addictive and destroy your mind.

- appeal to numbers—citing a number or popular opinion as evidence that something is right or wrong

    When The Beatles first came to the United States, tens of thousands of parents throughout the nation believed The Beatles and their music would have a negative effect on their children.

- either/or—offering only two alternatives when others might exist

    As for rock music, either we can ban it and protect our children's minds and morals, or we can allow it to destroy them, song by song. Since it is our responsibility to keep our children safe, we must ban rock music now!

- non sequitur—drawing a conclusion that does not clearly relate to the premise (which is assumed to be true)

    Hippies reject mainstream expectations such as steady employment and the accumulation of material goods. My brother John is always looking for a job and lives in his car. Therefore, my brother is a hippie.

Recognize Logical Fallacies

A. Read the following passages from Reading 1 and, with a partner, identify the logical fallacy in each.

1. The straight world is a jungle of taboos, fears, and personality games. People in that jungle prey on each other mercilessly. Therefore, to survive in any jungle requires good protective coloring: the camouflage of respectable appearance.

2. It has been demonstrated over and over again throughout history by the best possible people that very little is required for happiness. It is the fight for money and possessions and the prestige they bring that sets people at odds, and that is what makes the world hard.

3. We have been brainwashed by the advertising industry into being the most dissatisfied people in the world. We are told we must all be handsome or beautiful, sexually devastating, and owners of a staggering amount of recreational gadgetry or doomed to frustration. The result is that most of us are frustrated.

4. That danger [the hippies] moreover is felt clear up to city hall, that shrine of Squaredom. Why else, I submit, does the Health Department of this city have such a tender solicitude about the living conditions of human beings at the Haight when they have ignored the conditions at Hunter's Point, the Mission and the Fillmore?

5. We are the richest nation in the world, with the highest living standard. By our own fond illusions about prosperity we should also be the happiest. Are we? Suicides, racial violence, and the exodus of the young from comfortable homes suggest otherwise.

B. Read the following statements and identify the logical fallacy in each.

1. A recent poll showed that the majority of university students believe their professors require too much of them in terms of class work and homework.

2. The Internet is basically an information industry, and, like any industry, it needs to be regulated.

3. Cell phones should not be used in public places. In fact, 87 percent of people polled said that they are often bothered by rude cell phone users in stores, parks, and restaurants.

4. Cell phone use can cause cancer. A doctor who used a cell phone for nine years got brain cancer.

5. Plastic bags are like pesticides. They need to be eliminated because they are destroying the environment.

6. People who drive gas-guzzling vehicles are unpatriotic. Driving a gas-guzzling vehicle requires the country to import large quantities of oil from other countries. Money to these countries funds terrorist and drug-smuggling activities, many of which target this country.

C. Write statements of your own that contain a logical fallacy. The statements can be about any topic. Ask a partner to identify the error in reasoning in each.

1. _____

   _____

2. _____

   _____

3. _____

   _____

Identifying Text Structure—*Argument/Persuasion*

Argument: writing that persuades or convinces the reader to accept a particular view or belief

Writers often write with the purpose to persuade their readers. Using facts, statistics, examples, and even personal experiences as support, they hope to convince their readers to accept their ideas as presented. In Reading 1, the writer provides the reader background information on the U.S. counterculture of the 1960s. Following this is an explanation, the purpose of which is to convince the reader that the members of the mainstream culture react violently to the hippies because they don't understand them, and that the hippies are merely seeking self-realization. This defense of the counterculture by the writer follows the format for the text structure *argument/persuasion*.

Key Words—*Argument/Persuasion*

As the reader, it is your responsibility to weigh the evidence the writer offers and accept or reject it. This requires reading with a critical eye, looking for evidence that is presented objectively and logically. Successful arguments are those that are based on facts and that respect the reader's intelligence. Key words commonly used in the argument/persuasion pattern of organization are listed in the box below.

against	in favor of	disagree
argue	in fact	must, must not
con	oppose	ought to
for/pro	support	should, should not

Recognize Key Words

Read the paragraph and underline the key words that identify the text structure as argument/persuasion.

Partner or Burden?

The citizens of the United States have always prided themselves on holding the same values the Founding Fathers of this country held: self-reliance, independence, and competition. These members of mainstream society have also worked hard to instill these traits in their children. Members of the counterculture, however, disagree with the lifestyle led by American mainstream society. They oppose our lifestyle and want to change this country's culture. Since they do not support the way this country is run, they should not be allowed to collect welfare, food stamps, or use any social service this country provides to its citizens.

Use Key Words

Read the phrases below and then write sentences using the phrases and adding key words from the table above, to use in an essay of argument/persuasion.

1. mind-altering drugs / legalize _____

   _____

2. rock music / ban / radio airwaves _____

   _____

3. political issues / determine / citizens _____

   _____

4. individual freedom / restrict _____

   _____

5. self-reliance / teach / children _____

   _____

6. materialism / reject _____

   _____

7. competition / cooperation _____

8. mass media / promote / counterculture _____

READING 2	● **On Your Own**

In the first section of this chapter, you were introduced to drawing conclusions and to logical fallacies used in arguments. You practiced the skills and strategies of surveying, predicting, and summarizing with Reading 1. In this section you will practice these same skills with a new reading. You will also practice using context to guess the meaning of unfamiliar words.

Get Ready to Read

Check It Out

Read the following and guess whether they are book, song, movie, or television titles. On the line, write *B* for book, *S* for song, *M* for movie, and *T* for television. Discuss your answers with a partner.

_____ 1. *Laugh-In*

_____ 2. *The Harrad Experiment*

_____ 3. "Light My Fire"

_____ 4. *The Graduate*

_____ 5. "Get Back"

Survey and Predict

A. Using the following steps, survey Reading 2 and predict what the reading will be about.

1. Read the title.

2. Read the first paragraph and identify the main idea.

3. Read the headings.

4. Look for any graphic or visual aids in the reading.

5. Look for key terms in bold.

6. Read the last paragraph.

B. Write your prediction here: _____

_____

C. Now read the passage to see if your prediction is correct. Try to read as quickly as you can. Do not stop to look up words in your dictionary.

Reading 2

The Counterculture

"There's battle lines being drawn / Nobody's right if everybody's wrong," suggested a popular rock song of the period (1965–1968). Alienation from the Vietnam War was enhanced by the spread of countercultural values and youth-oriented lifestyles—components of a changing morality associated with the questioning of social authority and the spread of the "sexual revolution." Flaunting the breakdown of old barriers, rock songs such as the Rolling Stones' "Let's Spend the Night Together" directly described sexual longing. "Life was free and so was sex," novelist Sara Davidson later wrote in *Loose Change,* a novel set in Berkeley in the sixties.

Mass Media Role

Public fascination with new sexual standards and casual intimacy surfaced in books such as *The Harrad Experiment* (1967), a best-selling novel about a utopian sexual community of college students. It surfaced in Ian Fleming's popular James Bond series and in the **pulp fiction** of Jacqueline Susann, the most successful novelist of the period. Hollywood contributed to the shift in mores by replacing its 1930s production code with a rating system that permitted nudity and obscene language as well as "mature" themes. Television shows such as *The Smothers Brothers* and *Laugh-In* also broke precedent by joking about nonmarital sex, divorce, and **"uptight"** behavior. In country music, once the strong source of traditional morality, the widespread use of birth control pills and enhanced sexual frankness were reflected in the songs of superstars Tammy Wynette and Loretta Lynn.

As a psychedelic counterculture blossomed from Beat roots in San Francisco's Haight-Ashbury district,

the mass media discovered the "hippie." "I never hold back, man. I'm always on the outer limits of possibility," declared Haight rock vocalist Janis Joplin. Young cultural dissidents wore their hair defiantly long and dressed in a **free-form fashion** that included bells, feathers, bandanas, beads, and earrings. Many survived in **crash pads** or in shared housing by panhandling, making crafts, selling **"underground" newspapers**, and dealing drugs. Some, like the communal Diggers, started free kitchens and health clinics. The most important part of hippie culture involved its attempt to reject the mainstream's competitive individualism, materialism, and middle-class pretensions. Instead, the **alternative culture** prided itself on honest affection, physical pleasure, sharing, experimentation, and absolute inner freedom.

Middle-class Rebels

Few college students actually traveled to San Francisco during 1967's "Summer of Love" or identified themselves as hippies. Yet many sensed the counterculture's possibilities for social change and refashioned their private lives to emulate it. Many middle-class rebels believed their cultural lifestyles should reflect their political sensibilities. Thus, they left the cities to form thousands of rural **communes**. Others published underground comics and newspapers, produced **"guerrilla" theater** and alternative film documentaries, or created color-crazed **"pop art"** posters. Others sought expression in traditional disciplines such as musical composition, dance, poetry, or prose. Many more adopted antiestablishment attitudes. They spoke in "hip" language, wore blue jeans, and experimented with sexual freedom, marijuana, and rock music.

Pop Culture

"Psychedelic" or **"acid"** rock bands such as the Jefferson Airplane, the Grateful Dead, and Joplin's Big Brother and the Holding Company integrated electric guitars with elaborate light shows, developing the piercing "San Francisco" sound. As introspective lyrics and **"spaced-out"** musical styles spread to the Beatles and Rolling Stones as well as to Bob Dylan, the Byrds, Jimi Hendrix, and The Doors, performers sought to join high art with popular culture. The underground culture was highly irreverent. This was the mood captured in essayist Tom Wolfe's *The Electric Kool-Aid Acid Test* (1968). The book was a description of the exploits of writer Ken Kesey, whose Merry Pranksters traveled around the country in a psychedelically painted bus while promoting liberation through drugs, sex, and rock music. Satirical novels by Kesey, Kurt Vonnegut, and Thomas Pynchon won huge followings with absurdist portraits of **"straight" life** and social conventions. Youth culture received even wider exposure in provocative Hollywood films such as *Bonnie and Clyde* (1967), *The Graduate* (1967), and *Easy Rider* (1969).

Counterculture and Consumer Capitalism

Although radical activists insisted on the counterculture's hostility to **consumer capitalism**, the two forces were undeniably intertwined. Advertisers tied brand identity to youthful images and countercultural fantasies of liberation and revolution. By associating automobiles, carbonated beverages, cosmetics, and other products with the "rebellion" of the **"Now Generation,"** "hip" marketers encouraged the public to adopt changing styles and fashions as a way to satisfy psychological needs for authenticity and individuality. Pop artist Andy Warhol illustrated the compatibility of the two worlds by creating silk-screened representations of everyday commodities such as soup and soda cans. The purpose of art was to alter consciousness and explore new sensibilities and not to elevate formal culture above popular expression, lectured essayist Susan Sontag in her influential *Against Interpretation* (1964).

Feminist Movement

Radical feminists, however, remained hostile to the temptations of consumer capitalism. Drawing inspiration from the civil rights slogan "The Personal is Political," movement activists such as Casey Hayden and Mary King began to organize women against the male domination of SNCC (Student Nonviolent Coordinating Committee), SDS (Students for a Democratic Society), and other groups. Despite the radical community's support of equal rights, they asserted, New Left men reflected the establishment culture by assigning women office duties and other minor tasks. Feminists also complained that the male-oriented **sexual revolution** degraded women by treating them as playthings and objects of conquest.

While their male colleagues greeted their efforts with ridicule and open hostility, New Left women introduced "rap" sessions to share their complaints and address gender identity issues. In 1968, 200 radical feminists organized the first **women's liberation** demonstration. Calling themselves the Women's International Terrorist Conspiracy from Hell (WITCH), activists protested against "sexism" and capitalism's "objectification" of women's bodies. They picketed the Miss America Pageant and threw "instruments of torture" such as brassieres and high-heeled shoes into a "freedom trash can." Feminists focused on women's control of their own bodies with an agenda that included the right to legal abortions, distribution of birth control literature, and passage of tougher laws against rape and spousal abuse.

Key Concept Words

acid – (n.) slang for LSD, a hallucinogenic drug

alternative culture – (n.) counterculture

consumer capitalism – (n.) using mass-marketing techniques to influence the demand for goods by consumers/users

communes – (n.) communities in which people lived as a group and shared everything including work and earnings

crash pad – (n.) a place to stay temporarily

free-form fashion – (n.) clothing that does not follow a specific style

guerrilla theater – (n.) skits and songs about social issues conducted in public by political activists

Now Generation – (n.) term used to describe the young generation of the 1960s and '70s

pop art – (n.) art that developed from the popular culture of the 1960s

psychedelic – (adj.) affecting the senses through sight and sound; often used in reference to the effect of hallucinogenic drugs

pulp fiction – (n.) mass-market novels written for the general public

sexual revolution – (n.) the change in sexual behavior associated with the 1960s

spaced-out – (adj.) high or intoxicated from the effects of drugs

straight life – (n.) the mainstream culture; the life of those who followed traditional values

underground newspapers – (n.) alternative, independent newspapers published and associated with the counterculture of the 1960s

uptight – (adj.) very tense or nervous; often used to describe the members of mainstream culture

women's liberation – (n.) the feminist movement of the 1960s and '70s, which focused on the rights of women in both the personal and professional arenas

Glossed Words

absurdist – (adj.) exaggerated, so as to look or seem meaningless; **antiestablishment** – (adj.) against the mainstream or established culture; **dissidents** – (n.) those who disagree or object; **flaunting** – (v.) openly displaying or showing; **introspective** – (adj.) thoughtful, directed inward; **irreverent** – (adj.) disrespectful, rude; **mores** – (n.) accepted or shared values of a group or community; **obscene language** – (n.) vulgar or offensive language; **panhandling** – (n.) begging for money or food on the street; **picket** – (v.) to protest or demonstrate, usually carrying signs; **rebels** – (n.) revolutionaries; in the 1960s, members of the counterculture; **ridicule** – (n.) disapproval, derision, scorn; **satirical** – (adj.) works that ridicule or make fun of something or someone; **sexual longing** – (n.) sexual desire or yearning; **utopian** – (adj.) idealistic or imaginary

Summarizing

Share What You Read

Use two or three sentences to tell your partner what you thought the reading was about. Then listen to your partner's sentences. If you disagree, go back and find support for your summary. Write your summary statement below.

Summary: _____

_____

Check Your Comprehension

Read each phrase below and decide whether it is associated with *mainstream culture* or *counterculture*. Write the phrase in the chart under the correct heading.

sexual revolution	inner freedom	Miss America
Rolling Stones	blue jeans	high-heeled shoes
morality	consumer capitalism	feminism
beads and long hair	communes	establishment
materialism	marijuana	hippie
psychedelic	advertising brands	*Bonnie and Clyde*

Mainstream Culture	Counterculture

Academic Word List

 Scan and Define

A. Look at the ten words listed below. Scan the reading and underline the words from the list. Write the definitions for the words you know. Do not use a dictionary. The first one has been done for you.

1. commodities _products or goods for sale_____
2. compatibility _____
3. enhance _____
4. individualism _____
5. integrated (adj.) _____
6. lecture (v.) _____
7. mature (adj.) _____
8. oriented (adj.) _____
9. precedent _____
10. reject (v.) _____

B. Share your definitions with a partner and then with the rest of your classmates. As a group, try to complete the definitions for all ten words. Use a dictionary to check the definitions if you are unsure about them. Then complete the vocabulary activity.

Vocabulary Challenge

A. Using your dictionary, work with a partner to find the missing word forms and complete the chart. If no form exists, draw a line in the space. The first one has been done for you.

Noun	Verb	Adjective	Adverb
1. commodities	*commoditize*	---------	---------
2. compatibility			
3.	enhance		
4. individualism			
5.		integrated	
6.	lecture		
7.		mature	
8.		oriented	
9. precedent			
10.	reject		

B. Word analogies are pairs of words that share a relationship or have something in common. Look at the first pair of words and determine what they have in common. Then supply a word from the Academic Word List to complete the second pair. The first one has been done for you.

1. communal : collectivism :: independent : ___individualism___

2. child : young :: adult : _____

3. part : whole :: separated : _____

4. parent : advice :: professor : _____

5. people : harmonious :: software : _____

Using Context to Guess Meaning—*Surrounding Sentences*

While there are times when context clues in a sentence help you determine the meaning of an unfamiliar word or phrase, sometimes they are not enough. In that case, look to the surrounding sentences for extra help. They may provide a definition or an example that will clarify the meaning of the unfamiliar word.

Read the sentences and explanation below to see how surrounding sentences help explain the meaning of *hippie*.

*As a psychedelic counterculture blossomed from Beat roots in San Francisco's Haight-Ashbury district, the mass media discovered the "**hippie**." . . . Young cultural dissidents wore their hair defiantly long and dressed in free-form fashion that included bells, feathers, bandanas, beads, and earrings. Many survived in crash pads or in shared housing by panhandling, making crafts, selling "underground" newspapers, and dealing drugs.*

The surrounding sentences describe what a hippie looked like—long hair, clothing with bells and feathers and earrings—and acted like—shared houses, made crafts, sold drugs. The picture the sentences create offer a clue to the meaning of the word: Obviously, a *hippie* was someone very unlike the average citizen of the mid-1960s.

Guess Meaning from Context

Read the sentences below. Use the information in the surrounding sentences as well as your background knowledge and personal experience to write your own meaning of the words in bold. Then circle the letter of the answer that you think best defines the term as it is used in the passage.

1. "There's **battle lines** being drawn / Nobody's right if everybody's wrong," suggested a popular rock song of the period (1965–1968). Alienation from the Vietnam War was enhanced by the spread of countercultural vales and youth-oriented lifestyles—components of a changing morality associated with the questioning of social authority and the spread of the "sexual revolution."

   battle lines = _____
   a. the cause that joins two groups
   b. the issue that divides two sides
   c. the line that separates two countries

2. Public fascination with new sexual standards and casual intimacy surfaced in books. . . . Hollywood contributed to the shift in **mores** by replacing its 1930s production code with a rating system that permitted nudity and obscene language as well as "mature" themes. Television shows such as *The Smothers Brothers* and *Laugh-In* also broke precedent by joking about nonmarital sex, divorce, and "uptight" behavior.

   mores = _____
   a. the attitudes toward proper behavior of a culture
   b. the work-related customs and values of a culture
   c. the different types of entertainment of a culture

3. Yet many (college students) sensed the counterculture's possibilities for social change and refashioned their private lives to **emulate** it. Many middle-class rebels . . . left the cities to form thousands of rural communes. Others published underground comics and newspapers, produced "guerrilla" theater and alternative film documentaries, created color-crazed "pop art" posters. . . . Many more adopted antiestablishment attitudes, spoke in "hip" language, wore blue jeans, and experimented with sexual freedom, marijuana, and rock music.

   emulate = _____
   a. to support social change
   b. to imitate social change
   c. to achieve social change

4. Although radical activists insisted on the counterculture's hostility to **consumer capitalism**, the two forces were undeniably intertwined. Advertisers sought to tap expanded consumer tastes in a period of unprecedented prosperity by tying brand identity to youthful images and countercultural fantasies of liberation and revolution. By associating automobiles, carbonated beverages, cosmetics, and other products with the "rebellion" of the "Now Generation," "hip" marketers encouraged the public to adopt changing styles and fashions as a way of satisfying psychological needs for authenticity and individuality.

   consumer capitalism = _____
   a. advertisers using marketing techniques to influence what consumers want
   b. advertisers using marketing techniques to offer what consumers want
   c. advertisers using marketing techniques to find out what consumers want

5. Many people cannot understand the hippies' rejection of everything that is commonly expected of the individual in regard to employment and life goals: steady lucrative employment, and the accumulation through the years of possessions and money, building (always building) security for the future. It is precisely this **security hypochondria,** *this checking of bank book rather than pulses,* this worrying over budgets instead of medicine cabinets, that drive the youth of today away. It is this frantic concern with money that also drives the young into the Haight-Ashbury.

   security hypochondria = _____
   a. excessive protection of a person's money and property
   b. excessive illness as a result of trying to earn money
   c. excessive thinking about having and keeping money

6. We are the richest nation in the world, with the highest living standard. By our own fond illusions about prosperity, we should also be the happiest. Are we? Suicides, racial violence, and the exodus of the young from comfortable homes suggest otherwise. The terrible truth is that our prosperity is the bringer of **misery**.

   misery = _____
   a. feelings of unhappiness
   b. psychological problems
   c. discrimination against others

WRITING 1A ● Skills and Strategies

In this section, you will learn some skills and strategies associated with the writing process. It includes the grammar of adverb clauses, which is one of the grammatical structures used in the readings. In this section, you will practice the different steps in the writing process and will write an essay of argument/persuasion.

The Grammar of Adverb Clauses

Adverb clauses are dependent clauses that are connected to independent clauses. Subordinating conjunctions introduce adverb clauses, which can come before or after the main, independent, clause. If an adverb clause comes before the main clause, at the beginning of the sentence, a comma follows the adverb clause. Study the subordinating conjunctions and their use in adverb clauses in the chart on the following page.

Meaning	Conjunction	Adverb Clause
concession	although, even though, though	*Even though their lifestyle angered some people*, the hippies' new counterculture had some positive effects.
condition	if, even if, unless, only if	*If you moved to San Francisco*, people thought you were a hippie.
contrast	although, even though, though, while, whereas	Some young people followed the ways of the new counterculture *although others remained a part of the mainstream culture.*
reason / cause	as, because, since	*Because hippies often grew their hair long and dressed in bright-colored clothing*, people often feared them.
result / purpose	in order that, so that, so +adjective/adverb + that, such + noun + that	Some hippies published underground newspapers or produced alternative film documentaries *so that they could support themselves.*
time	after, as, as soon as, before, by the time, once, until, when, while	*Once women began to share their grievances and address gender identity issues,* they also began to work for tougher laws against rape and spousal abuse.

Recognize Adverb Clauses

Read the sentences below and underline the adverb clauses.

1. As introspective lyrics and "spaced-out" musical styles spread to The Beatles and Rolling Stones as well as to other musical groups, performers sought to fuse high art with popular culture.

2. Although radical activists insisted on the counterculture's hostility to consumer capitalism, the two forces were undeniably intertwined.

3. It is very likely that the hippie will go hungry and suffer exposure, and perhaps freak out though he considers these far less dangerous than the kind of dehumanization society tried to wreak on him before his rebellion.

4. While their male colleagues greeted their efforts with ridicule and outright hostility, New Left women initiated "rap" sessions to share their grievances and address gender identity issues.

5. The women's liberation demonstrators picketed the Miss America Pageant so that their message would be heard by millions of Americans.

Use Adverb Clauses

Woodstock Music Festival, 1969

Combine the two clauses using the subordinating conjunction in parentheses. You may have to change the order of the clauses and add or delete words and punctuation.

1. Some young people gravitated to the political movements of the sixties. Others were attracted to the counterculture. (while) _____

_____

2. Most of the attendees of Woodstock were not true hippies. The music festival demonstrated how deeply the counterculture had pervaded mainstream culture. (because) _____

_____

3. The concert ended. Four people were dead. (by the time) _____

_____

4. Many people could understand the counterculture. Guy Strait, a San Francisco-based journalist, explained it in a 1967 essay. (so that) _____

   _____

5. The hippie will go hungry and suffer exposure. He prefers this situation to living in the culture he escaped from. (even if) _____

   _____

6. As people with the highest standard of living in the world, we should be happy. Our prosperity is the bringer of misery. (although) _____

   _____

Sentence Essentials

Dependent Clauses: Adverb Clauses

In the previous *Sentence Essentials,* you learned about adjective clauses as one type of dependent clause. This section will focus on writing sentences using another type of dependent clause: the adverb clause.

Adverb clauses

- function as adverbs by modifying verbs or independent clauses

- express the relationship between the clauses (time, reason, result, etc.)

- are placed before or after the independent clause (most result/purpose clauses come after the independent clause)

- are connected to the independent clause with a subordinating conjunction

Using sentences that contain adverb clauses is another way to add variety and coherence to your writing.

Independent clause: *The mainstream community sometimes reacts angrily to the hippies.*

Adverb clause: *Because the hippies dress strangely*

Complex sentence: ***Because the hippies dress strangely,*** *the mainstream community sometimes reacts angrily to them.* **OR** *The mainstream community sometimes reacts angrily to the hippies* ***because they dress strangely.***

How to Form Adverb Clauses

First, determine the relationship between the two clauses. Then choose the correct subordinating conjunction; see The Grammar of Adverb Clauses in the previous section or the chart in Appendix 3 on page 283 for help choosing the correct conjunction. Add the conjunction to the clause that will modify the verb or the independent clause. Place the adverb clause before or after the independent clause. Place a comma after the adverb clause if it precedes the independent clause. See the example below.

Clauses to be connected: *The hippies reject mainstream employment and life goals.*

Their parents struggle to build security.

1. Determine the relationship between the clauses: contrast.

2. Choose the subordinating conjunction: *although* or *even though.*

3. Add the conjunction to the modifying clause: *Although* their parents struggle to build security.

4. Place the adverb clause before/after the independent clause: *Although their parents struggle to build security,* the hippies reject mainstream employment and life goals. **OR** The hippies reject mainstream employment and life goals *although their parents struggle to build security.*

Punctuation

Generally, when the adverb clause comes before the independent clause, a comma separates the two. When the adverb clause follows the independent clause, no comma is used. However, when using the subordinating conjunctions *while* and *whereas* to show contrast, it is common to insert a comma even if the adverb clause follows the independent clause.

Connect Clauses

Connect the two clauses with the subordinating conjunction in parentheses. You may have to change the order of the clauses and add or delete words and punctuation. The first one has been done for you.

1. you grew up during the 1960s / you are familiar with the hippie movement (if)
   If you grew up during the 1960s, you are familiar with the hippie movement

2. many of the people who attended weren't hippies / the Woodstock festival proved that the counterculture had become part of the mainstream culture (since) _____

3. many young people moved to San Francisco / they could become part of the hippie movement (so that) _____

4. people sometimes make major lifestyle changes / they understand what they need to be happy (once) _____

5. feminists had protested against gender discrimination / there would have been no changes in the laws (unless) _____

6. some people left the cities to form rural communes / they believed their cultural lifestyle should reflect their political awareness (because) _____

7. country music began to incorporate more sexual frankness into its lyrics / the same themes of sex and intimacy appeared in movies and novels (while) _____

8. advertisers and marketers targeted the public by combining images of youth with the counterculture / radical activists insisted they were against consumer capitalism (even though) _____

Choose the Subordinating Conjunction

Read the sentences and insert the correct subordinating conjunction from the chart on page 217 in the space. The first one has been done for you. Sometimes more than one answer is possible.

1. _____*While*_____ tickets to the Woodstock festival were sold before the concert, the festival eventually ended up being free.

2. Woodstock was hailed as a tribute to the counterculture _____ no one had anticipated how big an impact the festival would have on people.

3. _____ nearly half a million people peacefully coexisted for three days, Woodstock was called a festival of peace and love.

4. _____ the Woodstock festival began, many musical groups and musicians had been invited to perform.

5. The response would probably not be the same today _____ someone tried to organize an event similar to Woodstock.

6. Max Yasgur offered his farm as a site _____ the festival could take place.

Write Sentences Containing Adverb Clauses

A. Read the paragraph and choose at least two pairs of sentences that can be connected with subordinating conjunctions to form adverb clauses. Rewrite those sentences, making any necessary changes. Share your sentences with a partner.

Historical Events from 1968

The year 1968 was a pivotal year, historically, for people in the United States. There were many important events that occurred. Some deeply affected the country. For example, in April of 1968, Dr. Martin Luther King, Jr., was in Memphis, Tennessee. He was there to support the African-American sanitation workers. They were on strike. They were protesting poor working conditions and unequal wages. Dr. King was assassinated at his hotel on April 4th, 1968, by James Earl Ray. Also in April of 1968, President Lyndon Johnson signed the Civil Rights Act of 1968. It was an expansion of the Civil Rights Act of 1964. He signed the expansion. Discrimination based on race, religion, or national origin in housing would be prohibited. In early June of 1968, Robert F. Kennedy was in Los Angeles. He was campaigning as a candidate in the California primary election. He was assassinated on June 5th and died the next day. He was shot by Sirhan Sirhan. In September of that year, Women's Liberation groups protested the Miss America beauty pageant in Atlantic City, New Jersey. The reason for the protest was to draw attention to the commercialization of beauty and to the racism and the oppression of women that these groups believed the pageant symbolized. Finally, also in 1968, Shirley Chisholm was elected to the U.S. House of Representatives. It was an event of major political importance. She was the first African-American woman to be elected to Congress.

1. Pair 1 _____

_____

_____

2. Pair 2 _____

_____

_____

B. Write sentences that contain adverb clauses. The sentences can be about any topic.

1. _____

2. _____

3. _____

4. _____

Sentence Errors

Common errors (sentences marked with *) related to adverb clauses include

1. using a coordinating conjunction and a subordinating conjunction together. Do not use both conjunctions in the same sentence.

   *Although hippies stressed the positive aspects of their lifestyle, **but** there were negative aspects as well.*

   Although hippies stressed the positive aspects of their lifestyle, there were negative aspects as well.

2. using the subordinating conjunction with the wrong clause. Although *while* and *whereas* can be used with either clause and still have the same meaning, the other conjunctions cannot be interchanged without a change in meaning. The following sentences have different meanings: In the first sentence, *fear* is the cause and the effect is *not understand*; in the second sentence, *not understand* is the cause and the effect is *fear.* The second sentence makes more sense.

   Because they feared the hippies, many middle-class Americans did not always understand them.

   Because they did not always understand the hippies, many middle-class Americans feared them.

3. using the wrong verb tense. In adverb clauses of time, the verb tenses in both clauses are the same.

   *When people **will** think of the 1960s, they remember the days of the counterculture and the hippies.*

   When people think of the 1960s, they remember the days of the counterculture and the hippies.

4. using the incorrect punctuation. Place a comma after the adverb clause if it comes before the independent clause.

   Many mainstream people disliked the counterculture, because its values were in conflict with theirs.

   Many mainstream people disliked the counterculture because its values were in conflict with theirs.

   Because its values were in conflict with theirs, many mainstream people disliked the counterculture.

ACTIVITY 22

Spot the Error

Each sentence contains an error common to adverb clauses. Find the error and correct it. The first one has been done for you.

1. While hippies reject the values of their parents, yet they still need food, clothes, and a place to stay. _While hippies reject the values of their parents, they still need food, clothes, and a place to stay._

2. Members of the counterculture argue that we should be the happiest people in the world, because we are the richest nation in the world, and yet it is not true.
   _____
   _____

3. A member of the middle class wanted to "rebel" if he or she spoke in "hip" language, wore blue jeans, and experimented with sexual freedom, marijuana, and rock music. _____
   _____
   _____

4. You get a feeling for the youth culture at the time when you will watch movies such as *Bonnie and Clyde* or *The Graduate*. _____
   _____

5. Whereas many activists said they supported equal rights, but their actions actually reflected the establishment culture. _____
   _____

6. The American public was drawn to youthful images because advertisers tied those images to cars, drinks, cosmetics, and other products and found new sources of revenue. _____
   _____

7. After they will arrive in San Francisco, the hippies survive in crash pads or shared housing. _____
   _____

8. They don't become like their parents so that hippies will flee to Haight-Ashbury to be with others who share the same counterculture. _____
   _____

9. As young people looked up to the rock singers of the time it's no surprise they mimicked their behavior: growing their hair long, dressing in free-form fashion, and experimenting with drugs. _____
   _____
   _____

Making the Connection

Good readers take the time to survey a passage or an essay before they begin to read. They skim the introduction, looking for the thesis statement and its main points or controlling ideas to get an overview of the topic. They read the concluding paragraph, knowing that the writer has summarized the main points of the essay in this section as well. Good writers, therefore, use the conclusion to summarize the main points of their essay and to present their final comments on the topic.

Key Concepts 2: Reading and Writing Across the Disciplines

Get Ready to Write

Body and Support Sentences

The previous chapters introduced using quotations and facts as ways to support the thesis statement of an essay. Quotations from experts or from the article that is being discussed strengthen the essay. Using facts, including statistics, is another way writers provide support for their writing. Examples are another common means of providing support.

Examples as Support

Examples used as support are often based on the writer's own experience or knowledge. It is appropriate to use examples to support the thesis statement as long as they are relevant to the topic and sufficient in number. Offering one example as support is not sufficient. Phrases often used to introduce examples include *for example, for instance, specifically,* and *to illustrate.* Study the examples below.

Thesis statement: *Members of the counterculture rejected the traditional values of mainstream society.*

Example 1

Hippies rejected convention. For example, they refused to dress as their parents did, choosing instead to wear flamboyant and brightly colored clothing. They wore bold patterns and clothing decorated with beads and bells. They let their hair grow long. Hippies also embraced the "free love" attitude that accompanied the sexual revolution at the time. Specifically, they experimented with sex, and many had casual sex with multiple partners. Women taking the birth-control pill no longer had to worry about becoming pregnant; this, too, contributed to an increase in sexual freedom among members of the counterculture.

Example 2

Hippies rejected convention. For example, they dressed differently. Their behavior was different, too. For instance, they took part in the sexual revolution happening at the time.

The first example shows strong support for the thesis statement. It is relevant to the topic: it discusses the hippies' rejection of traditional values related to clothing and sex. It is also sufficient: it provides specific details about the hippie clothing style and about their sexual behavior. The second example, however, is weak. Although it is relevant to the topic and discusses the hippies' rejection of traditional values related to clothing and sex, it does not provide sufficient details about either. In order to use examples as support, the writer must provide examples that are both relevant and sufficient in number.

Relevant and Sufficient Examples

Read the examples below. Determine whether each example is relevant, sufficient, both, or neither. Circle your answer.

Thesis Statement: *Music in the 1960s ranged from folk music to rock 'n roll to psychedelic rock.*

1. The 1960s saw a variety of music in the United States. In the early 1960s, for example, folk music was very popular. One well-known folk singer was Bob Dylan. Bob Dylan eventually moved from folk music to rock 'n roll. The Beatles were also part of the rock 'n roll movement and, later, the psychedelic movement. Jimi Hendrix is an example of a psychedelic rock performer. His song "Purple Haze" is legendary psychedelic rock.

    a. relevant   c. relevant and sufficient
    b. sufficient   d. neither relevant nor sufficient

2. The 1960s saw a variety of music in the United States. In the early 1960s, for example, folk music was very popular and was often a form of social protest. Pete Seeger was a popular folk singer at that time as was the folk trio Peter, Paul, and Mary. By the mid-sixties, however, rock 'n roll had become enormously popular. Elvis Presley, for instance, had a tremendous impact on rock 'n roll music at that time. In addition, Ray Charles and Percy Sledge also joined the list of popular rock 'n roll artists. Psychedelic rock appeared in the late 1960s. Jimi Hendrix's rendition of the "Star-Spangled Banner" was classic psychedelic rock. The Doors and Jefferson Airplane were groups whose music was also classified as psychedelic rock.

    a. relevant   c. relevant and sufficient
    b. sufficient   d. neither relevant nor sufficient

3. The 1960s saw a variety of music in the United States. Many of the popular rock 'n roll bands came from England during the time of the "British Invasion" in the mid-1960s. For instance, The Beatles, Rolling Stones, The Dave Clark Five, and The Who were all British groups. There were also women rock 'n roll singers from England as well. Petula Clark is one of the most well-known singers of that time, for example.

    a. relevant   c. relevant and sufficient
    b. sufficient   d. neither relevant nor sufficient

4. The 1960s saw a variety of music in the United States. Before that, people were listening to the soft sounds of popular singers including, for example, Frank Sinatra, Dean Martin, Pat Boone and Perry Como. Popular women singers of that time were Rosemary Clooney and Billie Holiday. The younger generation was ready for a change, and the 1960s brought them that change.

    a. relevant   c. relevant and Sufficient
    b. sufficient   d. neither relevant nor sufficient

Provide Examples

Write your own examples of support. They may be about any topic.

1. _____

2. _____

3. _____

Conclusions

The conclusion of an essay is the writer's last opportunity to communicate with the reader. While the conclusion marks the end of the essay and leaves the reader with the writer's final thoughts about the topic, it may do so in various ways.

The concluding paragraph may

- restate the thesis
- summarize the main points
- call for action on the part of the reader
- make a prediction
- pose a question

The examples below demonstrate different types of conclusions. Although the essays would differ in development based on their thesis statements, the general topic addressed in each essay is *hippies as a part of the counterculture in the United States during the 1960s.*

Restate the Thesis

This country was founded by immigrants who, along with their dreams for a new life, brought their cultures and traditions with them when they came to the United States. It is our good fortune to share in the cultural contributions each group has made to this country's "melting pot." *The hippies and the counterculture they represent are included in that mix and, just as each culture has, have influenced mainstream U.S. culture.*

Summarize the Main Points

Many cultures can be identified by their dress, their values, and their customs. The counterculture is no different in that respect. *Their colorful dress* identifies them as hippies. *Their rejection of mainstream values*—owning a home and accumulating material goods and money—identifies them as hippies. They practice *their philosophy of living free* by avoiding the conventional; this, too, identifies them as hippies. Everything about them identifies them as a subculture, just one of many in this country.

Call for Action

Ours is a nation of myriad cultures. One is no better than the next. The hippies constitute a culture that may be different from the mainstream, but that does not mean they are inferior or that their culture is inferior. Despite their differences in dress and social or moral values and their view of what constitutes happiness, *we need to treat them with the same respect that members of all other cultures and subcultures in this country deserve and receive.*

Make a Prediction

It is only a matter of time before we see the effect this particular group will have on society. The hippies' refusal to get jobs and plan for the future will affect all hardworking Americans in this country. The hippies and other members of this so-called counterculture will have no place to live, no food to eat, no clothes to wear. *They will ultimately become a burden to the rest of society, who will be given the responsibility to house them, feed them, and clothe them.*

Pose a Question

This is a tumultuous time in our country. People are looking for an alternative lifestyle that will give meaning to their lives. *Is the lifestyle the hippies are pursuing that alternative? Will this counterculture continue and, over many decades, become the mainstream culture? Will it disappear, only to be replaced by another new alternative?* Only time will tell.

Writing a Conclusion

Read the thesis statements and main points below and, on a separate sheet of paper, write a concluding paragraph for each item.

1. Thesis statement: *The hippies and the mainstream held opposite views on several issues.*

Main points:

	Hippies	Mainstream
Dress	bright colors, feathers, beads	neutral colors, "fit in"
Values	reject security, possessions, money	own home, save money, send kids to school
Views	abandon inhibitions, pursue pleasure, "live free"	traditional views of marriage and family

2. Thesis statement: *The 1960s saw a variety of music being played in the United States.*

Main points:

Type of Music	Artist
Social protest (folk and rock music)	Bob Dylan; Joan Baez; Pete Seeger; Peter, Paul, and Mary
Sensuality and mysticism (rock music)	The Beatles; The Doors; The Grateful Dead
Classic rock	Jefferson Airplane; Jimi Hendrix; Janis Joplin
Motown Sound	Diana Ross and the Supremes; The Temptations; Marvin Gaye

3. Thesis statement: *The counterculture of the 1960s had different effects on specific groups of Americans.*

Main points:

Middle-class College Students	Mainstream Members of Society
sensed possibility for social change	felt values were being challenged
believed cultural lifestyle should reflect political sensibilities	viewed hippies as parasitic and immoral due to welfare abuse and theft
left the cities to form rural communes	disgusted by hippies' behavior: drug use, sexual freedom
published underground newspapers and comics	could not understand hippies' rejection of jobs, security
adopted antiestablishment attitudes	feared for own safety

Synthesizing

In the previous chapter, you synthesized information from a reading and statistics from a table to write a paragraph about voting that included the number of citizens registered to vote and the number who actually voted. In this chapter you will practice synthesizing information from two sources about the music of the 1960s. Before you begin the activity, review the steps in the process listed below.

1. Read the original source documents.

2. Choose the information that you want to include.

3. Paraphrase, summarize, or quote the information.

4. List any ideas of your own you want to include.

5. Put similar ideas together.

6. Organize the information in a logical order.

7. Rewrite the information as a paragraph, adding transitions and making other changes as necessary.

Practice Synthesizing

Follow the steps listed above to synthesize the information in the paragraphs below. The thesis statement has been provided for you and is at the end of the passages. Write your new paragraph on a separate sheet of paper.

Paragraph 1

Rock music was an integral element of the counterculture. Some artists, like Bob Dylan and Phil Ochs, used music as a tool of social protest. Others, like The Beatles, The Doors, and The Grateful Dead, celebrated sensuality and mysticism. In August 1969, almost 400,000 people attended Woodstock, a music festival in upstate New York. The peaceful crowd spent three days frolicking in the rain, having sex, and taking drugs. Since most of the attendees were not true hippies, Woodstock demonstrated how deeply the counterculture had pervaded mainstream culture.

Bob Dylan

Paragraphs 2 and 3

"There's battle lines being drawn / Nobody's right if everybody's wrong," suggested a popular rock song of the period (1965–1968). Alienation from the Vietnam War was enhanced by the spread of countercultural values and youth-oriented lifestyles—components of a changing morality associated with the questioning of social authority and the spread of the "sexual revolution." Flaunting the breakdown of old barriers, rock songs such as the Rolling Stones' "Let's Spend the Night Together" directly described sexual longing. In country music, once the strong source of traditional morality, the widespread use of birth control pills and enhanced sexual frankness were reflected in the songs of superstars Tammy Wynette and Loretta Lynn.

"Psychedelic" or "acid" rock bands such as the Jefferson Airplane, The Grateful Dead, and Joplin's Big Brother and the Holding Company integrated electric guitars with elaborate light shows, developing the piercing "San Francisco" sound. As introspective lyrics and "spaced-out" musical styles spread to The Beatles and the Rolling Stones as well as to Bob Dylan, The Byrds, Jimi Hendrix, and The Doors, performers sought to join high art with popular culture.

Thesis statement:

The 1960s included a variety of types of music: the folk music of social protest, the rock 'n roll of love and sexual freedom, and the psychedelic music of the drug culture.

How Did They Do That?

This section of the chapter focuses on essays of argument/persuasion. It begins with the characteristics of an argumentative/persuasive essay and describes its structure. In this section you will follow the steps in the writing process to identify the key elements in Reading 1, "What Is a Hippie?" by Guy Strait, to see how the writer used argumentation to develop the essay.

Essays of Argument/Persuasion

Essays of argument/persuasion

- are used to convince the reader to see and/or accept a specific point of view
- attempt to change the reader's thinking about a specific issue
- can address a controversial topic (gun control, euthanasia) or a belief (people should exercise and watch their diet)
- state a proposition and offer support for it
- support the thesis with sound/logical reasoning and relevant examples
- avoid using logical fallacies
- address the opposing view and refute/rebut it
- may include cause/effect, compare/contrast, or a combination of text structures
- use key words such as *support, oppose, in favor of, against, must, should*
- use facts, statistics, expert opinions, and quotes as support, and identify the source of the support

Parts of Argumentative/Persuasive Essays

The introduction and conclusion of an argumentative/persuasive essay are similar in format to other types of essays with the exception that the thesis statement is the proposition of the argument. The format and content of the body differ from other essays in that both sides of the argument are presented.

> **Proposition:** in an essay of argument/persuasion, the position the writer takes; what the writer wants the reader to believe or accept

The introduction

- begins with a hook to attract the reader's attention
- provides general information to explain the issue
- ends with the thesis statement that states the proposition, what the writer wants the reader to believe, accept, or do

The body

- addresses each point of the argument
- supports each point with facts, statistics, examples, expert opinions and quotes
- refutes/rebuts argument of the opposing view
- may offer main points first in separate paragraphs and then, in a separate paragraph, offer the opposing view and the refutation/rebuttal of each point

OR

- may offer the opposition's view and then the main points as a refutation; each point is addressed in a separate paragraph
- presents points in order from general → specific, weak → strong, or most → least important

The conclusion

- restates the proposition (thesis statement)
- restates the main points of the argument
- can include a call to action or make a prediction

Follow the Writer's Steps

Review Activity 28, *Follow the Writer's Steps,* in Chapter 3, which outlines the steps the writer took to develop an essay. Then read the following essay of argument/persuasion and complete the activity.

Forcing Cultural Change

The citizens of the United States have always prided themselves on holding the same values the founding fathers of this country held: self-reliance, independence, and competition. These members of mainstream society have also worked hard to instill the same values in their children. Members of the counterculture, however, disagree with the lifestyle led by American mainstream society. They oppose our lifestyle and want to change this country's culture. It is my view that neither this country nor its culture needs to be changed in any way.

Members of the counterculture argue that everyone ought to be actively involved in the country's politics. However, it is logistically impossible for everyone to become politically active. Nothing will ever be accomplished if everyone has a voice in every issue. While mainstream society supports its citizens' right to vote and the opportunity to run for political office, its members believe that decisions on critical issues should be made by the experts. These experts are the people we have elected to hold public office.

Members of the counterculture also support individual freedom. In fact, we, the members of mainstream society, favor individual freedom as well. However, individual freedom to them means taking drugs, having long hair, and not working a regular job to support themselves. For us, individual freedom means having the privacy to be left alone to do what we want. It means taking care of things the way we choose. The working members of society should not be forced to support people who choose not to work just because they are "doing their own thing." Those who support the counterculture should not be allowed to collect welfare. They should be denied food stamps and any social service this country provides to its citizens.

These members of the counterculture should stop trying to change this country. Our ancestors came here looking for freedom, and now the hippies and radicals oppose everything this country stands for and are trying to force us to change it. This country does not need to be changed. America, love it or leave it!

1. Circle the topic the writer brainstormed and used in the essay.

2. Underline the narrowed topic in the essay.

3. List some of the key words that identify the text structure. _____
   _____

4. Write the proposition (thesis statement) here. _____
   _____

5. Identify the writer's proposition as controversial topic or a belief. _____
   _____

6. Draw two lines under the topic discussed in each body paragraph.

7. Put parentheses around the opposing views the writer rebuts.

8. Identify the order the points are presented (general → specific, weak → strong,
   most → least important). _____

9. Identify the technique the writer used to conclude the essay. _____
   _____

WRITING 2 ● On Your Own

Essay of Argument/Persuasion

Write Your Essay

Choose an issue from your field of study or from a subject you are interested in and which can be expressed as a proposition in an essay of argument/persuasion. You may write about a controversial issue or about a belief. Examples of such topics are *steroid use; stem cell research; cloning; assisted suicide; salaries of professional athletes; amnesty for illegal immigrants; government laws regarding seat belts, cell phone use, or paying taxes; polluting the environment;* and *protecting endangered species.* Be sure to cite any outside source you use to provide facts, statistics, or quotes from experts. (Review Chapter 4 for the correct format.)

Follow the steps below to write an essay of argument/persuasion. You may choose to address the main points separately from your rebuttal of the opposing view, or you may offer the opposing view and your main points as refutation in the same paragraph. Your audience is your instructor and classmates. Your title will refer to the proposition you are supporting. After you finish writing your essay, read the sections on *Revising* and on *Editing and Proofreading* and complete the activities.

Refer to *Writing 2: On Your Own* in Chapter 3 for the steps to follow in writing your essay. In step 4, choose the text structure for argument/persuasion, which convinces or persuades the reader to accept a specific point of view. In step 9, writing the body paragraphs, each paragraph may address a main point of the argument or be the rebuttal of the opposing view OR each paragraph may be a combination of the opposing view and rebuttal.

ACTIVITY 29

Revising

Follow the Steps

A. Use the checklist to revise the essay of argument/persuasion you wrote.

Revising Checklist

1. Assignment
   - ☐ follows the assignment to write an essay of argument/persuasion
   - ☐ addresses the instructor and classmates as the audience
   - ☐ follows the ten steps listed in the assignment

2. Introduction
   - ☐ contains a hook to capture the reader's attention
   - ☐ contains some general statements or background information about the topic
   - ☐ contains a proposition (thesis statement) that states the writer's position on the topic
   - ☐ Proposition/thesis statement includes a controlling idea.
   - ☐ Proposition/thesis statement gives a clue to the text structure.

3. Body
   - ☐ Each paragraph addresses a main point of the argument or is the rebuttal of the opposing view. OR
   - ☐ Each paragraph is a combination of opposing view and rebuttal.
   - ☐ Each paragraph contains a topic sentence.
   - ☐ Each topic sentence is developed through general and specific support/details.
   - ☐ General and specific support/details are arranged in a logical order.
   - ☐ General and specific support/details follow the outline.
   - ☐ General and specific support/details are sufficient in number (not too many, not too few).
   - ☐ Facts, statistics, or quotes are cited correctly.

4. Conclusion
   - ☐ marks the end of the essay
   - ☐ offers the writer's final thoughts on the topic
   - ☐ restates the thesis, summarizes main points, calls for action and/or makes a prediction

B. Share your essay with a classmate. Ask your classmate to use the Revising Checklist to check your essay and give you some feedback. Make any changes to your essay that you feel are necessary. The changes you make should improve your essay.

Editing and Proofreading

The Final Steps

A. Follow the steps below to edit and proofread the essay of argument/persuasion you wrote.

Editing and Proofreading Checklist

1. Grammar

   ☐ Verb tenses are correct.

   ☐ Each subject agrees with its verb (singular/plural).

   ☐ Prepositions are correct.

   ☐ Pronouns are correct.

   ☐ No articles are missing (*a, an, the*).

2. Spelling

   ☐ All the words are spelled correctly.

   ☐ Abbreviations, if any, are used correctly.

   ☐ First word of each sentence begins with a capital letter.

   ☐ All proper nouns begin with a capital letter.

3. Punctuation

   ☐ All sentences end with a punctuation mark.

   ☐ Periods are after statements and question marks are after questions.

   ☐ Commas are used correctly in sentences containing coordinating and subordinating conjunctions.

   ☐ All quotations are punctuated correctly.

4. Sentences

   ☐ All sentences are complete.

   ☐ Each sentence has a subject and a verb.

   ☐ There are no fragments, run-on sentences, or comma splices.

   ☐ Sentences contain balanced or parallel grammatical structures.

5. Format

   ☐ Essay has a title.

   ☐ All paragraphs are in essay format (first line is indented or there is one blank line between paragraphs).

   ☐ All sentences are in paragraph format (not listed or numbered).

   ☐ Writer's name is on the paper.

   ☐ Paper is neat, clean, and legible (easily read).

B. Share your paragraph with a classmate. Ask your classmate to use the Editing and Proofreading Checklist to check your essay and mark any errors in grammar, spelling, punctuation, sentences, or format.

C. Fix any mistakes your essay contained. Proofread your essay one more time. Turn in your final draft to your instructor.

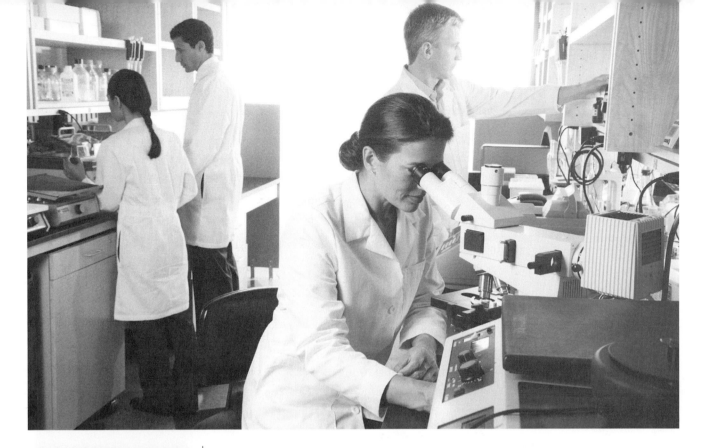

7 From the Physical Sciences: Physics

Included among the physical sciences are chemistry, geology, oceanography, and physics. Topics commonly addressed in physics courses range from Newton's Laws of motion to energy and heat to magnetic fields and forces. Understanding the basic principles of physics will increase your awareness of how physics affects your everyday life.

Using your general knowledge and experience, discuss the following questions with a partner or in a small group.

- How do scientists prove theories?
- What is an example of a *law* in physics?
- What are some ways energy is transferred as heat?

This chapter will help you understand some of the **key concepts** of physics such as

- the scientific method
- the process of conducting an experiment
- concepts of heat
- lab reports

Get Ready to Read

True or False

Read the following statements and decide if they are true or false. Share your answers with a classmate.

1.	Scientists observe, explain, and test phenomena (events).	TRUE	FALSE
2.	Scientific theories involve laws or principles in their explanations.	TRUE	FALSE
3.	Experiments do not need to test explanations of the results.	TRUE	FALSE
4.	One way to explain an event is by referring to another event that preceded it.	TRUE	FALSE
5.	The benefits of learning the scientific method are limited to science only.	TRUE	FALSE

Surveying and Predicting

Survey and Predict

A. Follow the steps below to survey Reading 1 below.

1. Read the title. Write it here. _____

2. Read the first paragraph. Write one or two words which tell the topic, what the paragraph is about. _____

3. Write the main idea here. _____
_____

4. Read the headings, the titles of the sections in the reading.

5. Look for any graphic or visual aids in the reading. Graphic aids are charts, graphs, pictures, maps, diagrams, etc.

6. Look for key (important) terms related to the topic. They are usually in bold.

7. Read the last paragraph. It is a summary of the entire reading.

B. Share your survey answers with a partner and discuss what you think the reading will be about. Then circle the number of the statement below that matches your prediction.

1. The passage will describe the three steps in the scientific method.

2. The passage will compare scientific theories to scientific hypotheses.

3. The passage will describe how scientists collect data.

C. Now read the passage to see if your prediction is correct. Try to read as quickly as you can. Do not stop to look up words in your dictionary.

Scientific Method

Science investigates natural phenomena of every conceivable sort—from the physical to the biological to the social. Scientists study everything from events occurring at the time of the formation of the universe to the stages of human intellectual and emotional development to the migratory patterns of butterflies. Judging by its subject matter, then, science is the study of very nearly everything.

Three-step Process

If we want to understand just what science is, we must look at science from a different perspective. We must ask ourselves, first, why scientists study the natural world, and then we must look at the way in which scientific inquiry is conducted, no matter what its subject. At its most basic level, **scientific method** is a simple three-step process by which scientists investigate nature. The three steps in the process are observing, explaining, and testing.

Observation

Observation is the first step in **scientific inquiry**. To insure observational accuracy, the following criteria must be satisfied.

1. Do we have a clear sense of what the relevant phenomena are? i.e., are key terms clearly specified?

2. Can we find a way to guarantee that nothing relevant is overlooked?

3. Have we separated observational fact from conjecture or assumption?

4. Have we considered any necessary comparative information?

5. Are our observations free of expectation and belief?

Many scientific observations concern **anomalies**—phenomena that do not square with well-established methods of explanation. Because they often pose a challenge to well-documented explanations, anomalies should be regarded with a healthy dose of skepticism. What this means is that observations pertaining to an alleged anomaly should look for data that suggest that the anomaly can be explained in some conventional way. Claims about an anomalous phenomenon should be accepted only when the phenomenon has been clearly documented and shown to have no conventional explanation.

Explanation

The second step in the process of scientific method is explanation. An explanation, in science, is an account of how or why something has come to be the case. Both **theories** and **hypotheses** involve explanations. Theories tend to be broad, unifying explanations while hypotheses are more limited in scope. Both can be tentative or well confirmed. Scientific explanations can make reference to causes, causal mechanisms, underlying processes, laws or function, all of which are summarized in Table 7.1.

Explanations often leave some explanatory questions about the **phenomenon** in question unanswered. To enrich an explanation of one type, other types of explanation may need to be given. **Correlations** alone explain very little unless they are accompanied by evidence that the correlated terms are either directly or indirectly linked.

Testing

Finally, testing is the third step in the process of scientific method. The basic strategy used to test an explanation is always the same. Isolate a prediction that will occur if an explanation is correct. Tests can be undertaken under laboratory conditions where circumstances will be arranged to yield a prediction, or in the real world by checking the prediction against the facts. In either case, the prediction must enable us to **reject** the explanation if it is wrong and to **confirm** it if it is correct. To accomplish this, any experiment must satisfy two criteria. First, it must rule out factors that could account for **predictive failure** even if the explanation is correct (the **falsifiability criterion**). Second, it must rule out factors that could explain **predictive success** even if the explanation is wrong (the **verifiability criterion**). By a similar experimental strategy, extraordinary **claims** and abilities can be tested. In such a test, care must be taken to insure that the predicted outcome is clear and measurable and that the **subject** or subjects believe they can perform under the conditions specified.

Becoming familiar with the basic methodology common to all good scientific research and learning to distinguish between legitimate and bogus applications of scientific method will lead you to think clearly and critically about the claims of scientists and charlatans alike to have advanced our understanding of the world about us.

Table 7.1   Ways of Explaining

Causes
To explain one thing or event by reference to another, antecedent thing or event. Example: *Debris from last night's windstorm caused the power outage.*

Causal Mechanisms
To explain by citing intervening causal factors, factors that explain the effects of a more distant cause. Example: *Debris from the storm severed several power lines thus causing last night's power outage.*

Laws
To explain an event by referring to a general law or principle of which the event is an instance. Example: *The fuel efficiency of a vehicle is determined in part by size and weight. This is because acceleration is directly proportional to force but inversely proportional to mass. Thus, the larger the object you want to move, the greater the force you need to apply, and so the more energy you need to expend.*

Underlying Processes
To explain something by reference to the working of its component parts. Example: *The chest pain and breathing difficulty symptomatic of pneumonia results from an infection of the lung tissues. The tiny air sacs of which the lungs are composed—called alveoli—fill with inflammatory fluid caused by the infection. As a result, the flow of oxygen through the alveolar walls is greatly impaired.*

Function
To explain something by reference to the role it fulfills in some larger enterprise. Example: *Many species of birds build their nests in high places—trees, cliffs, etc.—to protect their young from predators.*

Key Concept Words

anomalies – (n.) things or events that cannot be explained using established methods

claims – (n.) statements or assertions of something as fact

confirm – (v.) prove to be true

correlation – (n.) connection or correspondence between sets of data

falsifiability criterion – (n.) a test that is designed to rule out factors that could explain a failed prediction even if the explanation is correct

hypotheses – (n.) limited, more narrow explanations

phenomenon – (n.) event or occurrence

predictive failure/success – (n.) a prediction that enables one to reject an explanation if it is wrong and to confirm it if it is right

reject – (v.) not accept, discard

scientific inquiry – (n.) scientific method

scientific method – (n.) process used to investigate nature

subject – (n.) someone or something that undergoes an experiment or analysis

theories – (n.) broad explanations

verifiability criterion – (n.) a test that is designed to rule out factors that could explain a successful prediction even if the explanation is incorrect

Glossed Words

criteria – (n.) standards used to test or measure something (singular: criterion);
key terms –(n.) important words or expressions; **overlook** – (v.) to miss or not pay
attention to; **conjecture** – (n.) prediction, guess; **square with** – (v.) make sense with;
skepticism – (n.) doubt; **to come to be the case** – (v.) to happen, occur, result;
scope – (n.) extent, range; **tentative** – (adj.) not confirmed; **enrich** – (v.) to add to or give
more to; **yield** – (v.) to result in, give, produce; **bogus** – (adj.) fake, not real; **charlatan** – (n.)
a person who pretends to have knowledge about a subject but doesn't

Summarizing

Share What You Read

Use two or three sentences to tell your partner what you thought the reading was
about. Then listen to your partner's sentences. Next, read the following statements
and circle the number of the statement that best summarizes the reading.

1. The scientific method is used for experiments in the scientific world to explain
   phenomena.

2. There are many ways to explain theories and hypotheses: causes, underlying
   processes, and laws.

3. The scientific method is a process that involves observation, explanation, and
   testing.

Check Your Comprehension

Read the following statements. Circle all of the answers that make the statement true.

1. To make sure that observations are accurate, scientists
   a. specify key terms.
   b. separate facts from assumptions.
   c. eliminate comparative information.

2. Many scientific observations concern events that are not easily explained with
   established methods. When this situation occurs, scientists
   a. do not try to explain them.
   b. look for data that can explain them.
   c. accept them and document them.

3. Theories and hypotheses are similar in that both
   a. can be tentative or well confirmed.
   b. broad, unifying explanations.
   c. involve explanations.

4. "Deciduous trees lose their leaves in winter in order to protect themselves by
   conserving moisture and reducing the amount of energy they need to stay
   alive." This way of explaining a phenomenon makes reference to
   a. causal mechanisms.
   b. laws.
   c. function.

5. Testing an explanation in the process of scientific method means
   a. being able to confirm the explanation if it is correct.
   b. isolating a prediction that will occur if the explanation is correct.
   c. being able to reject the explanation if it is wrong.

6. The falsifiability criterion of a well-designed experiment
   a. rules out factors that could explain a failed prediction even if the explanation is correct.
   b. rules out factors that could explain a successful prediction even if the explanation is wrong.
   c. is the only criterion an experiment must satisfy.

7. The scientific method can be used to test extraordinary claims and abilities if
   a. the predicted outcome is clear.
   b. the predicted outcome can be measured.
   c. the subjects believe they can perform under the conditions specified.

8. Scientific explanations can make reference to
   a. causes.
   b. underlying processes.
   c. expectations and beliefs.

Academic Word List

Scan and Define

A. Look at the ten words listed below. Scan the reading and underline the words from the list. Write the definitions for the words you know. Do not use a dictionary. The first one has been done for you.

1. citing (n.) _mentioning, referring to, quoting_ _____

2. conceivable _____

3. factors _____

4. hypotheses _____

5. link (v.) _____

6. methods _____

7. process (n.) _____

8. relevant _____

9. undertake _____

10. vehicle _____

B. Share your definitions with a partner and then with the rest of your classmates. As a group, try to complete the definitions for all ten words. Use a dictionary to check the definitions if you are unsure about them. Then complete the vocabulary activity.

Vocabulary Challenge

A. Using your dictionary, work with a partner to find the missing word forms and complete the chart. If no form exists, draw a line in the space. The first one has been done for you.

Noun	Verb	Adjective	Adverb
1. citing, *citation*	*cite*	*cited*	---------
2.		conceivable	
3. factors			
4. hypotheses			
5.	link		
6. methods			
7. process			
8.		relevant	
9.	undertake		
10. vehicle			

B. Read the statements and then circle the correct answer or answers. Sometimes more than one answer is possible. The words from the Academic Word List are underlined. The first one has been done for you.

1. Factors are those elements that help explain the effects of an event. Which of the following would not be a <u>factor</u> in an auto accident?
   a. brake loss/loss of control
   b. excessive alcohol/unsafe driving
   c. make of car/color of car interior

2. Citing factors that explain the effects of a more distant cause is one type of scientific explanation. Which of the following can also be <u>cited</u>?
   a. statistics   b. writers   c. sounds

3. In science, correlations need to be accompanied by evidence that the correlated terms are linked, directly or indirectly. Which of the following is an example of a direct <u>link</u> to a town's loss of electricity?
   a. A tree falls on a power line during a windstorm.
   b. The wind knocks down power lines during a windstorm.
   c. A squirrel runs inside a transformer for safely and is electrocuted during a rainstorm.

4. In the late 1980s, hundreds of circular and semicircular indentations were discovered in the wheat and cornfields of southern England. There seemed to be no obvious explanation for the origin of these amazing figures.
   In science, to ensure observational accuracy, one of the criteria to be satisfied is finding a way to guarantee that nothing relevant is overlooked. In explaining crop circles, which of these facts might be considered overlooking a <u>relevant</u> part of a scientific observation?
   a. There were no footprints in the field.
   b. The crop circles were in the middle of a field.
   c. There were tractor lines nearby.

5. Both theories and hypotheses involve explanations. Theories tend to be broad, unifying explanations while hypotheses are more limited in scope. Both can be tentative or well confirmed. Which of the following would not be classified as a hypothesis?
   a. An object in a state of motion remains in that state of motion unless acted on by an external force.
   b. One's view of the world is determined by the language we speak.
   c. Crop circles are caused by a shift in the Earth's magnetic field.

Understanding Referents

Referents: nouns or pronouns that refer to nouns or phrases previously mentioned in a passage

Readers are able to understand and follow the ideas writers convey only when those ideas are presented logically. When ideas are presented in a logical order and the connection between ideas or sentences is clear, we say the passage has *coherence*. Using transitions is one way a writer adds coherence to a passage. Using referents—nouns or pronouns that refer or refer back to important nouns or phrases in the passage—is another way. Transitions and referents act as "signposts" to the reader and guide the reader through the passage. Readers use these signposts to follow the main idea and details the writer presents in the passage.

Read the sentences below. The words in bold are the key or important nouns or phrases. The underlined words are the referents, the words that refer to the important nouns or phrases.

Convection: In <u>this process</u>*, the temperature of a fluid is raised, and the* **fluid** *is moved from one point in space to another carrying the energy with* <u>it</u>.

In the sentence above, *this process* refers to the noun *convection*, and *it* refers to the noun *fluid*.

Judging by <u>its</u> *subject matter, then,* **science** *is the study of very nearly everything.*

In the sentence above, *its* refers to the noun *science*.

At <u>its</u> *most basic level,* **scientific method** *is a simple three-step process by which scientists investigate nature. The three steps in* <u>the process</u> *are observing, explaining, and testing.*

In the sentences above, both *its* and *the process* refer to the noun *scientific method*.

Common referents include *this, that, these, those,* subject/object/relative pronouns, and possessive adjectives.

ACTIVITY ❼   *Identify Referents*

A. Read the following sentences. Circle the key or important noun or phrase and underline the referent—the noun or pronoun used to refer to it.

1. Because they often pose a challenge to well-documented explanations, anomalies should be regarded with a healthy dose of skepticism. What this means is that observations pertaining to an alleged anomaly should look for data that suggest that the anomaly can be explained in some conventional way.

2. Theories tend to be broad, unifying explanations while hypotheses are more limited in scope. Both can be tentative or well confirmed.

3. One way of explaining an underlying process is to explain something by reference to the working of its compound parts.

4. The fuel efficiency of a vehicle is determined in part by size and weight. This is because acceleration is directly proportional to force but inversely proportional to mass.

5. The prediction must enable us to reject the explanation if it is wrong and to confirm it if it is correct. To accomplish this, any experiment must satisfy two criteria.

6. Any experiment must satisfy two criteria. First, it must rule out factors that could account for predictive failure even if the explanation is correct. Second, it must rule out factors that could explain predictive success even if the explanation is wrong.

B. Read the following sentences. Choose the correct referent and write the noun or pronoun it refers to.

1. The air above the fire in a fireplace is heated. *This / It* hot air is pushed up the chimney by the warm air in the room.

   Refers to: _____

2. Now, this air must be replaced from somewhere. *That / It* is usually replaced by cold air entering the house through leaks around doors and windows.

   Refers to: _____

3. Allowance must be made to provide this air, *which / who* can be provided by air ducts from the outside. In *these / this* way, the fire uses cold air from outside rather than warm air from inside.

   Refers to: _____

   Refers to: _____

C. Read the following sentences and determine whether the underlined referent is correct. If it is incorrect, make the correction.

1. If outside sources were used in conducting the experiment, <u>it</u> should be

   listed in the reference section.

2. These molecules "bump" into other molecules and start <u>them</u> moving faster.

3. Electromagnetic radiation carries energy, <u>which</u> can be absorbed by

   materials and may result in increased temperature.

4. The sense of feel in humans is based not so much on the temperature of

   an object in contact with the skin as on the rate of energy flow between the

   object and the skin. <u>These</u> explains why metal generally feels cold—it is a

   good thermal conductor, so <u>they</u> absorbs energy quickly from the skin.

5. The temperature of the black sock will rise faster in the presence of visible

   radiation from the Sun, due to <u>its</u> high radiative absorption.

Identifying Text Structure—*Process*

One of the most common types of text structure writers use is that of *process*. Anytime a writer explains how to do something or how something works, the reading will be divided into steps and presented chronologically or sequentially. In Reading 1, for example, the writer explains the three steps in the process of scientific inquiry. Each step is presented in sequence, and the writer provides examples to illustrate each of the steps.

Key Words—*Process*

Because process involves a method with steps and sequences, key words include chronological or time words. Some of the key words associated with the text structure process are listed in the chart below.

Process	Sequence	
how to	after / before	last
method	beginning with	meanwhile
phase	during	next
procedure	eventually	once X happens
process	for X amount of time	starting with
stage	finally	(at) the same time
step	first, second, third, etc.	then

Recognize Key Words

A. Read the following steps in the process of scientific inquiry. Using the key words as a guide, number the steps in the correct order.

_____ 1. An explanation is an account of how or why something has come to be the case.

_____ 2. Finally, testing is the last step in the process of scientific method.

_____ 3. The first step in scientific inquiry is observation.

_____ 4. The basic strategy used to test an explanation is always the same.

_____ 5. A number of criteria must be satisfied to insure observational accuracy.

_____ 6. Explanation is the next step in the process.

B. Go back to Reading 1 and find three examples of key words that show the text structure of process. Write them below.

1. _____

2. _____

3. _____

Use Key Words

Read the following passage and circle the key word(s) that best complete(s) each sentence.

Is TV Making Your Child Fat?

There has been a dramatic increase in the number of Americans who are overweight and obese. One of the groups most at risk is children. These days, it seems that more children opt for sitting in front of the TV than for playing outside. At the same time they watch TV, most children tend to snack. Are the two related?

A group of researchers looking at (1) *how to / what to* slow down or reverse obesity in children received a grant from Healthy Children Institute to study the matter. The researchers decided to study what children ate while they watched TV in an effort to determine if the children's snacking contributes to a rise in obesity.

(2) *Beginning with / First,* researchers chose two groups of children for the study. All of the children were (3) *eventually / then* weighed and measured. Among the children, one group of children watched TV between 14 and 21 hours per week. The other group watched TV between 35 and 40 hours per week.

(4) *During / Meanwhile* the period of study, one year, researchers asked the children to document their weekly TV watching, including what, if any, food they ate while they watched TV. The children's parents verified that the information the children supplied was correct. The children were also weighed and measured once a week. This information was submitted to the researchers weekly throughout the study period. At this (5) *procedure / stage* in the study, the researchers had completed their observation.

Researchers (6) *eventually / then* compiled the data. They compared the different types of food the children had eaten: snack food, sweets, vegetables, fruit, and nuts. (7) *At the same time, / During* they also compared the different results for weekday and weekend TV watching. The final comparison in this (8) *method / phase* of the study was the comparison of weight and height changes for children in both groups.

(9) *Before / After* summarizing the results, researchers shared data that showed that children ate more while they were watching TV than if they were not. The data also indicated that children who watched TV more than 30 hours per week ate fewer vegetables and fruits than children who watched TV between 10 and 15 hours per week. (10) *Next, / Finally,* the results indicated that the children who watched the most TV gained the most weight.

These results seem to indicate that there is a connection between watching TV and obesity. However, more studies with a larger number of participants need to be conducted. In addition, researchers need a more reliable method to verify that the information supplied by the children and their parents is accurate. Plans for another study are already underway.

In the first section of this chapter, you were introduced to referents and the pattern of process. You practiced the skills and strategies of surveying, predicting, and summarizing with Reading 1. In this section you will practice these same skills with a new reading. You will also review the strategies for using context to guess the meaning of unfamiliar words.

Get Ready to Read

Show What You Know

Read the following statements and put an X in front of the ones that you believe or know to be true about lab reports. Discuss your answers with a partner.

_____ 1. Lab reports are commonly written in chemistry, physics, and engineering courses.

_____ 2. One section in a lab report contains all of the data that has been collected.

_____ 3. The conclusion of a lab report consists of an analysis or interpretation of the data.

_____ 4. The step-by-step process followed in an experiment is called the *method*.

_____ 5. Outside sources used must be cited in the reference section of a lab report.

Survey and Predict

A. Using the following steps, survey Reading 2 and predict what the reading will be about.

1. Read the title.

2. Read the first paragraph and identify the main idea.

3. Read the headings.

4. Look for any graphic or visual aids in the reading.

5. Look for key terms in bold.

6. Read the last paragraph.

B. Write your prediction here: _____

_____

C. Now read the passage to see if your prediction is correct. Try to read as quickly as you can. Do not stop to look up words in your dictionary.

Reading 2

The Science of Lab Reports

Students enrolled in undergraduate college courses submit lab (laboratory) reports detailing experiments or projects completed for chemistry, physics, or engineering courses. Although the specific format of lab reports is often determined by the individual school or department, a lab report usually comprises five or six components. The **objective** of the lab report states the aims of the experiment and includes any hypothesis being tested. The **method** outlines the materials used and the step-by-step process followed to conduct the experiment. The **results** are typically the raw data that have been collected: facts, measurements, readings, etc. This information is usually presented in the form of a table or graph. Following the results is the **conclusion**. The conclusion is a summary of the results (raw data) and provides an analysis or interpretation of the data. A **discussion** follows the conclusion and states what the results mean. Finally, if outside sources were used in conducting the experiment, they are listed in the **reference** section.

The following selection, taken from a textbook that explores the physics of everyday life, presents the concept of heat in physics, followed by examples of a mystery to be explained, magic (method) to be performed, and a myth to be debunked, all using the physics concept of heat.

Concepts of Heat

Heat is one of the terms most commonly misused in colloquial conversation as well as in many textbooks. Heat is often referred to as a form of stored energy, but this is not true. Heat is a means by which we can transfer energy; it is not the stored energy itself.

So if heat is not stored energy, then what is the energy contained in a warm object? The correct description is **internal energy.**

The process by which the energy is transferred as heat is given as one of the following three in most textbooks:

Convection: In this process, the temperature of a fluid is raised, and the fluid is moved from one point in space to another, carrying the energy with it. Examples of convection include the water-based cooling system in an automobile engine and a forced-air heating system in a home. Natural convection refers to the rising of hot fluids due to the buoyant force. Convection can also occur due to wind, such as the convective cooling of one's skin as the air blows across it. Forced convection refers to movement of energy-carrying fluid due to mechanical means, such as in your automobile engine or your air conditioner.

Conduction: In this process, energy is transferred through a material without the actual transfer of **matter**. The molecules at one end of the material (in contact with a region of high temperature) start moving with increased **kinetic energy**. These **molecules** "bump" into other molecules and start them moving faster. This "bumping" moves down the material toward the cooler end. Examples include the warming up of the upper end of a spoon in a cup of coffee and the transfer of energy through the walls in a home, which can be countered by installing insulation in the walls.

Radiation: This process depends on electromagnetic **radiation**, the most familiar form of which is light. Electromagnetic radiation carries energy, which can be absorbed by materials and may result in increased temperature. Examples include the warmth one feels in front of a fireplace and the energy brought to Earth from the Sun.

Mystery to Be Explained

Why does a bare floor feel colder than a carpeted floor?

The sense of feel in humans is based not so much on the temperature of an object in contact with the skin as on the rate of energy flow between the object and the skin. This is why metals generally feel cold—they are good **thermal conductors**, so they absorb energy quickly from the skin. The bare floor and the carpet are at the same temperature, that of the room, but yet they do not feel the same temperature. The bare floor is a better thermal conductor than the carpet—hence it feels colder.

Magic (Method) to Be Followed

Black and White: The effects of color on radiation absorption can be easily demonstrated with socks. Insert thermometers into two socks, one white and one black. Record the initial temperatures. Now, place the socks under an intense light source or out in the Sun, making sure that each receives the same amount of radiation. After some time, read the temperatures again.

The black sock appears to be black because it absorbs almost all of the visible radiation incident upon it. The white sock appears to be white because it reflects much of the visible radiation incident upon it. Thus, the temperature of the black sock will rise faster in the presence of visible radiation from the Sun, due to its high **radiative absorption**. After several minutes in the Sun, the black sock should be several degrees warmer than the white sock.

Myth to Be Debunked

A fireplace is a heater for a home.

The air above the fire in a fireplace is heated. This hot air, which is less dense than warm air, is pushed up the chimney by the warm air in the room, carrying energy with it by convection. This air lost through the chimney must be replaced from somewhere. It is replaced with the warm air which enters the fireplace from the room in order to push the hot air up the chimney. Now, this air must be replaced from somewhere. It is usually replaced by cold air entering the house through leaks around doors and windows. The net result is that warm air from the house is going up the chimney and being replaced by cold air from outside. This is not obvious to the person sitting in front of the fire, due to the toasty feeling of the radiant heat, but, overall, the house is cooling off. This effect can be countered by putting glass doors on the fireplace, which will allow the radiant energy to pass through, but will cut off the convection flow from the room. The fire needs air, of course, so cutting off this convection flow will normally smother the fire. Allowance must be made to provide this air, which can be provided by air ducts from the outside. In this way, the fire uses cold air from outside rather than warm air from inside.

Key Concept Words

conclusion – (n.) a summary and analysis of the of results of an experiment

conduction – (n.) the transfer of energy as heat via molecules moving from a warmer end toward a cooler end

convection – (n.) the transfer of energy as heat via a fluid moving from one point to another

discussion – (n.) the significance or meaning of the results

internal energy – (n.) the energy contained in a warm object

kinetic energy – (n.) the energy of motion

matter – (n.) any substance that has weight and takes up space

method – (n.) the materials and steps used in an experiment

molecule – (n.) the smallest part of an element of a substance

objective – (n.) goal, purpose, aim of an experiment

radiation – (n.) the transfer of energy as heat via absorption

radiative absorption – (n.) ability to absorb energy transferred via rays or waves

reference – (n.) the section of a lab report that lists outside sources used in the experiment

results – (n.) the data collected in an experiment

thermal conductors – (n.) materials that absorb energy quickly

Glossed Words

undergraduate – (adj.) related to the first four years of college/university; **aims** – (n.) purposes or goals; **raw data** – (n.) facts, measurements, readings collected in an experiment; **debunk** – (v.) disprove or expose something as false or not true; **misused** – (v.) used incorrectly; **buoyant** – (adj.) able to float or rise; **countered** – (v.) opposed or stopped; prevented; remedied; **absorb** – (v.) to take in or soak up; **bare** – (adj.) uncovered; **reflect** – (v.) to give off, return or send back; **dense** – (adj.) compact, crowded together; heavy; **chimney** – (n.) structure through which smoke from a fire or furnace passes; **leaks** – (n.) spaces or holes which allow air or fluid to enter/leave; **toasty** – (adj.) warm; **smother** – (v.) to cut off oxygen to something; **ducts** – (n.) metal structures that carry heated or cold air through a building

Summarizing

Share What You Read

Use two or three sentences to tell your partner what you thought the reading was about. Then listen to your partner's sentences. If you disagree, go back and find support for your summary. Write your summary statement below.

Summary: _____

_____

Check Your Comprehension

Read the phrases related to the three processes by which energy is transferred as heat. Write the phrase in the chart under the correct heading.

1. temperature of fluid raised	5. cooling of skin as air blows across it	9. example: feeling warm by sitting in front of a fire
2. example: upper end of spoon in coffee warms up	6. insulation prevents this from occurring	10. molecules move with increased kinetic energy
3. most familiar form is light	7. example: water-based cooling system in car engine	11. can be natural or forced
4. energy transferred through material	8. energy absorbed by material	12. fluid moves, carrying energy with it

Convection	Conduction	Radiation

Academic Word List

Scan and Define

A. Look at the ten words listed below. Scan the reading and underline the words from the list. Write the definitions for the words you know. Do not use a dictionary. The first one has been done for you.

1. analysis *a study of the parts and their relationship to the whole* _____

2. data _____

3. energy _____

4. initial (adj.) _____

5. insert (v.) _____

6. occur _____

7. overall _____

8. submit _____

9. transfer (v.) _____

10. visible _____

B. Share your definitions with a partner and then with the rest of your classmates. As a group, try to complete the definitions for all ten words. Use a dictionary to check the definitions if you are unsure about them. Then complete the vocabulary activity.

Vocabulary Challenge

A. Decide whether the following statements are true or false based on the meaning of the underlined word. If a statement is true, put a *T* in the blank; if it is false, put an *F* in the blank. Share your answers with a partner and explain the reasons for your *False* answers.

_____ 1. If students are required to <u>submit</u> a physics research project, they give a written paper to their professor.

_____ 2. If students' grades are based on their <u>overall</u> performance in a class, the instructor looks at their assignments and tests but not at class participation.

_____ 3. If students are required to record their <u>initial</u> observation in a lab report, they must put the first letter of their first and last names in the report.

_____ 4. Placing a spoon in a cup of hot coffee will result in the upper end of the spoon becoming warm. The energy from the hot coffee is <u>transferred</u> to the spoon.

_____ 5. In a lab report, it is necessary to include the facts, measurements, and/or readings from the experiment. Recording the raw data provides an <u>analysis</u> of the data.

_____ 6. <u>Data</u> from which conclusions can be drawn can be measurements, temperature readings, speeds, or amounts.

_____ 7. What our eyes see is a reflection off a lower-temperature object. The reflection is of emitted energy from a high-temperature source. If all sources of high temperatures were removed, nothing would be <u>visible</u> to us.

_____ 8. If the mercury level of a thermometer drops before it begins to rise when it is <u>plunged</u> into a cup of hot coffee, then plunge means *insert*.

B. Circle the word that does not belong. The first one has been done for you. The words in bold are from the Academic Word List.

1. **occur**	happen	transpire	(accompany)
2. **transfer**	leave	move	conduct
3. **visible**	observable	transparent	perceptible
4. **energy**	power	force	heat
5. **overall**	part	complete	general
6. **submit**	give	present	disagree
7. **initial**	ultimate	first	beginning

Using Context to Guess Meaning—*Review*

In each chapter of *Key Concepts,* you have practiced strategies for guessing meaning from context. These strategies have included using contrasts, definitions and punctuation, synonyms and antonyms, inferences, examples, and surrounding sentences to determine the meaning of a word or phrase. In this chapter, you will review them all.

Strategy Review

Each sentence below contains an example of or a clue to one of the strategies you have practiced. Match the sentence in the left column with the appropriate strategy in the right column.

_____ 1. During convection, unlike during conduction, energy is transferred through a material and includes the actual transfer of matter.

    a. example

_____ 2. Chemistry refers to the science of composition, structure, and properties of matter.

    b. inference

_____ 3. Debris from the hurricane covered the roads. For example, downed trees, bent signs, and broken street lights were everywhere.

    c. punctuation

_____ 4. Dozens of people were sent to the hospital after a noxious gas was created during the chemistry lab experiment.

    d. contrast

_____ 5. Studying the snacking habits of obese or extremely overweight children was the focus of his research.

    e. definition

_____ 6. Molecules "bump" into each other, which results in increased kinetic, or moving, energy.

    f. synonym

Guess Meaning from Context

Read the short passages below. Use the strategies you have learned in this text to determine the meaning of the words in bold. Next to each word, write its meaning and the strategy or strategies (contrast, definition, punctuation, synonym, antonym, inference, example, surrounding sentences) you used to determine it.

1. Many scientific observations concern **anomalies**—phenomena that do not agree with well-established methods of explanation. Because anomalies are often a challenge to well-documented explanations, they should be regarded with **skepticism**. What this means is that observations about the anomaly should look for data that suggest that the anomaly can be explained in a conventional, traditional way. That is, anomalies should not be accepted without clear documentation that there is no conventional explanation for their occurrence.

   anomalies = _____

   skepticism = _____

2. Any experiment must satisfy two **criteria.** First, it must exclude from consideration factors that could account for predictive failure even if the explanation is correct (the falsifiability criterion). Second, it must also **rule out** factors than could explain predictive success even if the explanation is wrong (the verifiability criterion). By a similar experimental strategy, **extraordinary claims and abilities**, which refer to things that do not follow traditional scientific thinking, can be tested. Predicting the future or communicating with the dead are examples of such claims.

   criteria = _____

   rule out = _____

   extraordinary claims and abilities = _____

   _____

3. A lab report usually comprises five or six **components**. The objective of the lab report states the aims of the experiment and includes any hypothesis being tested. The method outlines the materials used and the step-by-step process followed to conduct the experiment. The results are typically the **raw data** that have been collected: facts, measurements, readings, etc. Following the results is the conclusion. The conclusion is a summary of the results (raw data) and provides an analysis or **interpretation** of the data. A discussion follows the conclusion and states what the results mean. Finally, if outside sources were used in conducting the experiment, they are listed in the reference section.

   components = _____

   raw data = _____

   interpretation = _____

4. Heat is one of the terms most commonly misused in **colloquial,** or informal, conversation as well as in many textbooks. Heat is often referred to as a form of stored energy, but this is not true. **Heat** is a means by which we can transfer energy; it is not the stored energy itself. So if heat is not stored energy, then what is the energy contained in a warm object? The correct description is **internal energy.**

colloquial = _____

heat = _____

internal energy = _____

WRITING 1A • ## Skills and Strategies

In this section, you will learn some skills and strategies associated with the writing process. It includes the grammar of modal auxiliaries, which is one of the grammatical structures used in the readings. In this section, you will practice the different steps in the writing process and will write a process essay.

The Grammar of Modals

Unlike other verbs, modal auxiliaries are not used alone. They are used with another verb and express attitudes or feelings rather than actions. Modals can convey, for example, the idea of permission or ability, of obligation or suggestion, or of possibility or advice. Study the modals and their meanings in the chart below.

Modal	Meaning
can	ability in the present; ask for permission (informal); make a request (informal)
may	make a request (formal); ask for permission (formal); express possibility
might	express possibility
could	ability in the past; make a request; make a suggestion; express possibility
should	give strong advice; express certainty
would	make a request; express preference (with *rather*); express desire (with *like*)
will	make a request; future certainty; make an offer to help
must	express obligation (affirmative); express prohibition (negative); express strong certainty
have to	express obligation (affirmative); express lack of obligation (negative)
shall	offer a suggestion; make an offer to help; express future (seldom used)

Recognize Modal Meaning

Read the following sentences and choose the meaning of the modal as it is used in the sentence.

1. Lab reports that use outside sources *must* contain a list of those sources in the reference section.
   a. obligation
   b. strong certainty

2. Heat is a means by which we *can* transfer energy.
   a. ability
   b. permission

3. A scientific anomaly *could* be the result of an error in observation.
   a. ability
   b. possibility

4. Observations pertaining to an alleged anomaly *should* look for data that suggest that the anomaly can be explained in some conventional way.
   a. advice
   b. certainty

5. Isolate a prediction that *will* occur if an explanation is correct.
   a. make a request
   b. future certainty

Use Modal Auxiliaries

Fill in the blanks with the correct modal auxiliary. Sometimes more than one modal may be correct.

1. Examples of convection include the water-based cooling system in an automobile engine. Convection _____ also occur due to wind, such as the convective cooling of one's skin as the air blows across it.

2. A black sock absorbs almost all of the visible radiation that strikes it. A white sock reflects much of the visible radiation that falls upon it. Thus, the temperature of the black sock _____ rise faster in the presence of visible radiation from the Sun.

3. After several minutes in the sun, the black sock _____ be several degrees warmer than the white sock.

4. A fireplace is not a heater for a home. The hot air above the fire is pushed up the chimney by the warm air in the room, carrying energy with it by convection. This air lost through the chimney _____ be replaced from somewhere. It is replaced with the warm air which enters the fireplace from the room.

5. The effect of cooling off the house _____ be countered by putting glass doors on the fireplace. These glass doors _____ allow the radiant energy to pass through, but they _____ cut off the convection flow from the room.

Sentence Essentials

Dependent Clauses: Noun Clauses

Previous sections of Sentence Essentials focused on writing sentences that contained adjective and adverb clauses, two of the three types of dependent clauses. This section addresses the third type: noun clauses.

Noun clauses

- function as nouns and can be subjects or objects
- can begin with a *wh*-word (*who, what, when, where, why, how,* etc.), *that,* or *if/whether*
- can follow certain adjectives and nouns

Noun clauses, depending on their function, are located at the beginning or at the end of a sentence and may follow some adjectives and nouns. Look at the examples below.

Why scientists study the natural world is an important question to ask.
                    subject
An important question to ask is **why scientists study the natural world.**
                                   complement
Scientists study **how or why something has come to be the case.**
                       object of the verb
Scientists help us learn about **why certain events occur in nature.**
                        object of a preposition
Researchers understand **that scientific observations may contain anomalies.**
                       object of the verb
They don't always know **if their theories will be confirmed.**
                       object of the verb
Scientists are upset **that little progress has been made.**
                   follows adjective *upset*
Through experiments in the lab, students confirmed the fact
that heat is not stored energy.
       follows noun *the fact*

Identify Noun Clauses

Read the sentences and underline the noun clauses. Identify the function of the noun clause as well. The first one has been done for you.

1. A discussion follows the conclusion and states <u>what the results mean.</u>

   function: *object of verb*

2. This is why metals generally feel cold—they are good thermal conductors.

   function: _____

3. Place the socks under an intense light source, and make sure that each receives the same amount of radiation.

   function: _____

4. The net result is that warm air from the house is going up the chimney and being replaced by cold air from outside.

   function: _____

5. Why a bare floor feels colder than a carpet can be explained by the theory of thermal conduction.

   function: _____

6. Whether to use a fireplace or not depends on your intention: to heat your home or to enjoy its beauty.

   function: _____

Types of Noun Clauses

Noun clauses with *that*

- are most often used after verbs and adjectives
  We **know** *that* heat is transferred in one of three ways.
  I am **certain** *that* the kitchen has a convection oven.
- often omit *that* when they are objects of the verb
  We **know** *(that)* heat is transferred in one of three ways.
- are commonly used with *It* in the subject position
  It is possible *that* our lab experiment won't work. vs. ***That*** our lab experiment won't work is possible.
- are used after some nouns
  I agree with the **statement** *that* a fireplace is a poor heater for a home.

Noun clauses with *wh-* words

- use sentence word order: subject + verb
  I don't understand *how* **heat radiation works.**
  　　　　　　　　　　　　　subject + verb
  Why the **experiment failed** remains a mystery.
  　　　subject + verb
- are often embedded in polite requests or questions
  Can you explain *how* the process of conduction works **once more, please?**
  Does the lab report state *which* steps they followed in the experiment?

Noun clauses with *if/whether*

- use sentence word order: subject + verb
  I don't know *if* our **lab report follows** the correct format.
  　　　　　　　　　　subject + verb
- sometimes include the phrase *or not*
  I don't know *whether* our lab report is correct **or not**.
  I wonder *if* we'll be graded on the lab report format **or not**.
- are often embedded in polite requests or questions
  Can you tell me *whether* the lab will be open this evening?
  Do you know *if* your sources were listed in the lab report?

Complete Noun Clauses

Read the statements below and fill in the blanks with noun clauses. The noun clauses can be about any topic.

1. Most college students believe that _____.

2. How _____ is a mystery to me.

3. Can you tell me if _____?

4. I didn't realize that _____.

5. It's a fact that _____.

6. Do you know who _____?

7. What _____ is the most important thing on my mind right now.

8. I will never understand why _____.

9. Do you know whether _____?

Indirect or Reported Speech

Noun clauses are commonly used in indirect speech to report what other people have said or written. In academic writing, indirect or reported speech is used when paraphrasing, summarizing, or citing sources. It requires use of a "reporting verb" and oftentimes a change in verb tense. Look at the examples below.

Original Statement	Indirect/Reported
Children who **watch** a lot of TV **do not eat** many vegetables.	Researchers *find* that children who **watch** a lot of TV **do not eat** many vegetables. **OR** Researchers *have found* that children who **watch** a lot of TV **do not eat** many vegetables.
There **seems** to be a connection between watching TV and obesity.	Results *showed* that there **seemed** to be a connection between watching TV and obesity.
Plans for another study **have** already **begun**.	The research institute *reported* that plans for another study **had** already **begun**.
Participants **will record** their activities for a year.	Researchers *noted* that participants **would record** their activities for a year.

Common reporting verbs include: *announce, ask, agree, claim, explain, note, remark, report, say, show, state, tell, think, warn,* and *write.*

In general, if the reporting verb is in the simple present or present perfect tense, then the verb in the noun clause is in the simple present or present perfect tense as well. If the noun clause expresses a general statement of fact or truth, the verb often stays in the present tense even if the reporting verb is in past.

If the reporting verb is in the past tense, then the verb in the noun clause changes as follows:

```
simple present → simple past
present continuous → past continuous
simple past → past perfect
past continuous → past perfect continuous
present perfect → past perfect
past perfect → past perfect
```

If the reporting verb is in the past tense, then the modal verb in the noun clause changes as follows:

```
will + verb → would + verb
can + verb → could + verb
may + verb → might + verb
must + verb → had to + verb
should + verb → should + verb
```

Change Statements to Indirect Speech

Rewrite the statements, adding a reporting verb and changing verb tenses when necessary. The first one has been done for you.

1. The chest pain and breathing difficulty of pneumonia result from an infection of the lung tissues. (doctor / state) _The doctor stated that the chest pain and_ _breathing difficulty of pneumonia resulted from an infection of the lung tissues._

2. Debris from last night's windstorm caused the power outage. (officials / note)
   _____
   _____

3. The fuel efficiency of a vehicle is determined in part by size and weight. (automotive engineer / report) _____
   _____

4. Many species of birds will build their nests in high places to protect their young from predators. (biologist / remark) _____
   _____

5. Factors that account for predictive failure have been ruled out. (lab director / announce) _____
   _____

6. Metals are good thermal conductors, so they absorb energy quickly. (physics instructor / explain) _____
   _____

Direct Speech

Direct speech means using a speaker's or author's exact words. In academic writing, it is common to quote a source from an academic article, journal, book, or web site when it is used as support for one's writing. Quoting a source requires the use of quotation marks and commas to set off the words of the speaker or writer. You can quote a phrase, a sentence, or multiple sentences. Look at the examples below.

Physics, according to *Webster's New World Dictionary,* is "a science that deals with matter and energy and their interactions."

Albert Einstein once said, "Imagination is more important than knowledge."

Stephen Carey, author of *A Beginner's Guide to Scientific Method,* states in the preface of his book, "If anything deserves to be called the scientific method, it is the simple but profoundly fundamental process wherein new ideas are put to the test— everything from the most rarefied and grand theoretical constructs to the claims of the experimenter to have discovered some new fact about the natural world." (p. viii)

In each example, the exact words of the speaker or writer were set apart from the rest of the sentence with quotation marks.

Punctuation

When using direct speech, follow these guidelines:

- Put quotation marks around the words that you cite.
  The official stated, "Debris from last night's windstorm caused the power outage."
- Insert a comma between the reporting verb and the quotation.
  She claimed, "The phenomena cannot be accounted for."

- Put end punctuation inside the quotation marks.

  The committee member asked, "What do the test results show?"

- Capitalize the first word of the quote.

  *The physicist warned, "**W**e are dealing with extreme radiation absorption."*

- Quotations that are split or divided require two sets of quotation marks; the second half of the quote does not begin with a capital letter. If the second half is a complete sentence, however, begin with quotation marks and a capital letter.

  "The sense of feel in humans is based not so much on the temperature of an object in contact with the skin," said the instructor, "as on the rate of energy flow between the object and the skin."

  "The sense of feel in humans is based not so much on the temperature of an object in contact with the skin," said the instructor. "The sense of feel is based more on the rate of energy flow between the object and the skin."

Punctuate Direct Speech

Rewrite the statements and insert quotation marks, commas, end punctuation, and capital letters where necessary. The first one has been done for you.

Albert Einstein

1. If the human race is to continue for another million years, we will have to boldly go where no one has gone before said Stephen Hawking, a famous British physicist. "If the human race is to continue for another million years, we will have to boldly go where no one has gone before," said Stephen Hawking, a famous British physicist.

2. Albert Einstein, who developed the theory of relativity, once said I never think of the future. It comes soon enough. _____

3. There's [sic] two possible outcomes: if the result confirms the hypothesis, then you've made a measurement said Italian-American physicist Enrico Fermi. If the result is contrary to the hypothesis, then you've made a discovery. _____

4. The optimist thinks this is the best of all possible worlds. The pessimist fears it is true said J. Robert Oppenheimer, who is called the Father of the Atomic Bomb. _____

5. We have no right to assume that any physical laws exist, or if they have existed up to now, or that they will continue to exist in a similar manner in the future claimed Max Planck, a German physicist. _____

6. Nothing in life is to be feared stated Marie Curie, a French physicist. It is only to be understood. _____

7. If I have seen further than others said Isaac Newton it is by standing upon the shoulders of giants. _____

Making the Connection

Good readers interact with the text they are reading. They locate the thesis statement and use its controlling idea to predict how the writer will present the information. As they read each paragraph, they identify the topic sentence, which introduces the main point of the paragraph. They evaluate the support for the main points as they read and use transitions in the reading to guide them from one idea, sentence, or paragraph to the next. Readers are able to do this, however, only if the writers have taken care to plan and organize their paragraphs and essays. It is not enough to have good ideas and sufficient support if they are not presented in a unified, logical way.

| WRITING 1B | ● The Process |

Get Ready to Write

Unity

Writing has unity when the writer introduces an idea and discusses only that idea. An essay has unity when all of the paragraphs in an essay focus on the topic presented in the thesis statement and when each paragraph develops one aspect of the controlling idea. Similarly, a paragraph has unity when all of the sentences in the paragraph focus on the topic presented in the topic sentence and when each sentence develops and supports the topic sentence.

In the paragraph below, the topic sentence is underlined. Read the paragraph and decide whether the paragraph has unity, that is, whether each sentence in the paragraph is related to the topic sentence.

A fireplace is not an efficient way to heat a home. The heated air above the fire is pushed up the chimney by the warm air in the room and carries energy with it. Next, the air lost through the chimney is replaced with more warm air from the room as it continues to push the heated air up the chimney. Eventually the warm air in the room is replaced by cold air entering the house through leaks around the doors and windows. One way to stop the leaks is to caulk around the openings. The result is that warm air from the house is going up the chimney and being replaced by cold air from outside.

This paragraph does not have unity; it contains one sentence that does not develop or support the topic sentence: *One way to stop the leaks is to caulk around the openings.* Although the sentence is related to the one that precedes it because it mentions leaks, it is not related to the topic sentence.

Evaluate Unity in Paragraphs

Read the following paragraphs. Underline the topic sentence in each paragraph and decide whether the paragraph has unity. Cross out any sentences that are unrelated to the topic sentence.

1. The effects of color on radiation absorption can be easily demonstrated with socks. Insert thermometers into two socks, one white and one black. Record the initial temperatures. Now, place the socks out in the Sun, making sure that each receives the same amount of radiation. It is probably not a good idea to conduct this experiment on a cloudy day. After some time, read the temperatures again. The black sock appears to be black because it absorbs almost all of the visible radiation incident upon it. The white sock appears to be white because it reflects much of the visible radiation incident upon it. Thus, the temperature of the black sock will rise faster in the presence of visible radiation from the Sun, due to its high radiative absorption. After several minutes in the Sun, the black sock should be several degrees warmer than the white sock. The same results will occur with a white sock and a navy blue sock.

   Unity: Yes   No

2. The process of energy transfer known as conduction explains why a bare floor feels colder than a carpeted floor. The sense of feel in humans is based not so much on the temperature of an object in contact with the skin as on the rate of energy flow between the object and the skin. This is why metals generally feel cold—they are good thermal conductors, so they absorb energy quickly from the skin. The bare floor and the carpet are at the same temperature, that of the room, but yet they do not feel the same temperature. The bare floor is a better thermal conductor than the carpet—hence it feels colder.

   Unity: Yes   No

3. In the process of convection, the temperature of a fluid is raised, and the fluid is moved from one point in space to another, carrying the energy with it. Examples of convection include the water-based cooling system in an automobile engine and a forced air heating system in a home. Many homes nowadays have convection ovens, which cook food faster and at a lower temperature than conventional ovens. Food baked in a convection oven also bakes more evenly. *Natural* convection refers to the rising of hot fluids due to the buoyant force. Convection can also occur due to wind, such as the convective cooling of one's skin as the air blows across it. *Forced* convection refers to movement of energy-carrying fluid due to mechanical means, such as in your automobile engine or your air conditioner.

   Unity: Yes   No

4. Heat is one of the terms most commonly misused in colloquial conversation as well as in many textbooks. Heat is often referred to as a form of stored energy, but this is not true. Heat is a means by which we can transfer energy; it is not the stored energy itself. Stored energy is actually called *potential energy*. It can be converted into other forms of energy. So if heat is not stored energy, then what is the energy contained in a warm object? The correct description is *internal energy.*

   Unity: Yes   No

Coherence

Writing has coherence when ideas move smoothly from one to the next. A paragraph has coherence when all of the sentences are connected and presented in a logical order. Similarly, an essay has coherence when all of the paragraphs are connected and presented in a logical order. There are a number of techniques writers use to give coherence to their writing. They include

- using the correct text structure or combination of text structures (patterns of organization)
- placing ideas in logical order (via an outline) before writing the paragraph or essay
- repeating key words and ideas
- using pronouns to refer to key nouns mentioned earlier (referents)
- using transitions to connect ideas, sentences, and paragraphs
- keeping verb tenses consistent
- keeping a consistent point of view

Identify Cohesive Elements

The paragraph below has coherence. Some of the elements that give it coherence are underlined. Read the paragraph and, on a separate sheet of paper, identify as many of the techniques the writer used as you can.

The Science of Lab Reports

Students enrolled in undergraduate college courses <u>submit</u> lab (laboratory) reports detailing experiments or projects completed for chemistry, physics, or engineering courses. Although the specific format of <u>lab reports</u> is often determined by the individual school or department, it usually comprises five or six components. The objective of the <u>lab report</u> states the aims of the experiment and <u>includes</u> any hypothesis being tested. The method <u>outlines</u> the materials used and the step-by-step process followed to conduct the experiment. The results <u>are</u> typically the raw data that have been collected: facts, measurements, readings, etc. <u>This information</u> is usually presented in the form of a table or graph. <u>Following the results</u> is the conclusion. <u>The conclusion</u> is a summary of the results (raw data) and provides an analysis or interpretation of the data. A discussion follows <u>the conclusion</u> and states what the results mean. Finally, if outside sources were used in conducting the experiment, they are listed in the reference section.

    Were you able to identify them all? "The Science of Lab Reports"

- uses a combination text structure of definition (what a lab report and its components are) and process (the order the components appear)
- states there are five or six components and then proceeds to list each in order from first to last
- repeats the key words *lab report, the results,* and *conclusion*
- uses the pronouns *it* and *this* to refer back to *lab report* and *raw data* respectively
- uses the transition word *following* to refer to one component (*results*) and introduce the next (*conclusion*); the transition word *finally* brings the paragraph to a conclusion
- uses verbs in simple present tense throughout the paragraph
- keeps the point of view in third person

Coherence does not occur automatically when you write. Because most of the techniques listed on the previous page focus on individual parts of your essay or paragraph, they are usually a part of the revision process. One exception, however, is the first technique listed: use correct text structure. Your thesis statement will often help you decide which text structure or pattern of organization to use. Another exception is the second technique listed: place ideas in logical order. This step occurs early in the writing process, after you have formed your thesis statement and brainstormed your ideas for support but before you have begun to write. Outlining your ideas is the best way to ensure they are in logical order.

Use Correct Text Structure

Common text structures include argument/persuasion, cause/effect, classification, compare/contrast, definition, description, exemplification, literary analysis or reaction, narration, and process. The topic and the ideas you have brainstormed about it will often lead to the appropriate text structure. In addition, the controlling idea in the thesis statement often offers a clue to the format of the essay development.

Identify Text Structure

Read the topics and thesis statements below, all of which are related to science. Then choose an appropriate text structure for an essay. There may be more than one answer possible for some topics or thesis statements.

1. Science investigates physical, biological, and social phenomena.
   - a. cause/effect
   - b. process
   - c. classification

2. different ways to explain how or why something has occurred
   - a. narration
   - b. reaction
   - c. exemplification

3. predictive failure and predictive success
   - a. compare/contrast
   - b. cause and effect
   - c. definition

4. scientific method and crop circles
   - a. definition
   - b. description
   - c. argument/ persuasion

5. The scientific method is a simple three-step method by which scientists investigate nature.
   - a. compare/contrast
   - b. process
   - c. description

6. A scientific anomaly is a phenomenon that poses a challenge to well-documented explanations.
   - a. definition
   - b. exemplification
   - c. argument/ persuasion

7. how scientists develop theories
   - a. process
   - b. cause/effect
   - d. exemplification

Place Ideas in Logical Order

Oftentimes, the text structure you choose will help determine the logical order of your ideas. In a narrative or process essay, for example, the logical order will be chronological or time order. In a descriptive essay, ideas are often presented according to spatial order: left to right, front to back, top to bottom. Other types of order are order of importance (most → least), order of familiarity (most → least), order of complexity (simple → complex), and order of specificity (general → specific).

Place Ideas in Logical Order

Read the controlling ideas and choose the appropriate logical order for an essay.

Logical Order		
chronological (time)	familiarity	spatial
complexity	importance	specificity

_____ 1. heat as a means by which energy is transferred

_____ 2. cells, tissues, organs, systems in the human body

_____ 3. fields of science you can study: biology, volcanology, ichthyology, geography

_____ 4. setting up a scientific laboratory

_____ 5. how science is used in everyday life: following a recipe, growing plants, cooling a hot room, making ice cubes

_____ 6. meanings of scientific terms: theory, data, research, hypothesis, testing

Cohesive Devices: Key Words, Synonyms, and Pronouns

Repeating key words or ideas adds coherence to your writing. It contributes to the flow of ideas and keeps the reader informed. Instead of repeating key words, you can also substitute synonyms or pronouns for them. Keep in mind that a pronoun refers back to an earlier noun; if the reference to the specific noun is not clear, the reader will be confused. Compare the two paragraphs below. Which one has more coherence?

Paragraph 1

The second step in the process of scientific method is explanation. In science, it is an account of how or why something has come to be the case. Both theories and hypotheses involve them. Theories tend to be broad, unifying explanations while hypotheses are limited in scope. They can be tentative or well confirmed. They can make reference to causes, causal mechanisms, underlying processes, laws, or function.

Paragraph 2

The second step in the process of scientific method is explanation. An explanation, in science, is an account of how or why something has come to be the case. Both theories and hypotheses involve explanations. Theories tend to be broad, unifying explanations while hypotheses are limited in scope. Both can be tentative or well confirmed. Scientific explanations can make reference to causes, causal mechanisms, underlying processes, laws, or function.

The second paragraph has more coherence. The key word *explanation* is used five times in the paragraph. In addition, the synonym *account* is substituted for the word in the definition. In the first paragraph, the word *explanation* is used twice. Pronouns are substituted for the word three times and are sometimes confusing. In the sentence *Both theories and hypotheses involve them*, what does *them* refer to? It is unclear. In the second paragraph, repeating the key word *explanation* in the sentence *Both theories and hypotheses involve explanations* adds coherence to the paragraph.

Recognize Cohesive Devices

Read the sentences and underline the repeated key words, ideas, synonyms, and pronouns that contribute to coherence. Compare your answers with a partner's.

1. Many scientific observations concern anomalies—phenomena that do not square with well-established methods of explanation. Because they often pose a challenge to well-documented explanations, anomalies should be regarded with a healthy dose of skepticism. What this means is that observations pertaining to an alleged anomaly should look for data that suggest that the anomaly can be explained in some conventional way.

2. Testing is the third step in the process of scientific method. The basic strategy used to test an explanation is always the same. Isolate a prediction that will occur if an explanation is correct. Tests can be undertaken under laboratory conditions where circumstances will be arranged to yield a prediction, or in the real world by checking the prediction against the facts.

3. Students in undergraduate college courses submit lab reports detailing experiments or projects completed for chemistry, physics, or engineering courses. Although the specific format of lab reports is often determined by the individual department, a lab report usually comprises five or six components. The objective of the lab report states the aims of the experiment and includes any hypothesis being tested. The method outlines the materials used and the step-by-step process followed to conduct the experiment. The results are the raw data that have been collected: facts, measurements, and readings. This information is usually presented in the form of a table or graph. Following the results is the conclusion. The conclusion is a summary of the results and provides an analysis of the data. A discussion follows the conclusion and states what the results mean.

Use Cohesive Devices

Read the paragraph and improve its coherence by filling in the blanks with the key words, synonyms, or pronouns given. Some words will be used more than once.

convection	the fluid	this process

A. The Process of Convection

Convection is one of three common processes by which energy is transferred as heat. In (1) _____, the temperature of a fluid is raised, and (2) _____ is moved from one point in space to another, carrying the energy with it. Examples of (3) _____ include the water-based cooling system in an automobile engine and a forced air heating system in a home. *Natural* convection refers to the rising of hot fluids due to the buoyant force. (4) _____ can also occur due to wind, such as the convective cooling of one's skin as the air blows across it. *Forced* convection refers to movement of energy-carrying fluid due to mechanical means, such as in your automobile engine or your air conditioner.

energy	molecules	them

B. The Process of Conduction

Conduction is another type of process in which energy is transferred as heat. In this process, (1) _____ is transferred through a material without the actual transfer of matter. The molecules at one end of the material (in contact with a region of high temperature) start moving with increased kinetic energy. These (2) _____ "bump" into other (3) _____ and start (4) _____ moving faster. This "bumping" moves down the material toward the cooler end. Examples include the warming up of the upper end of a spoon in a cup of coffee and the transfer of (5) _____ through the walls in a home, which can be countered by installing insulation in the walls.

electromagnetic radiation	it	one	sock	this process

C. The Process of Radiation

Radiation is the third method by which energy is transferred as heat. (1) _____ depends on electromagnetic radiation, the most familiar form of which is light. (2) _____ carries energy, which can be absorbed by materials and may result in increased temperature. For example, if two socks, a black one and a white (3) _____, are placed under an intense light source or out in the Sun, the black sock appears to be black because (4) _____ absorbs almost all of the visible radiation incident upon it. The white sock appears to be white because (5) _____ reflects much of the visible radiation incident upon (6) _____. Thus, the temperature of a black sock will rise faster in the presence of visible radiation from the Sun, due to its high radiative absorption. After several minutes in the Sun, the black sock should be several degrees warmer than the white (7) _____.

Use Transitions

Transitions are another cohesive device writers use to connect ideas in their writing. Transitions such as *first, second,* and *last,* for example, signal the reader to expect a sequence of related ideas. *Therefore, thus,* and *consequently* alert the reader to a cause/effect relationship among ideas. Writers use the transitions *similarly, likewise, in contrast,* and *nevertheless* to introduce comparison and/or contrast among ideas. While writers use transitions to connect sentences, ideas, and paragraphs, they are careful not to overuse them. Do not use a transition word to connect each sentence in a paragraph; repeat a key word or idea, or use a synonym or pronoun instead. Below is a list of common transition words and connectors and their meanings. See Appendix 3 on page 283 for a more comprehensive list.

Transition/Connector	Meaning
likewise, similarly, the same as	comparison
but, however, on the other hand	contrast
as a result, consequently, for this reason, thus, therefore	cause/effect
afterward, first, second, third, next, subsequently, then, when	time order or sequence
for example, for instance, to illustrate, specifically	example
category, classified	classification or division
in addition, moreover, furthermore	additional information

ACTIVITY 30

Recognize Transitions and Connectors

Read the paragraphs and underline the transitions or connectors.

1. Archimedes' Principle

Archimedes' principle states that when an object is immersed in a fluid, it feels an upward (buoyant) force equal to the weight of the fluid displace by the object. Submarines are beautiful examples of Archimedes' principle in action. When floating, the overall density of the submarine is less than that of water, the same as for a normal ship. When the diving process is initiated, water is allowed to flood into holding tanks in the submarine. As a result, the density of the submarine becomes greater than that of water, and the submarine sinks. With fine control over the overall density, the submarine can travel at a given depth in the water.

2. Why Ocean Waves "Break"

Depth and speed are two factors involved in the explanation of why ocean waves "break." For water waves traveling in deep water, the depth of water plays little role in the wave speed. In shallow water, however, the wave speed depends on the depth of the water. When a wave approaches the shallow water of the beach, it slows down, causing the amplitude (size) to increase. In very shallow water, therefore, the "top" of the wave is in deeper water than the "bottom" of the wave. As a result, since the speed depends on depth, the top of the wave is moving faster than the bottom, and the wave "breaks."

3. Cats

How do cats land on their feet when they fall? One popular theory claims that the rotation is done in two steps. First, the cat twists its body with its hind legs extended and its front legs pulled in. Thus, the front half of the body has a smaller moment of inertia and rotates through a larger angle than the back half. Next, the cat pulls its hind legs in and extends its front legs and twists the other way. This time, the front rotates through a smaller angle than before, and the back half is brought around. As a result, there is a rotation of the body without there ever having been a net angular momentum ("amount" of rotational motion).

ACTIVITY 31

Use Transitions

Choose the correct transition in parentheses to join sentences or ideas.

1. Airplane Travel

It takes a different amount of time to fly east to west than it does to fly west to east between the same two points. The difference in flight times arises because there is usually a prevailing wind blowing with a component from west to east across the United States. (1) *When / After* an airplane is flying toward the east, the prevailing wind helps the airplane. When flying west, (2) *furthermore, / however,* the airplane has to fight the headwind. (3) *In addition, / Thus,* the westward velocity of the airplane with respect to the ground is smaller than the corresponding eastward velocity, and it takes longer to fly west than to fly east.

2. Cars and Trees

Which is worse for the driver of a car: hitting an identical car traveling at the same speed head-on or hitting a large, solid tree? Imagine the effect on the driver's momentum if the driver hits the tree. The front of the car becomes immobile and the rest of the car crushes toward the front. (1) *As a result, / On the other hand,* the driver is brought to rest in a short period of time. (2) *Likewise, / Next,* think about the driver hitting the other identical car traveling at the same speed. Since the cars have the same mass and the same speed (in opposite directions), the net momentum of the system of the cars is zero. (3) *Furthermore, / However,* the net momentum of the system of any similar portions of the cars, such as the grills, is also zero. (4) *Thus, / Then,* the front of the car becomes immobile and the rest of the car crushes toward the front. Again, the driver is brought to rest in a short period of time. In fact, it is the same period of time as if the driver hit the tree. Thus, the change in momentum and, (5) *afterward, / therefore,* the forces on the driver's body are the same in both cases.

Consistency: Verb Tense and Point of View

Generally, writers do not shift tenses between and among sentences and paragraphs. Doing so confuses the reader. Do not change tenses in your writing unless the action requires it. Some general guidelines for using specific tenses follow.

Verb Tense

Present tense is commonly used to

- make statements of general truth
- report facts
- offer definitions
- explain steps in a process
- describe characteristics or behaviors
- give descriptions
- report data or statistics
- share theories or hypotheses
- make generalizations

Past tense is commonly used to

- report historic events
- narrate stories or time lines
- retell information or events
- summarize information
- introduce a source
- discuss fiction
- detail biographies
- explain case studies

Writers typically indicate a change or shift in verb tense by introducing a time marker: *yesterday, in 2005, usually, next year,* etc. These markers reduce any confusion the reader might have as a result of a sudden shift in verb tense.

Consistent Verb Tense

Scan the readings from previous chapters listed below. Then work with a partner and, on a separate sheet of paper, indicate the verb tense used and suggest why the writer might have chosen to use that tense. If there is a shift in verb tense, offer an explanation for the shift as well.

1. Chapter 1, Reading 1: "Taking Objective Tests"

2. Chapter 2, Reading 2: "Ethnographic Research: Its History, Methods, and Theories"

3. Chapter 3, Reading 2: "Managing a Socially Responsible Business"

4. Chapter 4, Reading 2: "Six Dead After Church Bombing"

5. Chapter 5, Reading 1: "Weighted Voting Systems"

6. Chapter 6, Reading 2: "The Counterculture"

7. Chapter 7, Reading 2: "The Science of Lab Reports"

Consistency: Point of View

As with verb tense, writers do not shift points of view between and among sentences and paragraphs. As the writer, it is not necessary for you to include phrases such as *I think* or *I am going to talk about* in your essay. The reader assumes the essay contains your beliefs or opinions. In addition, do not shift from first person *I* or *we* to second person *you* to third person *he, she,* or *they* in your writing. A sudden shift in point of view confuses the reader.

First person is commonly used when writing narratives about the writer's personal experiences. Writers of fiction also use the first person to tell their story from the character's point of view. Second person is used to write about processes or to give advice or instructions. Third person is commonly used in academic writing where the focus is on a specific topic or subject. This point of view is commonly used in summaries, analyses, and arguments, for example. When writing in the third person, it is sometimes easier to use the plural *they* instead of *he or she.*

Consistent Point of View

Scan the readings from previous chapters listed below. Then work with a partner and, on a separate sheet of paper, indicate the point of view used and suggest why the writer might have chosen to use it. If there is a shift in point of view, offer an explanation for the shift as well.

1. Chapter 1, Reading 2: "Taking Subjective Tests"

2. Chapter 2, Reading 1: "The Essence of Anthropology"

3. Chapter 3, Reading 1: "Organizations Can Influence Employees' Ethical Conduct"

4. Chapter 4, Reading 1: *The Story of an Hour* and Reading 2a: "Ballad of Birmingham"

5. Chapter 5, Reading 2: "Computing Probabilities in Simple Experiments"

6. Chapter 6, Reading 1: Guy Strait, "What Is a Hippie?"

7. Chapter 7, Reading 1: "Scientific Method"

How Did They Do That?

This section of the chapter addresses two types of essays: those that combine two or more patterns of organization and those that explain or describe a process. The focus of the section, however, is on process essays, and their characteristics and structure are outlined. In this section you will also follow the steps in the writing process to identify the key elements in Reading 1, "Scientific Method," to see how the writer used process to develop the essay.

Essays with Combined Text Structures

Although writers usually have a specific text structure or pattern of organization in mind when planning their essays, rarely do they follow only one method. More often than not, an essay will include two or more patterns of organization. A student who conducts a lab experiment and then writes a report, for example, will generally use a *process* pattern of development but might also use the following text structures in specific sections of the report:

Lab Report Components and Possible Text Structures

Objective → purpose of the experiment explained with **definition**

Method → steps in the experiment developed with **process** and explained with **description, narration,** and/or **cause/effect**

Results → data from experiment organized with **classification/division**

Conclusion → results of experiment explained with **description** or **summary**

Discussion → meaning of results explained with **definition, summary,** or **analysis**

Reference → sources used listed using **description**

Combined text structures are used in many types of essays. For instance, essays of argumentation may combine patterns of definition, summary, and compare/contrast. Essays of classification might combine patterns of definition and exemplification. Essays of cause/effect might use both description and exemplification. The pattern or patterns needed to develop your essay will become apparent as you develop your thesis statement and as you outline and organize your ideas. Because using the correct pattern or combination of patterns contributes to the coherence of your writing, it is important not to skip any of the steps in the writing process.

Process Essays

Process essays

- are one of two types: instructional/directional or informational/analytical
- explain how to do or make something (instructional/directional)
- explain how something works or happens (informational/analytical)
- follow a step-by-step or sequence format
- are organized chronologically (time order)

- use key words such as *first, second, next, then, before, after that, later, finally, at the same time*
- use the second person *you* and the imperative/command verb form (instructional/directional)
- lead the reader to a product or specific results (instructional/directional)
- offer the reader a better idea or understanding of how something functions or was developed (informational/analytical)

Parts of a Process Essay

The introduction

- begins with a hook to attract the reader's attention
- includes preparation information and materials needed (instructional/directional)
- provides general information related to the process (informational/analytical)
- ends with a thesis statement that refers to the process being explained

The body

- addresses each step in the process
- can contain one or more steps in each paragraph
- keeps related steps together
- is organized chronologically
- explains each step or sequence in order
- explains terms that the reader might not know
- offers advice (instructional/directional)

The conclusion

- explains the final result(s)
- offers final comments
- can make a prediction

Examples of Processes

Instructional/Directional	Informational/Analytical
how to assemble a desk	how a hurricane forms
how to prepare for a job interview	how the human digestive system works
how to comparison shop	how language changes over time
how to apply for citizenship	how a computer works
how to register for classes	how a president is elected

Review Activity 28 in Chapter 3, which outlines the steps the writer took to develop an essay. Then refer to Reading 1, "Scientific Method," in this chapter to complete the activity

1. Circle the topic the writer brainstormed and used in the essay.

2. Underline the narrowed topic in the essay.

3. List some of the key words that identify the text structure. _____
_____

4. Write the thesis statement here. _____
_____

5. Identify the writer's process as instructional/directional or informational/
analytical. _____

6. Draw two lines under the topic discussed in each body paragraph.

7. Identify the order the steps are presented. _____
_____

8. Identify the technique the writer used to conclude the essay. _____
_____

WRITING 2 | **On Your Own**

Essay of Process
Write Your Essay

Choose a topic from your field of study that interests you and which can be explained in an essay of process. You may write an instructional/directional or informational/analytical process essay. Examples of instructional/directional topics are *how to install a computer program, how to research a topic on the Internet, how to balance/reconcile a bank statement/checking account, how to prepare low-fat meals, how to treat and bandage a sprain, how to prune/plant a tree/bush, how to repair a leaky faucet,* or *how to prepare for a job interview.* Examples of informational/analytical topics are *how a mountain/lake/river is formed, how the digestive/circulatory/skeletal system of the body works, how a tornado/flood/hurricane/tsunami occurs, how pollutants get into the drinking water, how color wheels work,* or *how a bill becomes a law.*

Follow the steps below to write an essay of process. Your audience is your instructor and classmates. Your title will refer to the process you are explaining or describing. After you finish writing your essay, read the sections on *Revising* and *Editing and Proofreading* and complete the activities.

Refer to *Writing 2: On Your Own* in Chapter 3 for the steps to follow in writing your essay. In step 4, choose the text structure for process, which explains the steps in how to do/make something or how something happens/occurs. In step 8, writing the introduction, include general information about the process or preparation information, including a list of needed materials.

Revising

Follow the Steps

A. Use the checklist to revise the essay of process you wrote.

Revising Checklist

1. Assignment
   - ☐ follows the assignment to write an essay of process
   - ☐ addresses the instructor and classmates as the audience
   - ☐ follows the ten steps listed in the assignment

2. Introduction
   - ☐ contains a hook to capture the reader's attention
   - ☐ contains some general statements or background information about the topic
   - ☐ contains a thesis statement related to the topic of the essay
   - ☐ Thesis statement includes a controlling idea.
   - ☐ Thesis statement gives a clue to the text structure.

3. Body
   - ☐ Each paragraph addresses a step in the process that is being explained.
   - ☐ Each paragraph contains a topic sentence.
   - ☐ Each topic sentence is developed through general and specific support/details.
   - ☐ General and specific support/details are arranged in chronological order.
   - ☐ General and specific support/details follow the outline.
   - ☐ General and specific support/details are sufficient in number (not too many, not too few).

4. Conclusion
   - ☐ marks the end of the essay
   - ☐ offers the writer's final thoughts on the topic
   - ☐ explains the final results or makes a prediction

B. Share your essay with a classmate. Ask your classmate to use the Revising Checklist to check your essay and give you some feedback. Make any changes to your essay that you feel are necessary. The changes you make should improve your essay.

Editing and Proofreading

The Final Steps

A. Follow the steps below to edit and proofread the essay of process you wrote.

> ### Editing and Proofreading Checklist
>
> 1. Grammar
>   - ☐ Verb tenses are correct.
>   - ☐ Each subject agrees with its verb (singular/plural).
>   - ☐ Prepositions are correct.
>   - ☐ Pronouns are correct.
>   - ☐ No articles are missing (*a, an, the*).
> 2. Spelling
>   - ☐ All the words are spelled correctly.
>   - ☐ Abbreviations, if any, are used correctly.
>   - ☐ First word of each sentence begins with a capital letter.
>   - ☐ All proper nouns begin with a capital letter.
> 3. Punctuation
>   - ☐ All sentences end with a punctuation mark.
>   - ☐ Periods are after statements and question marks are after questions.
>   - ☐ Commas are used correctly in sentences containing coordinating and subordinating conjunctions.
> 4. Sentences
>   - ☐ All sentences are complete.
>   - ☐ Each sentence has a subject and a verb.
>   - ☐ There are no fragments, run-on sentences, or comma splices.
>   - ☐ Sentences contain balanced or parallel grammatical structures.
> 5. Format
>   - ☐ Essay has a title.
>   - ☐ All paragraphs are in essay format (first line is indented or there is one blank line between paragraphs).
>   - ☐ All sentences are in paragraph format (not listed or numbered).
>   - ☐ Writer's name is on the paper.
>   - ☐ Paper is neat, clean, and legible (easily read).

B. Share your paragraph with a classmate. Ask your classmate to use the Editing and Proofreading Checklist to check your essay and mark any errors in grammar, spelling, punctuation, sentences, or format.

C. Fix any mistakes your essay contained. Proofread your essay one more time. Turn in your final draft to your instructor.

APPENDIX 1 ● Academic Word List

Chapter 1

Reading 1		Reading 2	
allocate*	focus	aid*	image
alternatively*	grade	analyze	individual
approach*	instructor	anticipating	irrelevant*
assigned*	objective	appendix	item
available	option	approach	major
chapter	overlapping*	aspect*	process
contrast	require	contradictory*	quote
definitely*	section	contribute*	respond*
definition	specific*	create	task*
eliminate	strategies	crucial*	theme
ensure*	survey*	demonstrate	trace*
error	topic	error*	
expert*			

Chapter 2

Reading 1		Reading 2	
approach	insight	abandoned	major
assist	interpretation	analysis	obvious*
communication	investigate*	assumption	odds*
complexities	issue	challenge*	overseas
cultural	maintained	coherent	primarily*
data	participant	complex	pursuing
diversity	perspective*	comprise*	reliable
equip*	phenomena*	contrary	reluctant
evolutionary	physical	emerge*	residing
feature*	practitioner	evidence	scope*
focus*	recover	expand	selecting
formulate*	reliable*	feature	similarities
generation	research	final	site
global	respond	framework	theories
hypotheses	significant	function	traditional
ignoring	theories	fundamental	underlying*
impact*	unique*	image	unfounded
individual	variation	instance	validity
		justify*	visual
		location	widespread*

*Used in vocabulary exercise

Chapter 3

Reading 1		Reading 2	
appropriate*	legal*	alter*	expanded
awareness	negative	analysis	financial
code*	participant	annual	fund
corporate	policy	aspect	globe
created	positive	assumption	impact
distributed	potential*	beneficial*	internal*
emphasize	priorities	communities	investigator
environmental	regulatory	compensation	investors*
establish*	resolve*	components*	justified
ethics*	response	consist*	negative
foundation	role*	constructing	odd*
goal	securities	consume*	percent
guideline	series	corporate	predict
illustrate*	summary*	culture	regulator
image	technique	decade	reinforce*
involved		definition	required
		eliminate	resource
		emphasis	securities
		energy	traced
		equation	violate
		ethical	voluntary
		exclusively	welfare*

Chapter 4

Reading 1		Reading 2	
abandonment*	perception	adult	individual
approach*	persistence*	apparently*	induce*
assure*	physical	area	injuries*
brief*	relax*	assemble	inspector
enable*	reveal*	civil*	method
impose*	significance	commit	occupant
indicate	suspension*	enforcement	occurrence*
intelligences		establishment	reinforce
		expert	release*
		federal*	route
		finally*	survivors*
		identified	trigger*

*Used in vocabulary exercise

Chapter 5

Reading 1		Reading 2	
affect*	method	approximately*	occur
amendments*	minimum	comprise	outcome
assigned	outcome*	compute*	percentage
assume*	plus*	conduct*	precise*
constitutional	principal*	consist	region*
crucial	proportional	definition	sequence*
denote*	requirement	finally	series*
final	sequence	furthermore*	task
instance	similar	hence*	theory
legislative	status	illustrate	time-consuming
major*	sufficient*	interpret*	
margin*	unique		

Chapter 6

Reading 1		Reading 2	
abandonment	neutral*	attitude	legal
accumulation	notions*	authority	liberation
assurance	odds	coordinating	mature*
capable	participate	code	media
challenge	perspective	colleague	minor
community	philosophy	commodities*	oriented*
constant*	precisely	compatibility*	period
conventional	principle	consumer	precedent*
culture	pursuit	contributed	promote
demonstrate	reaction*	convention	psychological
element*	rejection	despite	published
expose*	require	domination	radical
goal	security	enhance*	reject*
ignore*	seek*	exploit	revolution
individual	sexuality	exposure	sexism
inhibitions*	submit	gender	shift
integral*	survive	generation	sought
jobs	traditional	identify	styles
negative	welfare	individualism*	survive
		initiate	theme
		integrated*	unprecedented
		involved	widespread
		lecture*	

*Used in vocabulary exercise

Chapter 7

Reading 1		Reading 2	
accompanied	involve	analysis*	interpretation
accuracy	isolate	comprise	method
challenge	link*	concept	normally
circumstance	mechanism	conclusion	objective
citing*	methods*	contact	obvious
conceivable*	migratory	data*	occur*
conduct	perspective	energy*	overall*
confirm	phenomena	finally	process
conventional	pose	format	project
criteria	principle	hence	region
document	process*	hypothesis	selection
enable	proportional	incident	source
energy	relevant*	initial*	submit*
evidence	role	insert*	summary
factors*	scope	intense	transfer*
function	specified	internal	visible*
guarantee	underlying		
hypotheses*	undertake*		
instance	unifying		
intervening	vehicle*		

*Used in vocabulary exercise

APPENDIX 2 • Brainstorming Methods

Brainstorming means generating a list of ideas for topics and/or support. During brainstorming, the writer lists all of the ideas that come to his or her mind when thinking about a topic. It is the first step in writing. Without ideas, you have nothing to write about.

Points to remember about brainstorming

1. Brainstorming takes more than one or two minutes. The more time you devote to brainstorming, the more ideas you will generate.

2. Brainstorming does not include evaluating your ideas. If you stop to evaluate your ideas before writing them down, you are not brainstorming.

3. Brainstorming is not the same as writing your paragraph or essay. It is the first step in the process. You will not use all of the ideas that you brainstormed in your paragraph or essay.

4. After you brainstorm topics, you go back and evaluate them, choosing those ideas that might be suitable for your writing. All of the other ideas, the ones you don't use, are discarded.

5. Sometimes, while you are brainstorming, you will generate ideas that will later become support or details for your writing. As you evaluate your ideas, note which ones might be good details to include in your writing.

Types of brainstorming

There are many ways to generate ideas, and the best way is the one that helps you generate the most and/or the best ideas. Below are some examples of different types of brainstorming.

1. Generating a list—this is the most common type of brainstorming. You simply write down everything that comes into your mind and generate a list of ideas. Later you go back and evaluate the items on your list, choosing those that are the best.

Brainstormed list for the topic *Success in College*

good reading skills	keeping up with work
know how to take notes	using the library
study for an exam	choosing a major
good teachers	getting a tutor if I need one
classes not too big	good grades
have a good computer	asking teacher for help
don't waste time	study groups
attending class every day	schedule for studying
doing assignments	time management

2. Creating a web or cluster—this is another common type of brainstorming. Place your topic in the center of the web/cluster and then generate your ideas, connecting related ideas to one another.

Brainstormed web/cluster for the topic *Success in College*

3. Free writing—this type of brainstorming is sometimes mistaken for the actual writing of a paragraph or essay. However, it is brainstorming: generating your ideas. In free writing, you write almost as if you are writing in a journal, i.e., you write your ideas in sentences and write whatever comes to mind about your topic. Later, during the evaluation process, you go back and search for ideas in what you have written.

Key Concepts 2: Reading and Writing Across the Disciplines

Brainstormed free writing for topic *Success in College*

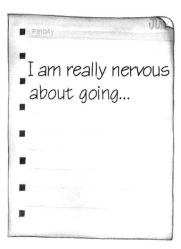

I am really nervous about going to college. I'm so afraid that I won't know what to do or how to study. What if I get bad grades on all my tests? I'll be so depressed and humiliated. I can feel the stress already. I wonder if anyone else feels this way. Well, I'll just have to make sure that I'm prepared. I have good reading skills. When I read, I can always figure out what the main idea is. I just have to make sure that I am prepared for class by reading the chapter or assignment before class meets. I'm not really worried about writing. I always get pretty good grades in writing. The thing is, writing takes time, so I have to make sure I don't wait till the last minute to start my writing. I'm strong in math, so that shouldn't be a problem for me. The good thing about math is that the homework doesn't seem so time-consuming as maybe a reading class would be. I think that if I'm going to succeed, I'll really have to manage my time. Everything kind of keeps coming back to that.

4. Questioning—this type of brainstorming does not work for every topic and so is not used as often as the other types of techniques. As with most questions, you will generate more ideas if you use *wh-* questions (who, what, where, when, how, why) instead of yes/no questions. After you brainstorm your list of questions, you answer them. Your answers will contain the ideas you evaluate and eventually write about.

Brainstormed questions for the topic of *Success in College*

What does it mean to be successful in college?

Why are some people successful and others not?

Who is successful in college?

What types of students succeed in college?

Do only smart people succeed?

What kind of skills do people need to do well?

How good do your reading skills have to be in college?

Do you do a lot of reading in college?

How much reading do you have to do?

Is there a lot of writing in college?

How much writing do you have to do?

What kinds of writing do you have to do?

Who can help you get those skills if you don't have them or if they aren't very good?

Where can you learn about the skills you will need to succeed in college?

Where can you go for help if you need it?

When do most people decide to go to college?

When do most students study at college – during the day or at night?

Does it make a difference what time of day you study?

How long do students usually study for tests?

What do I do with my brainstorming results?

Once you have finished brainstorming, you begin to evaluate your ideas. You go over your list of ideas and cross out any that seem unrelated to the topic. Cross out ideas which are boring or too difficult to write about. Also cross out ideas which are too narrow to develop into a paragraph. The chances are that one of your ideas will appeal to you more than the others will. This is the idea you want to develop into a topic sentence for your paragraph or into a thesis statement for your essay. Be sure to scan your list of brainstormed ideas for details that might help support your topic sentence. Next, organize your ideas and, if necessary, brainstorm additional details. Once you have your topic sentence and supporting details organized, start writing your first draft.

Additional brainstorming techniques

If you are brainstorming ideas for a specific type or pattern of writing—comparison/contrast, for example—there are graphic organizers you can use. See the following examples.

1. This Venn diagram graphic organizer is good for brainstorming and organizing comparison/contrast writing. In one circle you list all the ideas that apply only to Topic A. In the other circle, you list all the ideas that apply only to Topic B. In the center, where the circles overlap, you list the ideas that Topic A and Topic B have in common.

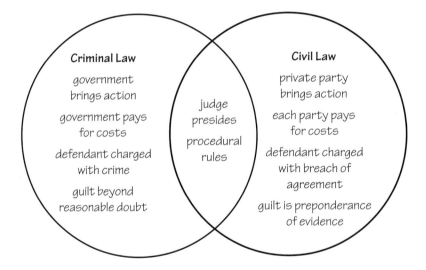

2. In this T-structure, all the points related to Topic A are listed on the left, and those related to Topic B are listed on the right. Similarities and differences can then easily be compared, and the focus of the paragraph or essay can highlight whichever predominates, the similarities or differences.

Criminal Law	Civil Law
government brings action	private party brings action
government pays for costs	each party pays for costs
defendant charged with crime	defendant charged with breach of agreement
guilt beyond a reasonable doubt	guilt is preponderance of evidence
judge presides	judge presides
follow procedural rules	follow procedural rules

3. In this flow chart, the topic is heart disease. The causes of heart disease are listed on the left; the effects of heart disease are listed on the right. It is possible to have different configurations for cause/effect essays: one cause and one effect, one cause and multiple effects, multiple causes and one effect, and multiple causes and multiple effects.

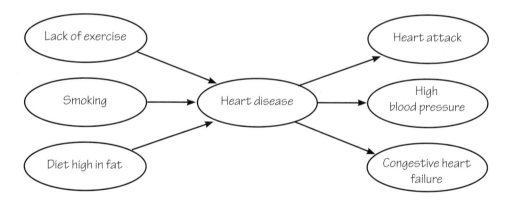

4. In this chart, the topic is cell phone use. The first column contains the support for banning cell phone use in school. Because essays of argument/persuasion need to consider the opposing view, the second column lists support for allowing cell phone use in school. The third column lists the writer's rebuttal for the opposition's view.

Proposition: Cell phones should be banned from schools.

Support for Argument	Opposition to Argument	Rebuttal for Opposition
1. are a distraction for students	1. emergencies	1. in an emergency, the school can be contacted
2. used to cheat on tests	2. in-between classes/ lunch time is free time	2. won't restrict their use of phones to just those times; students can text without looking—even while the phone is in their pocket
3. phones are stolen		
4. can be used to organize gang meetings		
5. can be used to take pictures of people without their permission	3. tracking device if child is missing	3. may or may not work; could be thrown away or used to create a false trail
6. disrupt class when they ring		
	4. makes parents feel safer	4. it doesn't mean that children are safer

Conjunctions

Conjunctions join or connect words, phrases, and clauses. See the following charts for the different types of conjunctions.

Coordinating Conjunctions

Coordinating conjunctions connect words, phrases, or clauses that are equal in importance.

Coordinating Conjunction	Use and Meaning
for	introduces reason (more formal than *because*)
and	introduces another idea or more information
nor	introduces another idea or more information (negative)
but	introduces contrast
or	introduces an alternative
yet	introduces contrast
so	introduces the result

Example sentences

1. People listened when he spoke, **for** he was the authority on the subject.

2. There are many ways to brainstorm ideas, **and** all of them are effective.

3. I don't have the time to help her with her math today, **nor** do I have the energy.

4. Most people are making an effort to conserve energy, **but** we still have a long way to go.

5. We can travel by train to California next month, **or** we can get there by plane.

6. She's explained this economic principle to me several times, **yet** I still don't understand it.

7. He's always been great at math, **so** he decided to major in accounting in college.

Subordinating Conjunctions

Subordinating conjunctions connect dependent and independent clauses and show the relationship between the two; the conjunction introduces the dependent clause.

Subordinating Conjunction	Use and Meaning
although even though though	concession
if even if unless only if	condition
although even though though whereas while	contrast
as because since	reason or cause
in order that so that so + adjective/adverb + that such + noun + that	result or purpose
after once as until as soon as when before whenever by the time while	time

Example sentences

1. **Although** the new academic advisor is not very friendly, she's not rude.
2. We aren't going to make our flight **unless** the security line is short.
3. **Whereas** I prefer to vacation at the beach, my family prefers to go to the mountains.
4. **Since** it was too early to go to the mall, we stopped at a restaurant and had breakfast.
5. He left himself a voicemail message **in order that** he would remember to bring the latest version of his report with him the next day.
6. They formed a study group for their business class **so that** they could divide up the work and meet to review for tests.
7. **As soon as** the snow starts melting, people start smiling and feeling better, knowing that winter is almost over.
8. I listen to the classical music station **whenever** I have the chance.

Conjunctive Adverbs / Transitional Words

Conjunctive adverbs are words or phrases which connect independent clauses or which introduce an independent clause. Because they show the relationship between ideas, sentences, and paragraphs, and add coherence to one's writing, many conjunctive adverbs are used as transitional devices.

Conjunctive Adverb / Transition	Use and Meaning
also besides furthermore in addition moreover	introduces another idea or more information
in that case otherwise	introduces a condition
however in contrast instead nevertheless nonetheless on the contrary on the other hand	introduces a contrast or concession
for example for instance in fact in other words that is (i.e.) to illustrate	introduces an explanation or example
accordingly as a result consequently for that reason hence therefore thus	introduces a result
afterward finally first last meanwhile next second then	introduces a sequence
also likewise similarly	introduces a similarity

Example sentences

1. I really didn't like the characters in the latest novel I read; **furthermore**, the plot made absolutely no sense.

2. She practices yoga for its health benefits; **moreover**, she says it's also a way for her to meet new people with whom she has something in common.

3. Please let me know if you plan to use your ticket for the concert; **otherwise**, I'll give it to someone else.

4. Lillian wants to live out in the country, away from the city; **however**, her husband prefers to live in the city because of his interest in art and the theater.

5. We hadn't planned to buy a new car until next year; **nevertheless**, when our old one broke down again last week, we bought a new one.

6. For some reason, Ella thinks her supervisor doesn't like her; **on the contrary**, her supervisor admires her and speaks highly of her.

7. I'm thinking about going back to school to study medicine because it's what I want to do; **on the other hand**, I don't know if I want to spend the next seven years of my life in med school.

8. Jason was let go from his job. **In other words,** he was fired.

9. He waited too long before he made a plane reservation; **consequently**, he couldn't get a flight to the conference.

10. I have to work late every night this week and on the weekend as well; **thus**, I won't be able to see you as planned.

11. Samantha practiced the piano for years. **Finally,** her perseverance was rewarded with a music scholarship to a four-year university.

12. Anita's brothers all worked for the family business; **likewise,** Anita expected to join the family team after she finished college.

Key Words

Key words act as signals: they give the reader an indication of the way a writer has organized a paragraph or essay. The key words listed below are commonly used with the text structure noted.

Key Word			Text Structure
against argue con for / pro should / should not	in favor of in fact oppose support	disagree must / must not ought to	argument / persuasion
because / because of cause for since result	as a result of reason thus consequence	therefore due to effect as	cause / effect
category classify comprise consist of	divided into division sort part	type of kind group	classification / division
alike also and compared to differ from	in contrast to instead likewise same similar	too unlike versus whereas while	compare / contrast
mean refer to	such as be defined as	is / are	definition
as an example as an illustration consider for example (e.g.)	for instance imagine that in the case of specifically	such as to demonstrate to illustrate	exemplification / illustration
impact on influence issue	option recommend warrant	answer benefit solution	problem / solution
how to method phase procedure process stage step for X amount of time	beginning with during eventually finally first second before after	third last meanwhile next once X happens starting with at the same time then	process / sequence
based on basically in general	generally many overall	some usually	summary

APPENDIX 4 • Additional Writing Topics

Chapter 1 – Timed Writing

- compare and/or contrast objective and subjective tests
- list five terms that might be used on an essay exam and explain/offer examples of each
- show how reading test questions can affect a student's grade on an exam
- discuss the advantages of using outlines in the writing process
- evaluate the use of objective tests by college professors
- argue for or against open-book tests (or take-home tests)

Chapter 2 – Summary

- literature: a short story or novel
- history: a historical period (the Industrial Revolution, the Gold Rush, the 1920s)
- debate of an issue
- political science: platforms of a specific political party
- business: the history of a company (Microsoft™, American Express™, Starbucks™)
- the culture of a specific country or group of people

Chapter 3 – Cause/Effect

- physics: the cause/effect of static electricity
- chemistry: the cause/effect of ozone depletion
- music: the cause/effect of a specific type of music on its audience
- history: the cause/effect of World War I or II, or another war
- computer science: the cause/effect of computer viruses
- sociology: the cause/effect of immigrating to another country

Chapter 4 – Reaction/Response

- literature: short story, novel, poem
- art: painting, sculpture, pottery, photograph

- music: classical, rock 'n roll, country, traditional/folk, blues, reggae, opera, hip hop/rap
- business: advertisement, commercial, sales technique
- everyday object: computer, espresso machine, automobile, bicycle, radio, television, watch, toothbrush

Chapter 5 – Exemplification/Illustration

- the expression "clothes make the man"
- a person who is a true leader, a true friend, a good parent
- influence that music has on a person
- role models for children
- the ferocity/violence of weather
- holidays are the worst days of the year

Chapter 6 – Argument/Persuasion

- using animals for testing/research of new products
- school vouchers or school choice
- gay marriage
- polygamy
- amnesty for illegal immigrants
- seatbelts and motorcycle helmets—law or free choice?

Chapter 7 – Process

- physics: how gravity works, how energy is transferred, how rain clouds form
- government: how a president is elected, how a bill becomes law
- how to adapt to a new culture
- how to become a citizen
- how to prepare for an interview
- how to study for a test
- how hurricanes, tornadoes, or earthquakes occur

Academic Word List: a list of words that will help prepare students for study at a college or university

analysis: a study of a specific topic and the components of which it is made

antonym: a word that means the opposite of another word

appositive: a word or phrase that describes or gives more information about a topic

argument/persuasion: a style of writing in which the writer attempts to convince the reader to accept a particular viewpoint

audience: the readers of a piece of writing

body: the main part of a paragraph or essay, it contains the support for the topic sentence or thesis statement

brainstorming: generating ideas for topics and/or support, listing all the ideas that come to mind when thinking about a topic

cause/effect: a style of writing in which the reasons for and/or the results of specific actions are offered/explained

cited works: a list of sources the writer has referred to or used in his/her work

classification: a style of writing in which items are first grouped or categorized according to their common or shared characteristics or traits and then analyzed

clause: a group of words containing a subject and a verb

clustering: grouping similar items or ideas

coherence: used to describe writing that is clear and logical; writing that follows a logical order

comma splice: a writing error; two independent clauses (sentences) combined with only a comma

compare/contrast: a style of writing in which two or more items are shown to be similar or different

controlling idea: indicates what the writer will address when discussing the main idea; the specific aspects of the main idea that will be addressed in the writing

definition: a style of writing in which the meaning of a term or concept is explained

detail: support or evidence for the statements the writer makes; major details support the topic sentence, and minor details provide more information and may include facts, statistics, or examples

draft: a piece of writing that is still in progress and that is not yet final or ready to be submitted

drawing a conclusion: using all the information presented in a piece of writing in order to make a judgment about a topic or viewpoint that has been presented

edit: to correct errors or rewrite unclear statements in a piece of writing

elements: parts of a whole; in literature, elements include *character, setting, tone, theme,* and *word choice,* for example

emphatic order: the order in which ideas are presented: smallest to largest, most well-known to least well-known, most important to least important, etc.

exemplification: a style of writing in which examples are used to clarify or define concepts and provide explanation

fact: a piece of information that is known to be true and that can be proved

fallacy: a statement used as support in writing but that contains an error in reasoning or logic

figurative language: language that describes through the use of analogies, metaphors, similes, or symbols; it explains or compares dissimilar items or represents something with more than one meaning

fragment: a writing error; an incomplete sentence, often lacking a subject or verb

free writing: a brainstorming technique in which the writer puts down, in sentence form, ideas as they occur in his or her mind

gloss: short for *glossary,* a list of terms and their meanings/definitions

graphic aid: a visual image such as a chart, graph, diagram, or picture that accompanies a piece of writing

heading: a group of words that summarizes a section of writing; usually in bold font

inference: drawing a conclusion from indirect evidence or support the writer offers

listing: a brainstorming technique in which the writer puts down, in list form, ideas as they occur in his or her mind

main idea: the topic of a piece of writing; an implied main idea is not stated or directly written

opinion: the writer's personal view or feelings about a subject based on his or her knowledge or interpretation of the facts on a subject

outline: an organized list that summarizes the main ideas of a piece of writing

parallelism: balancing the grammatical structures used in writing by pairing similar parts of speech—nouns with nouns, adjectives with adjectives, for example

paraphrase: to restate a writer's ideas in your own words

pattern of organization: rhetorical or academic style, text structure; a specific way of writing to show cause and effect, comparison and contrast, definition, narration, etc.

predict: to anticipate what comes next in a piece of writing

problem/solution: a style of writing in which a problem is stated and possible solutions are offered; a preferred solution is often suggested in the conclusion

process: a style of writing in which the steps to a procedure or method of doing something are outlined

proofread: to look for errors in grammar, spelling, punctuation, and format in a piece of writing

purpose: the reason for writing: to persuade, inform, or entertain

qualifiers: words that limit or restrict meaning; *all, always, never, none, only* are examples

reaction/response: a style of writing in which the writer shares a personal reaction to something; a piece of literature, a movie, or a news article, for example

referent: nouns or pronouns that refer or refer back to important nouns or phrases in a passage

revise: to make changes or corrections in or rewrite a piece of work

rewrite: to revise, to make changes or corrections in a piece of work

run-on sentence: a writing error; two independent clauses (sentences) combined without any connectors or punctuation

scan: to find specific information in a text by reading quickly

spatial order: presenting information according to place or area; for example, *on the left, on the right, above, below*

subheading: a group of words that summarizes a section of writing

summarizing: using your own words to give a brief overview of a text or lecture

summary: a style of writing in which only the most important pieces of information are presented

survey: to look at the parts of a text in order to get a general view or idea of the topic

synonym: a word that means the same thing as another word

synthesizing: integrating, combining, or blending information from two or more sources

text structure: pattern of organization or method of development writers use to express their ideas; examples include cause/effect, compare/contrast, definition, narration, etc.

thesis statement: in an essay, the sentence or statement that contains the main and controlling ideas that will be presented

time order: presenting information chronologically, in the order in which events occurred

tone: the attitude the writer has about the subject: serious, optimistic, critical, informative, etc.

topic: the general or main idea a piece of writing will discuss or focus on

topic sentence: in a paragraph, the sentence or statement that contains the main and controlling ideas that will be presented; for example, in the sentence *Thinking is a purposeful mental activity*, the main idea is *thinking* and the controlling idea is *a purposeful and mental activity.*

transition: a word or phrase that connects ideas, sentences, or paragraphs, resulting in a smooth flow of ideas between them

unity: used to describe writing that contains ideas that are all related to the topic; typically, each paragraph contains ideas related to one topic

Term	Definition	Example
analyze	show how one or more parts of a whole works or what it means	**Analyze** the behavior of the main character in the short story *The Story of an Hour*.
apply	show how a theory or principle works in a specific process/situation	**Apply** Newton's Law to the situation in which a book falls off the edge of a table.
argue	express a point of view and defend it with facts, examples, etc.	**Argue** for or against the merits of the Patriot Act.
compare	show how two or more things are similar	**Compare** the two major political parties in the United States.
contrast	show how two or more things are different	**Contrast** the three branches of the U.S. government.
criticize	offer the positive and negative sides of an issue	**Criticize** the issue of amnesty for illegal immigrants.
define	give the meaning and examples of its use	**Define** *surrealism* and give examples of it as an art type.
describe	tell how something happened or what it looks like by providing specific details	**Describe** the events leading up to World War II.
discuss	provide the details of a situation and the resultant effect	**Discuss** managerial opportunities in Fortune 500 companies for women and minorities.
evaluate	state the positive and negative aspects of an event or situation and provide your opinion	**Evaluate** the popularity of reality shows on television.
explain	give reasons how or why an event or situation occurred/occurs/will occur	**Explain** the effects of global warming on future plant life.
illustrate	provide examples that show how X is related to the topic/subject	**Illustrate** the ways computers have influenced students' performance in school.
justify	provide examples or reasons for a specific event or situation	**Justify** the use of school vouchers.
list/enumerate	state the reasons an event or situation happened/occurred or the characteristics of something	**List/Enumerate** the causes of inflation.
relate	explain how two or more things are connected	**Relate** the increase in registered voters to the passage of the Civil Rights Act of 1964.
show	provide examples to explain an event or situation	**Show** how education has increased the life expectancy rate for U.S. males.
state/specify	explain or give the main points of an event or situation using specific details	**State/Specify** the common causes of depression among the elderly.
summarize/outline	provide the main or most important ideas related to the subject/topic	**Summarize/Outline** the causes of the increase in divorce rates.
support	offer reasons or proof for a specific position on a subject or topic	Explain the reasons for U.S. sanctions against Cuba and **support** the keeping/lifting of the embargo.
trace	explain the step-by-step process that led up to a specific event or situation or that led to a change in something	**Trace** the role of women in the U.S. political arena since the 1950s.

In Chapter 4, guidelines and examples for citing sources using the MLA style were used. Below are examples for citing the same sources using the APA style.

Basic APA Format—Books, Articles, Newspaper

A. Book—Author

Author, A. (Year of publication). *Title of book: Capital letter for a subtitle.* Location: Publisher.

Leyendo, G. (2005). *Introduction to the elements of literature.* Miami: Onshore Books.

B. Edited Book—No Author

Editor, A., & Editor, B. (Eds.) (Year of publication). *Title of book: Capital letter for a subtitle.* Location: Publisher.

Jones, B., & Smith, D. (Eds.) (2003). *Womenspeak: An anthology of short stories by feminist writers.* Boston: Voice of Women, Inc.

C. Edited Book—Author

Author, A. (Year of publication). *Title of book: Capital letter for a subtitle.* (E. Editor, Ed.). Location: Publisher.

Small, J. (1999). *Famous women writers: A new look at old themes.* (L. Johnson, Ed.). Chicago: Independent Books.

D. Article

Author, A. (Year of publication). Title of article. *Title of Periodical, volume number* (issue number), pages.

Dell, F. (2003). Literature of today. *Journal of Literary Issues, 6* (4), 66–73.

E. Newspaper

Author, A. (Year of publication, Month day). Title of article. *Title of Newspaper,* p. of section.

Wales, L. (2007, May 23). Academic skills at work. *Our County News,* p. 3A.

Electronic Resources

F. Web Site

Title of document. (Date of publication). Retrieved month day, year, from http://web address

Key life concepts. (2006). Retrieved April 3, 2008, from http://www.keylifeconcepts.org./lessons/learned

G. Online Periodical

Author, A. (Date of publication). Title of article. *Title of Online Periodical, volume number* (issue number if available). Retrieved month day, year, from http://www.web address

Ellis, B. & Green, H. (2002). Cite that quote! *Online Sources: Using Them Correctly, 15.*

Retrieved October 18, 2005, from http://www.onlinesources.com/quotes/correct

Text Credits

Chapter 1

Prove Understanding, first essay question, p. 3: From SHIPMAN. *INTRODUCTION TO PHYSICAL SCIENCE 10E*, 10E. © 2003 Brooks/Cole, a part of Cengage Learning, Inc. Reproduced by permission. www.cengage.com/permissions; *Prove Understanding, second essay question, p. 30; Show Relationships, second essay question, p. 30:* From FERRARO. *Cultural Anthropology*, 7E. © 2008 Wadsworth, a part of Cengage Learning, Inc. Reproduced by permission. www.cengage.com/permissions; *Show Relationships, first essay question, p. 30:* From HYSER/ARNDT. *Voices of the American Past*, 3E. © 2005 Wadsworth, a part of Cengage Learning, Inc. Reproduced by permission. www.cengage.com/permissions.

Chapter 2

Reading 1, p. 43; Activity 10, p. 50; Reading 2, pp. 52-53: From HAVILAND/PRINS/WALRATH. *Cultural Anthropology*, 12E. © 2008 Wadsworth, a part of Cengage Learning, Inc. Reproduced by permission. www.cengage.com/permissions; *Activity 7, p. 47; Activity 32, pp. 68-69; Activity 33, pp. 69-70:* From FERRARO. *Cultural Anthropology*, 7E. © 2008 Wadsworth, a part of Cengage Learning, Inc. Reproduced by permission. www.cengage.com/permissions.

Chapter 3

Reading 1, p. 79; "Social Responsibility," p. 83; Activity 7, Part B, "Regulation of the Internet," p. 85; Reading 2, pp. 88-89: From GITMAN/MCDANIEL. *Instructor's Edition for Gitman/McDaniel's Future of Business, 6th*, 6E. © 2008 South-Western, a part of Cengage Learning, Inc. Reproduced by permission. www.cengage.com/permissions; *Activity 7, "Online Pharmaceuticals," "Online Pharmacies," "Fighting Spam," "The Remaking of the American University," and "Romantic and Electronic Stalking," pp. 83-85:* From HALBERT/INGULLI. *CyberEthics*, 2E. © 2005 South-Western, a part of Cengage Learning, Inc. Reproduced by permission. www.cengage.com/permissions.

Chapter 4

"The Lama," p. 128: Copyright © 1931 by Ogden Nash. Reprinted by permission of Curtis Brown, Ltd. *"Dug through rubble after 1963 church bombing," p. 129:* Used with permission of The Associated Press Copyright © 2008. All rights reserved. *Reading 2a, p. 133:* Reprinted by permission of the Dudley Randall Literary Estate. *Reading 2b, p. 135-136:* Six Dead After Church Bombing (9/16/1963) © United Press International, Inc. All rights reserved.

Chapter 5

Reading 1, pp. 167–168; Activity 10, p. 196; Reading 2, pp. 178-179; Activity 16, Part B, p. 181: From PARKS/MUSSER/TRIMPE/MAURER. *A Mathematical View of Our World (with CD-ROM and iLrn Student, Personal Tutor with SMARTHINKING Printed Access Card) (Hardcover)*, 1E. © 2007 Brooks/Cole, a part of Cengage Learning, Inc. Reproduced by permission. www.cengage.com/permissions; *Figure 7, p. 191:* www.census.gov; *Figure 11, p. 194:* www.census.gov/prod/2006pubs/p20-556.pdf.

Chapter 6

Introduction, Reading 1, p. 201: From BELMONTE. *Speaking of America: Readings in U.S. History, Vol. II: Since 1865.* © 2007 Wadsworth, a part of Cengage Learning, Inc.

Photo Credits

Chapter 1

Chapter 2

Chapter 3

Chapter 4

Chapter 5

Chapter 6

Chapter 7

NOTES

NOTES

NOTES

NOTES

NOTES

NOTES